**PRACTICE
MAKES
PERFECT**™

Trigonometry

PRACTICE
MAKES
PERFECT™

Trigonometry

Carolyn Wheater

Mc
Graw
Hill

New York   Chicago   San Francisco   Lisbon   London   Madrid   Mexico City
Milan   New Delhi   San Juan   Seoul   Singapore   Sydney   Toronto

ISBN   978-0-07-176179-6
MHID   0-07-176179-9

e-ISBN 978-0-07-178509-9
e-MHID   0-07-178509-4

Library of Congress Control Number 2011928642

Interior design by Village Bookworks, Inc.

Contents

Preface

Math has a lot in common with music, dance, and sports. There are skills to be learned and a sequence of activities you need to go through if you want to be good at it. You don't just read math, or just listen to math, or even just understand math. You do math, and to learn to do it well, you have to practice. That's why homework exists, but most people need more practice than homework provides. That's where *Practice Makes Perfect: Trigonometry* comes in.

The study of trigonometry starts with material you've learned in geometry and expands upon it, giving you both more powerful tools for very practical applications and more analytical approaches to the concepts. It merges all this with the skills you acquired in algebra, asking you to think about solving equations and graphing functions. The exercises in this book are designed to help you acquire the skills you need, practice each one individually until you have confidence in it, and then combine various skills to solve more complicated problems.

You can use *Practice Makes Perfect: Trigonometry* as a companion to your classroom study, for that extra experience that helps you solidify your skills. You can use it as a review of concepts you've learned previously, whether you're preparing for an exam or you're taking an advanced course and feel you need a refresher.

With patience and practice, you'll find that you've assembled an impressive set of tools and that you're confident about your ability to use them properly. The skills you acquire in trigonometry will serve you well in other math courses, like calculus, and in other disciplines, like physics. Be persistent. You must keep working at it, bit by bit. Be patient. You will make mistakes, but mistakes are one of the ways we learn, so welcome your mistakes. They'll decrease as you practice, because practice makes perfect.

Trigonometry

Right triangle trigonometry

Trigonometry, or "triangle measurement," developed as a means to calculate the lengths of the sides of right triangles and was based on similar triangle relationships. The fundamental ideas of trigonometry will be extended well beyond right triangles, but for now, we'll look at right triangles and measure the angles in them in degrees.

Angle measurement: degrees

The traditional system for measuring angles in geometry is degree measure. The measurement of an angle involves the amount of rotation between the two sides of the angle. A full rotation, or full circle, is 360°. A half rotation is 180°, the measure of a straight angle. Because the three angles of any triangle total 180°, each angle in the triangle must be less than 180°. Angles that measure less than 90° are acute angles, angles of exactly 90° are right angles, and angles greater than 90° and less than 180° are obtuse angles.

Two acute angles are complementary if the sum of their measures is 90°. Each angle in the pair is the complement of the other. Two angles are supplementary if their measures total 180°. Each angle is the supplement of the other.

EXERCISE
1·1

Classify each angle as acute or obtuse.

1. 42°   4. 83°   7. 174°   10. 11.6°

2. 110°   5. 96°   8. 39°

3. 17°   6. 108°   9. 7°

Give the complement (if possible) and the supplement of each angle.

11. 47°   14. 89°   17. 151°   20. 13.8°

12. 130°   15. 92°   18. 40.5°

13. 19°   16. 123°   19. 9.2°

Degrees, minutes, seconds

In geometry, it's unusual to talk about fractions of a degree, and when you do, it's usually by a simple fraction or a decimal. In trigonometry, you'll sometimes need a level of precision that can only be accomplished by measuring fractions of a degree. While this is sometimes done by fractions or decimals, it's also common to break a degree into 60 parts called minutes ($1° = 60'$), and a minute into 60 parts called seconds ($1' = 60''$ so $1° = 3,600''$).

EXERCISE

1·2

Convert each measurement to decimal form.

1. 22°45'
2. 18°12'
3. 39°48
4. 137°27'
5. 96°51'
6. 81°6'45"
7. 1°43'12"
8. 178°22'30"
9. 11°7'30"
10. 78°22'36"

Convert each measurement to degree-minute-second form.

11. 25.3°
12. 18.75°
13. 37.1°
14. 135.545°
15. 94.735°
16. 86.9°
17. 3.25°
18. 167.6°
19. 19.25°
20. 74.3°

Bearings

Because trigonometry is frequently used in navigation, information about an angle is often given in terms of bearings. A bearing first specifies a starting direction, usually north or south, then gives a number of degrees (and possibly minutes and seconds) to rotate, followed by the direction of rotation. A bearing of N 30° W tells you to start facing north and turn 30° toward the west.

EXERCISE

1·3

Point A is 100 meters due west of point B. The bearings of point C from point A and from point B are given. Find the measures of the angles of △ABC.

1. From *A*: N 23° E   From *B*: N 36° W
2. From *A*: N 14° E   From *B*: N 45° W
3. From *A*: N 62° W   From *B*: N 81° W
4. From *A*: S 4° W   From *B*: S 72° W
5. From *A*: S 55° E   From *B*: S 12° E
6. From *A*: N 22° E   From *B*: N 17° W
7. From *A*: N 78° E   From *B*: N 29° W
8. From *A*: S 64° E   From *B*: S 63° E
9. From *A*: S 64° E   From *B*: S 63° E
10. From *A*: N 19° W   From *B*: N 89° W

Angle of elevation and angle of depression

In many trigonometry problems, you'll hear about the angle of elevation or the angle of depression. If you imagine standing looking straight ahead and then raising your eyes to look up at an object, the angle between your original horizontal gaze and your line of sight to the object above is the angle of elevation. On the other hand, if you're in an elevated position, looking straight ahead, and shift your gaze down to an object below, the angle between your original horizontal gaze and your line of sight to the object below is the angle of depression. Since the horizontal lines are parallel, a little basic geometry shows that the angle of elevation is equal to the angle of depression.

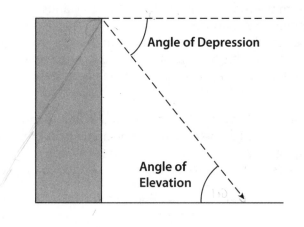

EXERCISE 1·4

Find the specified angle(s).

1. From a point 200 yards from the foot of a building, the angle of elevation to the top of the building is 37°. Find the measures of the angles of the triangle formed by the building, the ground, and the line of sight to the top of the building.

2. The angle of depression from the top of a lighthouse to a ship at sea is 12°48'. Find the measures of the angles of the triangle formed by the lighthouse, the sea, and the line of sight to the ship.

3. The angle of depression from the top of a tower to an observer on the ground is 37°. Find the angle of elevation from the observer to the top of the tower.

4. The ground, a 90 foot tower, and the line of sight to the top of the tower from a point 25 yards away from the base of the tower form a right triangle. If the acute angles of the triangle are 50° and 40°, what is the angle of depression from the top of the tower to an observer on the ground?

5. From point *F*, 500 meters from the foot of a cliff, *B*, the angle of elevation to the top of the cliff, *T*, is 54°27'. From the top of the cliff, *T*, the angle of depression to a point *N*, 200 meters from the foot of the cliff, is 74°3'. Find the measure of ∠*FTN*.

6. From a plane *P* at an altitude of 2,500 feet, a pilot can see a tower 5 miles ahead. The angle of depression to the top of the tower, *T*, is 4°58' and the angle of depression to the bottom of the tower, *B*, is 5°24'. Find the measure of ∠*PBT*.

7. From the Top of the Rock, the observation deck at Rockefeller Center (call it T), 850 feet above street level, a visitor can look north and see Central Park. If the visitor looks down at the northern edge of the park, N, the angle of depression is 2°58'. If the visitor looks to the southern edge of the park, S, the angle of depression is 12°57'. Find ∠NST.

8. When ready for launch, the space shuttle, with its fuel tanks, stands 184 feet high. From a point level with the launch pad, 1 mile away, the angle of elevation to the highest point of the shuttle assembly is 2°. From another point, on the beach south of the launch site, the angle of elevation to the highest point of the shuttle assembly is about 0°10'. Find the measure of the angle formed by connecting the beach viewing site to the highest point on the shuttle to the 1 mile viewing site.

9. In ideal weather, from the top of the Eiffel Tower, which stands 324 meters high, it is possible to see a point on the horizon 67.5 kilometers away. A tourist at the top of the Eiffel Tower on such a perfect day looks out at that distant horizon and the angle of depression is 0°16'30". The tourist then shifts his gaze 3°50'30" to look down at the Jardin du Luxembourg, 4.5 kilometers away. What is the angle of depression from the top of the Eiffel Tower to the Jardin du Luxembourg?

10. The London Eye reaches a height of 135 meters, and from the top, it is possible for a rider to see Buckingham Palace, 1.9 kilometers away, at an angle of depression of 4°3'. If a rider at the top shifts her gaze up 2°54', she will be able to see Windsor Castle, 6.6 kilometers away. What is the angle of depression from the top of the London Eye to Windsor Castle?

Similar triangles

In geometry, you studied similar triangles. Triangles with corresponding angles congruent and corresponding sides in proportion have the same shape but different sizes. They appear as enlargements or reductions of one another.

Similar right triangles

When you begin to consider similarity in right triangles, you immediately know that the right angles are congruent. If you also know that an acute angle of one right triangle is congruent to an acute angle of the other, you can be certain that the third angles are congruent as well, and the triangles are similar. If the triangles are similar, the corresponding sides are in proportion.

If you look at two right triangles, each with an acute angle of 25°, you can quickly prove that the two triangles are similar. In fact, all right triangles containing an angle of 25° are similar, and you might think of them as a family. Throughout the family of 25° right triangles, the corresponding sides are in proportion. If you call the legs a and b and the hypotenuse c,

$$\frac{a \text{ in one triangle}}{a \text{ in the second triangle}} = \frac{b \text{ in one triangle}}{b \text{ in the second triangle}} = \frac{c \text{ in one triangle}}{c \text{ in the second triangle}}$$

If you focus on any two of those ratios, so that you have a proportion, and apply a property of proportions that you learned in algebra, you can say

$$\frac{a \text{ in one triangle}}{b \text{ in one triangle}} = \frac{a \text{ in the second triangle}}{b \text{ in the second triangle}}$$

$$\frac{a \text{ in one triangle}}{c \text{ in one triangle}} = \frac{a \text{ in the second triangle}}{c \text{ in the second triangle}}$$

$$\frac{b \text{ in one triangle}}{c \text{ in one triangle}} = \frac{b \text{ in the second triangle}}{c \text{ in the second triangle}}$$

In any right triangle in this family, the ratio of the side opposite the 25° angle to the hypotenuse will always be the same; likewise, the ratios of other pairs of sides will remain constant throughout the family. Trigonometry takes advantage of that fact and assigns a name to each of the possible ratios.

Trigonometric ratios

If the three sides of the right triangle are labeled as the hypotenuse, the side opposite a particular acute angle, A, and the side adjacent to the acute angle A, six different ratios are possible. The six ratios are called the sine, cosine, tangent, cosecant, secant, and cotangent, and are defined as

$$\sin A = \frac{\text{opposite}}{\text{hypotenuse}} \qquad \csc A = \frac{\text{hypotenuse}}{\text{opposite}}$$

$$\cos A = \frac{\text{adjacent}}{\text{hypotenuse}} \qquad \sec A = \frac{\text{hypotenuse}}{\text{adjacent}}$$

$$\tan A = \frac{\text{opposite}}{\text{adjacent}} \qquad \cot A = \frac{\text{adjacent}}{\text{opposite}}$$

Notice that three of the ratios are reciprocals of the other three. The cosecant is the reciprocal of the sine, the secant and the cosine are reciprocals, and the cotangent is the reciprocal of the tangent. It's also true that the tangent is equal to the sine divided by the cosine:

$$\frac{\sin A}{\cos A} = \frac{\text{opposite}}{\text{hypotenuse}} \div \frac{\text{adjacent}}{\text{hypotenuse}} = \frac{\text{opposite}}{\cancel{\text{hypotenuse}}} \times \frac{\cancel{\text{hypotenuse}}}{\text{adjacent}} = \frac{\text{opposite}}{\text{adjacent}} = \tan A$$

A similar argument shows that the cotangent is equal to the cosine divided by the sine.

If $\angle A$ and $\angle B$ are the acute angles of right $\triangle ABC$, the side opposite $\angle A$ is adjacent to $\angle B$ and the side opposite $\angle B$ is adjacent to $\angle A$, but the hypotenuse is always the hypotenuse. This means that $\sin \angle A = \dfrac{BC}{AB} = \cos \angle B$, $\cos \angle A = \dfrac{AC}{AB} = \sin \angle B$, and $\tan \angle A = \dfrac{BC}{AC} = \cot \angle B$.

In more general terms, because the two acute angles of a right triangle are complementary, the sine of an angle is the cosine of its complement, and the tangent of an angle is the cotangent of its complement. In fact, the "co" in cosine (and cotangent and cosecant) comes from the "co" in complementary. The cosine is the complementary sine, or the sine of the complement. The cosecant is the secant of the complement, and the cotangent is the tangent of the complement.

Special right triangles

Isosceles right triangles and 30°-60°-90° right triangles pop up in enough different circumstances that you probably learned the relationships of the sides by memory. The isosceles, or 45°-45°-90°, right triangle has legs of equal length and a hypotenuse equal to that length times the square root of 2. If the legs of the isosceles right triangle measure 8 centimeters, the hypotenuse will be $8\sqrt{2}$ centimeters. If the hypotenuse is 14 inches, the legs will be $\dfrac{14}{\sqrt{2}} = \dfrac{14\sqrt{2}}{2} = 7\sqrt{2}$.

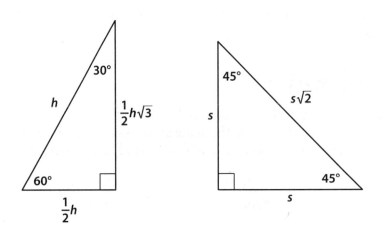

In the 30°-60°-90° right triangle, the shorter leg, opposite the 30° angle, is half as long as the hypotenuse, and the longer leg, opposite the 60° angle, is half the hypotenuse times the square root of 3. If the hypotenuse is 10 centimeters, the shorter leg is 5 centimeters and the longer leg is $5\sqrt{3}$ centimeters. If you know the shorter side, tack on a $\sqrt{3}$ to get the longer side but double the short leg to get the hypotenuse. If the short leg is 3 centimeters, the longer leg is $3\sqrt{3}$ centimeters and the hypotenuse is 6 centimeters. To find the other sides when you're given the longer leg, divide by $\sqrt{3}$ to get the shorter leg and then double the shorter leg to get the hypotenuse. In a 30°-60°-90° right triangle with a longer leg of 18 centimeters, the shorter leg is $\dfrac{18}{\sqrt{3}} = \dfrac{18\sqrt{3}}{3} = 6\sqrt{3}$ centimeters and the hypotenuse is $12\sqrt{3}$ centimeters.

Because you know the relationships of the sides of those triangles, you can easily determine the values of the trigonometric ratios for angles of 30°, 45°, and 60°:

	sin	cos	tan
30°	$\dfrac{1}{2}$	$\dfrac{\sqrt{3}}{2}$	$\dfrac{\sqrt{3}}{3}$
45°	$\dfrac{\sqrt{2}}{2}$	$\dfrac{\sqrt{2}}{2}$	1
60°	$\dfrac{\sqrt{3}}{2}$	$\dfrac{1}{2}$	$\sqrt{3}$

Find the missing sides of each 45°-45°-90° right triangle.

1. △ABC with hypotenuse AC measuring $7\sqrt{2}$ inches

2. △XYZ with leg XY measuring 4 centimeters

3. △ARM with hypotenuse AM measuring 12 feet

4. △LEG with leg EG measuring $5\sqrt{6}$ meters

5. △RST with hypotenuse RT measuring $8\sqrt{14}$ centimeters

Find the missing sides of each 30°-60°-90° right triangle.

6. △XYZ with hypotenuse XZ measuring 50 meters

7. △ABC with shorter leg AB measuring 9 centimeters

8. △RST with longer leg ST measuring $7\sqrt{3}$ inches

9. △CAT with shorter leg CA measuring $14\sqrt{6}$ feet

10. △DOG with hypotenuse DG measuring $4\sqrt{21}$ centimeters

Find the indicated ratios from memory.

11. sin 45°

12. tan 30°

13. cos 60°

14. tan 45°

15. sec 60°

16. csc 30°

17. cot 60°

18. cos 45°

19. sin 30°

20. sec 45°

Finding sides

With these six ratios, it is possible to solve for any unknown side of the right triangle, if another side and an acute angle are known, or to find the angle if two sides are known. You just need to choose a ratio that incorporates the side you know and the side that you want to find, and substitute the values you know. Then you'll have to look up the sine, cosine, or tangent of the angle. Once upon a time, students had to rely on tables to look up the values of the ratios for each family of right triangles, but now the sine, cosine, and tangent of an angle can be found with a few keystrokes on your calculator.

In right $\triangle ABC$, hypotenuse AC is 6 centimeters long and $\angle A$ measures $32°$. To find the length of the shorter leg, first make a sketch to help you visualize the triangle. The shorter leg will be opposite the smaller angle. If one of the acute angles is $32°$, the other is $58°$, so you need to find the side opposite the $32°$ angle, or side BC. If you use the $32°$ angle, you need a ratio that includes the opposite side and the hypotenuse. You can choose between sine (sin) and cosecant (csc), but since your calculator has a key for sin but not for csc, sine is more convenient:

$$\sin 32° = \frac{BC}{AC} = \frac{x}{6}$$

From your calculator, you can find that

$$\sin 32° \approx 0.53$$

so

$$0.53 = \frac{x}{6}$$

and

$$x \approx 3.2$$

EXERCISE

1·6

Solve the following.

1. In right $\triangle RST$, $\angle S$ is a right angle and $RT = 24$. If $\angle T$ measures $30°$, find the length of RS.

2. Given $\triangle XYZ$ with $\angle Y$ a right angle and hypotenuse XZ equal to 42. If $\angle X = 56°$, find the length of side YZ to the nearest tenth.

3. In right $\triangle ABC$ with right angle at C, $\angle A = 46°36'$ and side AC is 42 feet. Find the lengths of the other two sides.

4. In right $\triangle ABC$ with right angle at C, $\angle B = 76°30'$ and side BC is 80 feet. Find the lengths of the other two sides.

5. In right $\triangle XYZ$ with right angle at Y, $\angle X = 32°$ and side YZ is 58 meters. Find the lengths of the other two sides.

6. From onboard a ship at sea, the angle of elevation to the top of a lighthouse is $41°$. If the lighthouse is known to be 50 feet high, how far from shore is the ship?

7. A ladder 28 feet long makes an angle of $15°$ with the wall of a building. How far from the wall is the foot of the ladder?

8. From the top of the ski slope, Elise sees the lodge at an angle of depression of $18°30'$. If the slope is known to have an elevation of 1,500 feet, how far does Elise have to ski to reach the lodge?

9. From a point 85 feet from the base of the schoolhouse, the angle of elevation to the bottom of a flagpole on the roof of the schoolhouse is $38°30'$. Find the height of the schoolhouse.

10. If the angle of elevation to the top of the flagpole in question 9 is $54°36'$, how tall is the flagpole?

11. The angle of depression from the top of a security tower to the entrance to a plaza is 42°. If the tower is 20 feet high, how far is it from the entrance to the base of the tower?

12. From the seats in the top deck of a baseball stadium, the angle of depression to home plate is 22°. If the diagonal distance from home plate to the top deck is 320 feet, how high is the top deck?

13. When Claire is lying in bed watching television, the angle of elevation from her pillow to the TV is 23°. If Claire's TV is mounted on the wall 7.5 feet above the level of the bed, how far is her pillow from the wall?

14. If an observer notes that the angle of elevation to the top of a 162 meter tower is 38°24', how far is the observer from the tower?

15. In △ABC, AB = 13 feet and ∠A measures 29.5°. If △ABC is not a right triangle, find the altitude BD from B to AC.

16. In △ABC, as noted in question 15, AB = 13 feet, ∠A measures 29.5°, and △ABC is not a right triangle. If AC measures 22 feet and the altitude from B meets AC at D, find the length of AD.

17. In △ABC, as noted in questions 15 and 16, AB = 13 feet, ∠A measures 29.5°, and △ABC is not a right triangle. If ∠C = 18° and the altitude from B meets AC at D, find the length of BC.

18. △PQR has ∠Q = 32° and ∠R = 38°. If PR = 369 feet, find the length of the altitude PT from P to QR.

19. In △PQR, as noted in question 18, ∠Q = 32°, ∠R = 38°, and PR = 369 feet. Find the length of PQ.

20. Use the information in questions 18 and 19 to find the length of QR.

Finding angles

In addition to finding the other sides of a right triangle when you know one side and the angle measures, trigonometric ratios can be used to find the measures of the acute angles of the right triangle if you know the lengths of the sides. Knowing two sides is adequate, because you know that the Pythagorean theorem applies to the sides, so you could find the third side if necessary. You also know that one of the angles is 90°, so you only need to find one of the acute angles and subtract from 90° to find the other.

If you know the lengths of two sides of the right triangle, you can calculate one of the ratios. Which ratio will be determined by which sides you know. Once you know the ratio, you'll work backward to the angle. If you're working with tables of trigonometric ratios, that means poring through the tables, looking for the value of the sin, cos, or tan closest to the value you have to see what angle it belongs to. If you're using a calculator, it's a little easier.

Arcsin, arccos, arctan

Working backward means you know the sine (or cosine or tangent) of the angle and want to find the angle that has that sine. The common way to say "the angle whose sine is N" is arcsin N. The "arc" in arcsin comes from the fact that the measure of a central angle is equal to the measure of its intercepted arc. The name is saying "the arc (and therefore the angle) that has this sine." In the next chapter, when talking about trigonometric functions, you'll use the inverse function notation $\sin^{-1} N$ to denote the number whose sine is N. You'll see these two notations used interchangeably, although there actually is a subtle difference in their meaning.

Each of the trigonometric ratios has an inverse. Just as the angle whose sine is N can be denoted as arcsin N, the angle whose cosine is N can be indicated by arcos N and the angle whose tangent is N by arctan N. You'll find a way to enter each of the inverses on your calculator, usually as a second function or inverse function on the keys for sin, cos, and tan. The calculator keys may be marked with the inverse function symbols $\sin^{-1}$, $\cos^{-1}$, and $\tan^{-1}$.

If the legs of a right triangle measure 18 centimeters and 25 centimeters, you can find the measures of the acute angles by using the two known sides to find the tangent of one of the angles. The tangent of the smaller angle will be $\dfrac{18}{25}$, or the tangent of the larger angle will be $\dfrac{25}{18}$, but you can work with either one. To find the measure of the angle, use the $\tan^{-1}$ key on your calculator: $\tan^{-1}\dfrac{18}{25} \approx 35.75°$ or $35°45'$. The two acute angles of a right triangle are complementary, so the larger of the acute angles measures approximately $90° - 35°45' = 54°15'$.

EXERCISE
1·7

Solve the following.

1. Find the measures of the angles of a right triangle with legs of 16 inches and 35 inches.

2. Find the measures of the angles of a right triangle with a hypotenuse of 592.7 meters and a leg of 86.4 meters.

3. If the leg of a right triangle measures 349.2 centimeters and the hypotenuse measures 716.8 centimeters, find the measure of each of the acute angles.

4. Find the measures of the angles of a 3-4-5 right triangle.

5. Find the measures of the angles of a 5-12-13 right triangle.

6. A mountain slope rises 760 feet in a quarter mile on the horizontal. If 1 mile = 5,280 feet, what angle does the slope make with the horizontal?

7. If the sides of a rectangle measure 5 inches and 12 inches, what angle does the diagonal of the rectangle make with the longer side?

8. What is the angle of elevation of the sun at the instant a 68 foot flagpole casts a shadow of 81 feet?

9. In $\triangle ABC$, $AB = 25$ inches and altitude BD measures 16 inches. Find the measure of $\angle A$ to the nearest degree.

10. What angle does a stairway make with the floor if the steps have a tread of 9 inches and a rise of 7.5 inches?

11. In right $\triangle ABC$ with right angle at C, $AC = 22$ meters and $BC = 72$ meters. Find the measure of $\angle B$.

12. In right $\triangle XYZ$, leg $XZ = 35$ inches and leg $YZ = 16$ inches. Find the measure of $\angle X$.

13. If a 20 foot ladder is positioned to reach 15 feet up on the wall, what angle does the foot of the ladder make with the ground?

14. If the legs of a right triangle measure 349.2 meters and 716.8 meters, find the measures of the acute angles of the triangle.

15. Midville is 47.39 miles due north of Smalltown and 96.42 miles from Centerville. If Centerville is due west of Smalltown, find the bearing of Midville from Centerville.

16. Katrina's office building is exactly half a mile from City Hall, and she knows that the office building is 220 feet high. If Katrina stands on the roof of her office building and looks down at city hall, what is the angle of depression? (There are 5,280 feet in 1 mile.)

17. The diagonal of a rectangle measures 19 inches. If the shorter side of the rectangle measures 8 inches, find the measure of the angle between the diagonal and the longer side.

18. In football, the crossbar of the goal post is 10 feet high and is positioned at the end line, 10 yards beyond the goal line, so a field goal kicked from the 30-yard line must travel 40 yards. Find the angle of elevation of the crossbar from the 30-yard line.

19. Using the information in question 18, find the angle of elevation of the crossbar from the 20 yard line.

20. Using the information in question 18, find the angle of elevation of the crossbar from the 5 yard line.

Finding areas

In geometry, you learned that the area of a parallelogram is the product of its base and its height, $A = bh$, and that the area of a triangle is half the product of its base and its height, $A = \frac{1}{2}bh$. The problem you sometimes encountered in trying to use those formulas was that while you might know the lengths of the sides, you didn't always know the altitude, or height, and didn't have a convenient way to find it.

Thanks to right triangle trigonometry, that problem can sometimes be solved. If you know two sides of a triangle and the angle included between them, or two adjacent sides of a parallelogram and the angle included between them, it's possible to use trig ratios to find the height.

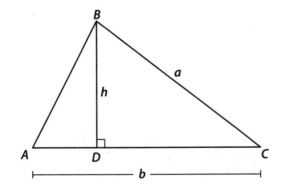

Look first at the triangle. You know the lengths of two sides, a and b, and the measurement of the angle between them, $\angle C$. Drop a perpendicular from vertex B to side b. If you can find the length of that altitude to side b, you can calculate the area. Because the perpendicular creates a right triangle, in which side a is the hypotenuse and the altitude, call it x, is the side opposite $\angle C$, you can find the height by using the trigonometric ratio $\sin C = \frac{x}{a}$ or $x = a \sin C$.

If you incorporate that new information into the area formula for a triangle, $A = \frac{1}{2}bh$, you get a new formula for the area of a triangle:

$$A = \frac{1}{2}bh$$
$$= \frac{1}{2}b \cdot a \sin C$$
$$= \frac{1}{2}ab \sin C$$

If you know two sides of a triangle and the angle included between them, the area of the triangle is half the product of the two sides and the sine of the included angle. A triangle with sides of 4 centimeters and 7 centimeters and an included angle of 50° has an area of

$$A = \frac{1}{2}ab \sin C$$
$$= \frac{1}{2}(4)(7)\sin 50°$$
$$= 14(0.766)$$
$$\approx 10.725 \text{ cm}^2$$

With a similar logic, you can modify the formula for the area of a parallelogram. Drop an altitude from one vertex to the opposite side. If you know the lengths of two adjacent sides, you can find the altitude because one of your sides forms the hypotenuse of the right triangle created by the altitude. If you call the side that forms the hypotenuse a and call the included angle $\angle C$, then the length of the altitude is $a \sin C$ and the area of the parallelogram is $A = ab \sin C$.

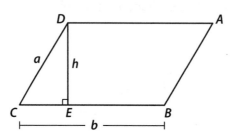

To find the area of a parallelogram with sides of 18 inches and 22 inches and an included angle of 60°, use the area formula

$$A = ab \sin C$$
$$= 18 \cdot 22 \sin 60°$$
$$= 396 \cdot \frac{\sqrt{3}}{2}$$
$$= 198\sqrt{3} \text{ in.}^2$$

Find the height of each triangle to the nearest tenth.

1. In △ABC, AB = 4 centimeters, BC = 6 centimeters, and ∠B = 57°. Find the altitude from A.

2. In △XYZ, XY = 6 inches, YZ = 14 inches, and ∠Y = 83°. Find the altitude from X.

3. In △DOG, DO = 9 feet, OG = 10 feet, and ∠O = 84°. Find the altitude from D.

4. In △CAT, CA = 12 meters, AT = 6 meters, and ∠A = 51°. Find the altitude from T.

5. In △RST, RS = 8.5 kilometers, ST = 3 kilometers, and ∠S = 102°. Find the altitude from R.

Find the height of each parallelogram to the nearest tenth.

6. In ▱ABCD, AB = 6 centimeters, BC = 9.4 centimeters, and ∠B = 105°. Find the altitude from A.

7. In ▱WXYZ, WX = 5 yards, XY = 8 yards, and ∠X = 30°. Find the altitude from W.

8. In ▱FROG, FR = 5 kilometers, RO = 5 kilometers, and ∠R = 150°. Find the altitude from F.

9. In ▱MATH, MA = 5 feet, AT = 5 feet, and ∠A = 62°. Find the altitude from M.

10. In ▱SODA, SO = 3 meters, OD = 10 meters, and ∠O = 57°. Find the altitude from S.

Find the area of each triangle to the nearest tenth.

11. In △RST, RS = 10, ST = 7.5, and ∠S = 121°. Find the area.

12. In △ARM, AR = 10, RM = 7.5, and ∠R = 84°. Find the area.

13. In △LEG, LE = 10, EG = 7.5, and ∠E = 30°. Find the area.

14. In △XYZ, XY = 12, YZ = 4, and ∠Y = 121°. Find the area.

15. In △ABC, AB = 12, BC = 4, and ∠B = 9°. Find the area.

Find the area of each parallelogram to the nearest tenth.

16. In ▱CHEM, CH = 2.8, HE = 3.5, and ∠H = 54°. Find the area.

17. In ▱LOVE, LO = 5, OV = 7, and ∠O = 75°. Find the area.

18. In ▱SOAP, SO = 1.5, OA = 11, and ∠O = 67°. Find the area.

19. In ▱NEXT, NE = 3, EX = 9, and ∠E = 140°. Find the area.

20. In ▱ABCD, AB = 3, BC = 4, and ∠B = 97°. Find the area.

Trigonometric functions  ·2·

Trigonometry, or triangle measurement, begins in the right triangle, but it doesn't have to be restricted to right triangles or to triangles at all. By introducing what are called the trigonometric functions, you can carry the ideas of triangle trigonometry into a broader world. By moving the right triangle onto the coordinate plane and observing the interaction between the triangle and a circle centered at the origin, you can define six trigonometric functions, based on the six trig ratios, but not tied to the right triangle. With those functions, it becomes possible to talk about the sine, cosine, and tangent (or other functions) of an angle of any size.

Radian measure

When you define a function, the domain of the function is the largest subset of the real numbers for which the rule has meaning. Up to this point, all the angles whose sine, cosine, or tangent you've calculated have been measured in degrees. To begin to talk about trigonometry in function terms, it is helpful to move to a different system of measurement called radian measure that allows you to talk about the domain of the trig functions as subsets of the real numbers.

A radian is the measure of a central angle whose intercepted arc is equal in length to the radius of the circle. Imagine that you cut a piece of string exactly the length of the radius of a circle and then place that string on the circumference of the circle. Draw two radii, one from the center to one end of the string and one from the center to the other end of the string. The central angle that results has a measurement of 1 radian.

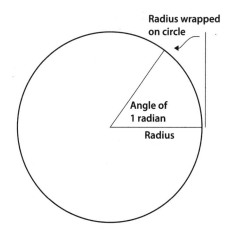

If you cut several strings that size and started to place them end to end around the circle, you'd find you can fit 6 of them, with a little bit of space left over. That's because the circumference of a circle is 2π times the radius. Your string is the same length as the radius, so 2π, or a little more than 6, of them fit around the circumference. There are 2π radians in a full rotation, π radians in a half rotation.

If you need to convert from degrees to radians or radians to degrees, you can use the proportion $\dfrac{\text{degrees}}{360°} = \dfrac{\text{radians}}{2\pi}$. Simply fill in the degree measure or radian measure that you know and a variable for the one you don't know and solve the proportion.

To find the radian equivalent of 135°, set up the proportion and put 135 in the degrees position. Then cross multiply and solve:

$$\frac{\text{degrees}}{360°} = \frac{\text{radians}}{2\pi}$$

$$\frac{135°}{360°} = \frac{r}{2\pi}$$

$$360r = 135 \cdot 2\pi$$

$$360r = 270\pi$$

$$r = \frac{270\pi}{360} = \frac{3\pi}{4}$$

The radian equivalent of 135° is $\dfrac{3\pi}{4}$ radians.

Common angles in radians

Just as you learned the relationships of sides in common right triangles, you'll find it helpful to know the radian equivalent of common angles:

$0° = 0$ radians	$30° = \dfrac{\pi}{6}$ radians	$45° = \dfrac{\pi}{4}$ radians
$60° = \dfrac{\pi}{3}$ radians		$90° = \dfrac{\pi}{2}$ radians

Don't become dependent on conversion, however. You want to work, and think, in radians. Learn to count around the circle, starting from the positive x-axis, by multiples of $\dfrac{\pi}{2}$, by multiples of $\dfrac{\pi}{3}$, by multiples of $\dfrac{\pi}{4}$, and by multiples of $\dfrac{\pi}{6}$. Develop a mental image of where each of the multiples falls.

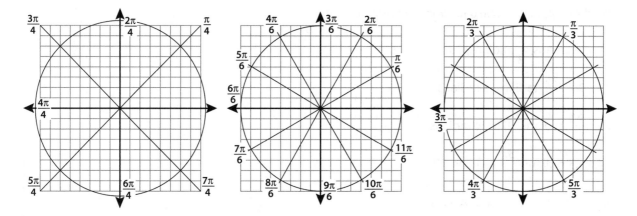

Learn to estimate where values like 3.2 radians or 2.5 radians will fall. Remember, half the circle is π, and π is a little more than 3, or approximately 3.14. So 3.2 is just beyond half a rotation. An angle of 2.5 radians is smaller, but how much smaller? If half a rotation is π, a quarter circle is half of π, so a little more than 1.5 radians. An angle of 2.5 radians will fall past the quarter circle but before the half circle, and closer to the half. Obviously, these are just approximations, but learning to make those estimates will help you work more comfortably with radians.

Comparing angles

One of the advantages of radian measure, from the point of view of defining functions, is that you're using real numbers. You may encounter measurements like 8.63 radians or −2.5 radians, but often radian measures will be multiples or fractions of π, because there are 2π radians in a full rotation.

To compare angle measurements like $\frac{2\pi}{3}$ and $\frac{3\pi}{4}$, simply compare the fractions: $\frac{2}{3} < \frac{3}{4}$ so $\frac{2\pi}{3} < \frac{3\pi}{4}$. To compare a measurement like $\frac{2\pi}{3}$ with something like 1.5 radians, remember that π is slightly more than 3, so $\frac{2\pi}{3}$ is a little more than 2 radians, while 1.5 radians is closer to $\frac{\pi}{2}$.

EXERCISE
2·1

Find the radian equivalent of each angle measure.

1. 40°
2. 135°
3. 270°
4. 330°
5. 450°
6. 120°
7. 225°
8. 300°
9. 765°
10. 2,025°

Find the degree equivalent of each angle measure.

11. $\frac{\pi}{4}-1$
12. $\frac{5\pi}{6}$
13. $\frac{5\pi}{3}$
14. $-\frac{3\pi}{2}$
15. $-\frac{7\pi}{4}$
16. $-\frac{7\pi}{2}$
17. $\frac{17\pi}{4}$
18. $\frac{17\pi}{6}$
19. $\frac{\pi}{12}$
20. $-\frac{5\pi}{9}$

Put the angle measures in order from smallest to largest.

21. 2 radians, $\dfrac{\pi}{3}$ radians, 75°

22. 94°, $\dfrac{5\pi}{6}$ radians, 3 radians

23. $\dfrac{5\pi}{4}$ radians, 220°, 4 radians

24. 5.5 radians, $\dfrac{3\pi}{2}$ radians, 280°

25. 12°, $\dfrac{\pi}{12}$ radians, 1.2 radians

Angles in standard position

An angle is in *standard position* if its vertex is at the origin and one of its sides, called the initial side, lies on the positive *x*-axis. The other side of the angle is called the terminal side. Think about the sides of the angle like the hands of a clock, one of which—the initial side—is stuck pointing to 3, and the other—the terminal side—is able to rotate. If the direction of rotation is counterclockwise, the measure of the angle between the two sides is considered to be positive. If the direction of rotation is clockwise, the measure of the angle is negative. Angles may be acute, right, obtuse, straight, or reflex (more than a straight angle). An angle may even be more than a full rotation, so it's quite possible to have an angle of 18.5 radians or $-\dfrac{17\pi}{3}$ radians.

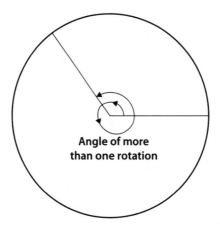

Angle of more than one rotation

Because the terminal side can rotate in different directions and can complete any number of rotations before reaching its final position, two angles in standard position may have different measurements yet share the same terminal side. One may be a positive angle while the other is negative, or one may include one or more full rotations while the other is less than a full rotation. Angles that share the same terminal side are called coterminal angles.

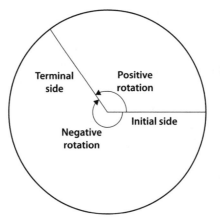

An angle of $\dfrac{2\pi}{3}$ in standard position has a terminal side in the second quadrant, as shown in the figure above. That ray is also the terminal side of an angle of $-\dfrac{4\pi}{3}$. One angle rotates in the positive direction and one in the negative direction, but both terminal sides wind up in the same place. Because we allow angles of more than a full rotation, that same side is also the terminal side of an angle that completes a full rotation in the positive direction plus $\dfrac{2\pi}{3}$, that is, an angle of $\dfrac{8\pi}{3}$. Start in standard position and move clockwise a full rotation and another $\dfrac{4\pi}{3}$ in this negative direction and you have an angle of $-\dfrac{10\pi}{3}$, which is also coterminal with $\dfrac{2\pi}{3}$. You're not limited to how many full rotations you can use, so there are infinitely many positive angles and infinitely many negative angles that are coterminal.

EXERCISE 2·2

Sketch an angle in standard position with the given measurement.

1. $\dfrac{\pi}{2}$
4. $\dfrac{2\pi}{3}$
7. $-\dfrac{5\pi}{3}$
10. $-\dfrac{9\pi}{2}$

2. $\dfrac{3\pi}{4}$
5. $-\dfrac{5\pi}{4}$
8. $\dfrac{11\pi}{4}$

3. $-\dfrac{\pi}{6}$
6. 5π
9. $-\dfrac{17\pi}{6}$

Find a positive angle and a negative angle coterminal with the given angle.

11. $\dfrac{\pi}{2}$
14. $-\dfrac{7\pi}{4}$
17. $\dfrac{11\pi}{9}$
20. $-\dfrac{13\pi}{6}$

12. $\dfrac{11\pi}{6}$
15. 3π
18. $-\dfrac{7\pi}{3}$

13. $-\dfrac{5\pi}{3}$
16. $\dfrac{5\pi}{6}$
19. $\dfrac{7\pi}{4}$

The unit circle

Imagine a circle on the coordinate plane, with its center at the origin and with a radius of 1. Such a circle is called a unit circle. You're going to look at central angles of the unit circle, specifically, angles in standard form. The unit circle has a particular property that will let you extend what you know about trigonometric ratios to larger angles.

Choose a point on the circle somewhere in the first quadrant. Connect the origin to the point and, from that point, drop a perpendicular to the x-axis. This creates a right triangle with a hypotenuse of 1.

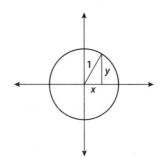

Call the angle at the origin between the positive x-axis and the hypotenuse θ. This angle is in standard position. Its initial side is the positive x-axis, along which one leg of the right triangle sits, and its terminal side contains the hypotenuse of the right triangle, a hypotenuse that measures 1 because it is the radius of the unit circle. The lengths of the legs of that right triangle are the x- and y-coordinates of the point you chose.

Apply what you know about right triangle trigonometry to this triangle, and something interesting emerges. If the point you chose is (x, y), then

$$\sin\theta = \frac{\text{opposite}}{\text{hypotenuse}} = \frac{y}{1}$$
$$\cos\theta = \frac{\text{adjacent}}{\text{hypotenuse}} = \frac{x}{1}$$
$$\tan\theta = \frac{\text{opposite}}{\text{adjacent}} = \frac{y}{x}$$

If you know the coordinates of the point where the terminal side of the angle intersects the unit circle, you know cos θ and sin θ, because they are the coordinates of that point. You can find tan θ by dividing the coordinates, and if you're interested in sec θ, csc θ, or cot θ, they're just the reciprocals.

If you're appropriately skeptical, you're probably wondering if this is just a coincidence of the point you chose, but more investigation will show you that it's not. You can repeat the experiment for any point along the unit circle in the first quadrant and get the same result.

What's important about this result is that it gives you a way to define the sine, cosine, and tangent of an angle θ, in standard position, whether it's acute, right, obtuse, or larger, and even if it's negative.

If θ is an angle in standard position and the terminal side of θ intersects the unit circle at the point (x, y), then you can define

$$\sin\theta = y \qquad\qquad \csc\theta = \frac{1}{y}$$

$$\cos\theta = x \qquad\qquad \sec\theta = \frac{1}{x}$$

$$\tan\theta = \frac{y}{x} \qquad\qquad \cot\theta = \frac{x}{y}$$

This gives you a method of finding the sine, cosine, or other values based solely on the point where the terminal side intersects the unit circle. No right triangles are required. Even angles that wouldn't fit in a right triangle can now be assigned a sine or cosine. If $\theta = \frac{5\pi}{4}$, the terminal side falls in the third quadrant, intersecting the unit circle at the point $\left(-\frac{\sqrt{2}}{2}, -\frac{\sqrt{2}}{2}\right)$. Using that point, you can determine that

$$\sin\frac{5\pi}{4} = -\frac{\sqrt{2}}{2} \qquad\qquad \csc\frac{5\pi}{4} = -\frac{2}{\sqrt{2}} = -\sqrt{2}$$

$$\cos\frac{5\pi}{4} = -\frac{\sqrt{2}}{2} \qquad\qquad \sec\frac{5\pi}{4} = -\frac{2}{\sqrt{2}} = -\sqrt{2}$$

$$\tan\frac{5\pi}{4} = 1 \qquad\qquad \cot\frac{5\pi}{4} = 1$$

EXERCISE
2·3

Determine the point at which the terminal side of the angle intersects the unit circle. Use special right triangle relationships where helpful.

1. $\frac{\pi}{4}$

2. $\frac{2\pi}{3}$

3. $-\frac{\pi}{2}$

4. $\frac{7\pi}{6}$

5. $-\frac{5\pi}{4}$

6. $\frac{14\pi}{3}$

7. $-\frac{11\pi}{6}$

8. $\frac{15\pi}{4}$

9. $-\frac{9\pi}{2}$

10. $\frac{7\pi}{4}$

Find the value of each expression.

11. $\sin\frac{\pi}{4}$

12. $\cos\frac{2\pi}{3}$

13. $\tan\frac{11\pi}{6}$

14. $\cos\left(-\frac{4\pi}{3}\right)$

15. $\sin\left(-\frac{\pi}{2}\right)$

16. $\tan\pi$

17. $\sin\frac{11\pi}{3}$

18. $\cos\frac{13\pi}{4}$

19. $\tan\left(-\frac{7\pi}{6}\right)$

20. $\cos\frac{19\pi}{2}$

Trigonometric functions

You've extended the idea of trigonometric ratios for the acute angles of a right triangle to a wider world in which it's possible to find the sine, cosine, and tangent and their reciprocals for any angle in standard position, if you know the point at which the terminal side of the angle intersects the unit circle. This in turn broadens your understanding of ideas like the sine from a ratio of two sides of a triangle to a function that assigns to every real number θ a value that we call $\sin \theta$ and that we define by the y-coordinate of that point on the unit circle. Now you can talk about trig functions rather than trig ratios.

Domains and ranges

Whenever you consider a new function, you want to think about the domain and range of the function. The domain is the set of all inputs, or values of the independent variable, for which the function is defined. The sine function and cosine function are defined for all real numbers, but the other trig functions, because of the denominators in their definitions, have restricted domains.

The sine and cosine functions are defined for all real numbers, so their domain is $(-\infty, \infty)$, and because each of them is equal to one of the coordinates of a point on the unit circle, each of them returns values between −1 and 1, so their range is $[-1, 1]$.

The functions that have x in the denominator of their definition, tangent and secant, are undefined where x is 0, or, put another way, where the cosine is 0. The cosine will equal 0 when θ is $\dfrac{\pi}{2}$ or $\dfrac{3\pi}{2}$ or $\dfrac{5\pi}{2}$ or any positive or negative odd multiple of $\dfrac{\pi}{2}$, or at $\dfrac{\pi}{2}$ and every π units clockwise or counterclockwise from there. The functions that have y in the denominator of their definition, cosecant and cotangent, are undefined where y is 0, or where the sine is 0. The sine will equal 0 at 0 and any multiple of π.

The range of the tangent and cotangent includes all real numbers. The secant and cosecant, because they are the reciprocals of the cosine and sine functions, respectively, have ranges made up of two intervals. The values of the sine and cosine range from −1 to 1. The reciprocals of those numbers range from 1 to ∞ on the positive side and from −1 to $-\infty$ on the negative side.

Function	Domain	Range
$\sin \theta$	$(-\infty, \infty)$	$[-1, 1]$
$\cos \theta$	$(-\infty, \infty)$	$[-1, 1]$
$\tan \theta$	All reals except $\pm\dfrac{(2n-1)\pi}{2}$, that is, except odd multiples of $\dfrac{\pi}{2}$	$(-\infty, \infty)$
$\csc \theta$	All reals except $\pm\dfrac{(2n-1)\pi}{2}$, that is, except odd multiples of $\dfrac{\pi}{2}$	$(-\infty, -1] \cup [1, \infty)$
$\sec \theta$	All reals except multiples of π	$(-\infty, -1] \cup [1, \infty)$
$\cot \theta$	All reals except multiples of π	$(-\infty, \infty)$

Beyond the unit circle

While the trigonometric functions are defined in terms of the point where the terminal side intersects the unit circle, it is possible to find the values of the trig functions if any point on the terminal side is known. If you know the point on the terminal side where it intersects the unit circle, you can go right to the definitions of the trig functions, but if the point you know is not on the unit circle, proportional thinking will still let you find the values of the functions. If you drop a perpendicular from your point to the x-axis, you create a right triangle that is similar to the one on which the definition relies.

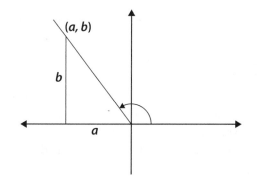

If (a, b) is a point on the terminal side of the angle and $r = \sqrt{a^2 + b^2}$, then

$$\sin\theta = \frac{b}{r} \qquad \csc\theta = \frac{r}{b}$$

$$\cos\theta = \frac{a}{r} \qquad \sec\theta = \frac{r}{a}$$

$$\tan\theta = \frac{b}{a} \qquad \cot\theta = \frac{a}{b}$$

The proportional relationships in similar right triangles assure that these definitions are equivalent to the unit circle definitions.

EXERCISE
2·4

Find the values of the six trig functions for each value of θ.

1. $\theta = \dfrac{\pi}{3}$

2. $\theta = -\dfrac{3\pi}{4}$

3. $\theta = \dfrac{7\pi}{6}$

4. $\theta = \dfrac{3\pi}{2}$

5. $\theta = -\pi$

6. $\theta = -\dfrac{13\pi}{6}$

7. $\theta = 8\pi$

8. $\theta = \dfrac{9\pi}{2}$

9. $\theta = \dfrac{11\pi}{6}$

10. $\theta = -\dfrac{7\pi}{3}$

Find the sine, cosine, and tangent of an angle in standard position if the given point is on the terminal side of the angle.

11. $(5,-5)$ 14. $\left(\sqrt{3},-2\right)$ 17. $(-2,5)$ 20. $(-2,-8)$

12. $(0,4)$ 15. $(4,0)$ 18. $(6,-3)$

13. $\left(-4,4\sqrt{3}\right)$ 16. $(8,3)$ 19. $(7,4)$

All-star trig class

The symmetries of the unit circle mean that many of the values of the trigonometric functions are repeated as you move around the circle, with a change of sign as you move from quadrant to quadrant. If you know the values of the six functions for the angles in the first quadrant and you understand how the signs change, you can find the trig functions of any angle in the $\frac{\pi}{6}$, $\frac{\pi}{4}$, $\frac{\pi}{3}$, or $\frac{\pi}{2}$ family.

When the terminal side of an angle falls in the first quadrant, the point where the terminal side intersects the unit circle has positive coordinates, and so all six trig functions of the angle have positive values. When the terminal side moves to the second quadrant, the *x*-coordinate is negative and the *y*-coordinate is positive. As a result, the sine and cosecant are positive, but all four other functions are negative. In the third quadrant, both coordinates are negative, so only the tangent and cotangent are positive. In quadrant IV, the *x*-coordinate is positive and the *y*-coordinate is negative, so the cosine and secant are positive, but the other functions are negative.

There is a variety of mnemonic devices to help you remember those signs. All of them refer to the quadrant labels in the figure below. They differ in how they suggest you remember the placement of the letters. You can remember ACTS, starting in quadrant I and moving clockwise, or CAST, if you prefer to move counterclockwise, but you'll have to start in quadrant IV. It's probably easier to take the quadrants in the traditional order, but since ASTC is hard to pronounce, take it as an acronym. Some people learn "all seniors take calculus," but since that's not always true, you might prefer "all-star trig class."

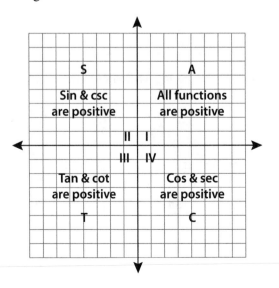

The A in the first quadrant tells you that, in that quadrant, all six trig functions are positive. The second quadrant gets an S because the sine and its reciprocal, the cosecant, are positive, but all the other functions are negative. The T in the third quadrant signals that the tangent and its reciprocal, the cotangent, are positive there, and the C in quadrant IV says that the cosine and its reciprocal, the secant, are the only positive functions in that quadrant.

If you combine your experience finding the six trig functions when you're given a point on the terminal side with your knowledge of the signs of the functions in different quadrants, you can take just a little bit of information and find all six trig functions for a particular value of θ.

Suppose you know that $\tan\theta = \dfrac{3}{4}$. You don't know the value of θ, and you don't know the point where the terminal side intersects the unit circle, but you do know that the ratio of the y-coordinate to the x-coordinate is $\dfrac{3}{4}$. The right triangle formed when you drop a perpendicular from the point on the unit circle to the x-axis will be similar to a 3-4-5 right triangle. You can almost find the other trig functions.

The only problem is that you don't know whether $\tan\theta = \dfrac{3}{4}$ because the terminal side of θ falls in quadrant I or because it falls in quadrant III. If θ is a first-quadrant angle, all six functions are positive. If θ falls in quadrant III, only the tangent and cotangent are positive, and the rest are negative. You need more information.

If you have the additional piece of information that $\csc\theta < 0$, you know that $\sin\theta < 0$, so the angle must fall in the third quadrant. Once you have that, you can say

$$\sin\theta = -\frac{3}{5} \qquad \csc\theta = -\frac{5}{3}$$

$$\cos\theta = -\frac{4}{5} \qquad \sec\theta = -\frac{5}{4}$$

$$\tan\theta = \frac{3}{4} \qquad \cot\theta = \frac{4}{3}$$

In this example, you knew that the triangle would be a 3-4-5 right triangle, but even if the sides of the triangle weren't a Pythagorean triple, you could use the two known sides in the Pythagorean theorem to find the third side.

If $\sin\theta = \dfrac{7}{8}$ and $\tan\theta < 0$, you know that the terminal side of θ will fall in the second quadrant. You know the six trig functions will have values the same as a right triangle with a leg of 7 and a hypotenuse of 8. Find the third side with the Pythagorean theorem:

$$a^2 + b^2 = c^2$$
$$7^2 + b^2 = 8^2$$
$$49 + b^2 = 64$$
$$b^2 = 15$$
$$b = \pm\sqrt{15}$$

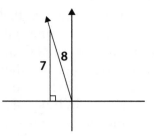

Draw the terminal side of θ in quadrant II and drop a perpendicular to make the right triangle. The hypotenuse is 8, the vertical side is 7, and the side along the x-axis will be $-\sqrt{15}$, negative because x-coordinates are negative in the second quadrant. You can find all six functions:

$$\sin\theta = \frac{7}{8} \qquad\qquad \csc\theta = \frac{8}{7}$$

$$\cos\theta = -\frac{\sqrt{15}}{8} \qquad\qquad \sec\theta = -\frac{8}{\sqrt{15}} = -\frac{8\sqrt{15}}{15}$$

$$\tan\theta = -\frac{7}{\sqrt{15}} = -\frac{7\sqrt{15}}{15} \qquad\qquad \cot\theta = -\frac{\sqrt{15}}{7}$$

Even if there are variables involved, you can still find representations for the six trig functions. If you know that θ is an angle in the fourth quadrant and its terminal side is the line $y = -2x$, you can sketch a graph of that line, choose a point on the line in quadrant IV, and drop a perpendicular to the x-axis. Call the length of the horizontal side x, and the vertical side will be $-2x$. Use the Pythagorean theorem to find the length of the hypotenuse:

$$a^2 + b^2 = c^2$$
$$x^2 + (-2x)^2 = c^2$$
$$5x^2 = c^2$$
$$\sqrt{5}x = c$$

Find the six trig functions, simplifying where you can:

$$\sin\theta = \frac{-2x}{\sqrt{5}x} = -\frac{2\sqrt{5}}{5} \qquad \csc\theta = \frac{\sqrt{5}x}{-2x} = -\frac{\sqrt{5}}{2}$$

$$\cos\theta = \frac{x}{\sqrt{5}x} = \frac{\sqrt{5}}{5} \qquad \sec\theta = \frac{\sqrt{5}x}{x} = \sqrt{5}$$

$$\tan\theta = \frac{-2x}{x} = -2 \qquad \cot\theta = \frac{x}{-2x} = -\frac{1}{2}$$

In some cases, you won't be able to simplify away all the variables. Suppose you know that θ is an angle in standard position in the first quadrant, and a point (x, y) on its terminal side also is a point on the line $y = x + 1$. That line can't be the terminal side because it doesn't pass through the origin, but if the point you're interested in is on that line, you can say that $(x, y) = (x, x+1)$. Build your right triangle with legs of x and $x + 1$ and find the hypotenuse:

$$a^2 + b^2 = c^2$$

$$x^2 + (x+1)^2 = c^2$$

$$x^2 + x^2 + 2x + 1 = c^2$$

$$2x^2 + 2x + 1 = c^2$$

$$\sqrt{2x^2 + 2x + 1} = c$$

Unless the radicand is a perfect square trinomial, which is unlikely, you're not going to get rid of the radical, and unless it has one of the legs as a factor, you're not going to see much to simplify. You can still find the six functions, however:

$$\sin\theta = \frac{x+1}{\sqrt{2x^2+2x+1}} = \frac{(x+1)\sqrt{2x^2+2x+1}}{2x^2+2x+1} \qquad \csc\theta = \frac{\sqrt{2x^2+2x+1}}{x+1}$$

$$\cos\theta = \frac{x}{\sqrt{2x^2+2x+1}} = \frac{x\sqrt{2x^2+2x+1}}{2x^2+2x+1} \qquad \sec\theta = \frac{\sqrt{2x^2+2x+1}}{x}$$

$$\tan\theta = \frac{x+1}{x} \qquad\qquad\qquad \cot\theta = \frac{x}{x+1}$$

EXERCISE 2·5

Determine in which quadrant the terminal side of θ falls.

1. $\sin\theta > 0$ and $\cos\theta < 0$

2. $\cos\theta < 0$ and $\tan\theta > 0$

3. $\tan\theta > 0$ and $\sec\theta > 0$

4. $\csc\theta < 0$ and $\csc\theta < 0$

5. $\csc\theta > 0$ and $\cot\theta < 0$

6. $\sec\theta > 0$ and $\sin\theta > 0$

7. $\tan\theta < 0$ and $\sec\theta > 0$

8. $\csc\theta < 0$ and $\cos\theta > 0$

9. $\tan\theta > 0$ and $\sin\theta < 0$

10. $\cos\theta > 0$ and $\cot\theta > 0$

Find the value of all six trig functions of θ from the information given.

11. $\sin\theta = \dfrac{5}{13}$ and $\tan\theta > 0$

12. $\cos\theta = \dfrac{3}{5}$ and $\csc\theta < 0$

13. $\tan\theta = \dfrac{12}{5}$ and $\sec\theta > 0$

14. $\sin\theta = -\dfrac{1}{4}$ and $\tan\theta > 0$

15. $\cos\theta = \dfrac{3}{7}$ and $\tan\theta < 0$

16. $\tan\theta = -\dfrac{8}{3}$ and $\csc\theta < 0$

17. $\sin\theta = \dfrac{2}{3}$ and $\cos\theta < 0$

18. $\sec\theta = \dfrac{5}{4}$ and $\tan\theta < 0$

19. $\cot\theta = -\dfrac{4}{9}$ and $\cos\theta < 0$

20. $\sec\theta = -\dfrac{13}{4}$ and $\tan\theta < 0$

Find the value of all six trig functions of θ in terms of x if necessary.

21. θ is an angle in the third quadrant whose terminal side is the line $y = 3x$.

22. θ is an angle in the second quadrant whose terminal side is the line $y = -\dfrac{1}{2}x$.

23. θ is an angle in the first quadrant. A point on the terminal side also lies on the line $y = 4 - x$.

24. θ is an angle in the fourth quadrant. A point on the terminal side also lies on the line $y = 2x - 3$.

25. θ is an angle in the third quadrant. A point on the terminal side also lines on the line $2x - y = 5$.

Graphs of trigonometric functions

The six trigonometric functions—sine, cosine, tangent, and their reciprocals—are periodic functions. Each of them repeats a certain pattern, over and over again, in a specified interval called the period. The repetition of values occurs because the functions are defined by values around the circle. Each time you go around the circle, you repeat the pattern.

Studying the graphs of trigonometric functions can help you understand the periodic nature of the functions and help you see how the trig functions model phenomena from the world around you. It can allow you to see the repetition and, as a result, help you solve trigonometric equations. The better you are able to visualize the repetitions of the periodic function, the faster you'll locate the multiple solutions possible for a trig equation.

In Chapter 4, you'll look at applications of the trig functions in different kinds of problems. You'll use periodic functions to model different kinds of behaviors, and you'll solve equations involving trig functions. Being able to sketch a graph can often be a great help in solving problems that are modeled by trig functions.

The more you explore the graphs of the trigonometric functions, the better you'll understand how the functions behave. You'll be able to sketch a graph quickly and anticipate the repetitions of the function. Once you're acquainted with the parent functions, the simplest case of each of the trig functions, you can sketch graphs of more complex functions by applying principles of translation, reflection, stretching, and compressing. Each of those changes shows up in a particular spot in the equation, and knowing where to look for them and how to interpret them will make your work easier.

Graphs of sine and cosine functions

You have to start with the parent graphs. The graphs of the trig functions are often referred to as waves because of their repetitive nature. The various trig functions have graphs of different shapes, but each is repetitive, periodic, and undulating, behaving somewhat like a wave. The graphs of $y = \sin\theta$ and $y = \cos\theta$ in particular rise and fall like waves on the ocean.

Sine

The most fundamental sine wave, $y = \sin x$, has the following graph. The horizontal axis represents θ, the rotation, and the vertical axis is $\sin\theta$, which was defined as the y-coordinate of the point where the terminal side crosses the unit circle. The sine function is defined for all real numbers, so the domain of $y = \sin x$ is $(-\infty, \infty)$. The y-coordinates of points on the unit circle vary between -1 and 1, so the range of $y = \sin x$ is $[-1, 1]$.

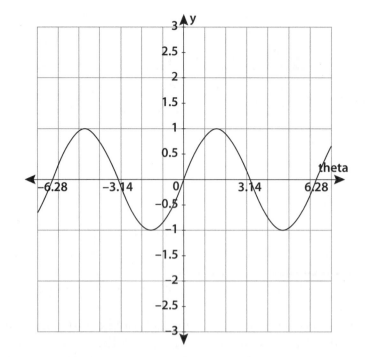

As you move around the unit circle in the positive direction, the y-coordinate increases from 0 to 1 as you move through the first quadrant, then decreases to 0 and then to -1 as you travel through quadrants II and III. As you rotate through the fourth quadrant, the y-coordinate increases from -1 to 0. The graph of $y = \sin x$ fluctuates from 0 to a high of 1, down through 0 to -1, and back to 0, in a space of 2π, one full rotation. The period of the sine wave, the time it takes to complete one full wave, is 2π, a full rotation.

As you investigate each of the parent graphs, you'll want to learn the general shape of the graph, but also locate a few key points on the parent graph. Once you know those key points, you can work transformations on those points, and the image points will help you define the new graph. You'll want to remember key points on this parent graph for the family of sine functions.

Think of $(0, 0)$ as the start of a wave, and $\left(\dfrac{\pi}{2}, 1\right)$ as the peak of the upward bump. The upward bump is complete at $(\pi, 0)$, and then the graph drops down to $\left(\dfrac{3\pi}{2}, 1\right)$ and then rises up to finish the full cycle at $(2\pi, 0)$.

Transformations

There are six possible alterations to the parent graph, but these show up as four numbers in the equation $y = a\sin\big(b(\theta - h)\big) + k$. The h and k represent translations, or rigid shifts. The number h is the horizontal shift, sometimes called the phase shift, and the k is the vertical shift. The vertical shift defines the midline of the graph. For the parent graph, the midline is the x-axis, and the graph rises above the midline and falls below it by equal distances.

Change $y = \sin\theta$ to $y = \sin(\theta - 3)$ and the graph will move 3 units to the right because the value of h is 3. Change $y = \sin\theta$ to $y = \sin(\theta + 2)$ and it will move 2 units left because h is -2. Moving left or right will change the x-coordinate of the key points.

Tacking on a constant at the end shifts the graph up or down $y = \sin\theta + 4$ moves the parent graph up 4 units, and $y = \sin\theta - 1$ shifts the parent graph down 1 unit. Translating the graph up or down will change the y-coordinate of your key points. Of course, a single equation may have more than one transformation and certainly may have both a horizontal and a vertical shift.

The numbers in the a and b positions do double duty. The absolute value of the number communicates one idea, while its sign tells you something else. If a is negative, the graph will be reflected across the x-axis. That will change the sign of the x-coordinates of the key points. If b is a negative number, the graph is reflected across the y-axis, and the sign of the y-coordinates of the key points changes.

You may find that it's sometimes hard to tell whether there's been a reflection across the x-axis or across the y-axis. The graph of the parent function $y = \sin\theta$, reflected across the x-axis, looks exactly the same as the graph of $y = \sin\theta$ reflected across the y-axis. For other graphs, that won't be the case, but there may be other curiosities. The parent graph $y = \cos\theta$, reflected across the y-axis, for example, will appear not to have changed at all because $y = \cos\theta$ is symmetric about the y-axis.

The absolute value of a, called the amplitude, tells you about vertical stretch or compression and defines the height of each bump on the sine wave. When $|a| > 1$, the graph is stretched, and the peaks get higher and the troughs lower. If $|a| < 1$, the graph is compressed, with peaks and troughs that are closer to the midline than those of the parent graph. The amplitude is a multiplier, affecting the y-coordinates of the key points.

The absolute value of b refers to horizontal stretch and compression. If $|b| > 1$, the graph is compressed because more than one full cycle must fit into the space of 2π. When $|b| < 1$, you complete less than one cycle in 2π, so the graph is stretched horizontally. Adjust your key points by dividing each of the x-coordinates by b.

Because stretching or compressing the wave horizontally will change the number of waves that fit in a space of 2π, the number in the b position is called the frequency. The product of the frequency and the period will always be 2π.

Cosine

The graph of $y = \cos\theta$ resembles the graph of $y = \sin\theta$ but is shifted, or translated, $\dfrac{\pi}{2}$ units to the left. The reason for that shift is that the cosine is the sine of the complement. The cosine of θ is the sine of $\dfrac{\pi}{2} - \theta$. The graph of $y = \cos\theta$ is the same graph as $y = \sin\left(\dfrac{\pi}{2} - \theta\right) = \sin\left(-\theta + \dfrac{\pi}{2}\right) = \sin\left(-1\left(\theta - \dfrac{\pi}{2}\right)\right)$. That's the graph of $y = \sin\theta$ shifted $\dfrac{\pi}{2}$ units right, but then reflected over the y-axis.

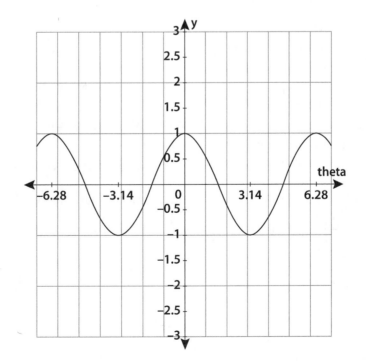

The key points to remember for the cosine wave are $(0, 1)$, $\left(\dfrac{\pi}{2}, 0\right)$, $(\pi, -1)$, $\left(\dfrac{3\pi}{2}, 0\right)$, and $(2\pi, 1)$.

The cosine wave "starts high," which means that the first key point you remember is actually the high point of the wave. Then the graph drops down through 0 to –1 and back up through 0, back to the high of 1 again. The parent graph makes that cycle in a space of 2π.

The values of a, b, h, and k change the shape and location of the wave as they did for the sine. The values of a and b concern reflection over the axes and stretching and compression. The values of h and k tell you how to translate the graph.

Shifting, stretching, compressing, and reflecting

The graph of $y = a\sin\big(b(\theta - h)\big) + k$ is determined by four numbers, a, b, h, and k, in the equation. The numbers h and k tell how the wave is translated from the position of the parent, with h indicating the horizontal translation and k the vertical shift. The value in the h position will be added to the x-coordinate of the key points, and the number in the k position will be added to the y-coordinate of the key points. The vertical shift, k, will raise or lower the midline of the wave.

The amplitude, a, tells the height of each peak and the depth of each trough from the midline. This represents a vertical stretch. An amplitude greater than 1 stretches the graph vertically, making each of the peaks taller than the parent. An amplitude less than 1 compresses the graph, making it shorter.

The frequency, b, tells the number of full wave patterns that are completed in a space of 2π. The period of the function, which is the length of a full cycle, is $\dfrac{2\pi}{b}$. The frequency and period are inversely related. As one increases, the other decreases, and their product is always 2π. Because increasing the frequency, b, decreases the period, it compresses the wave, and decreasing the frequency increases the period and stretches the wave.

Here are some examples of these adjustments, one change at a time.

- $y = \cos\left(\theta - \dfrac{\pi}{4}\right)$ Shift the graph of $y = \cos\theta$ $\dfrac{\pi}{4}$ units to the right. Add $\dfrac{\pi}{4}$ to the x-coordinate of the key points.

- $y = \cos(2\theta)$ Two full waves fit in the space between 0 and 2π. The period of the wave is π units. The wave has been compressed horizontally. Divide the x-coordinates of the key points by 2.

- $y = -\cos\theta$ The graph is reflected over the x-axis. Change the sign of the y-coordinates of the key points.

- $y = 3\cos\theta$ The graph is stretched vertically, so it rises to 3 and falls to –3. Multiply the y-coordinates of the key points by 3.

- $y = \cos\theta + 1$ Shift the graph up 1 unit and add 1 to the y-coordinates of the key points.

If you put all those changes into one equation, you'll get the equation $y = -3\cos\left(2\left(\theta - \dfrac{\pi}{4}\right)\right) + 1$ or $y = -3\cos\left(2\theta - \dfrac{\pi}{2}\right) + 1$. To sketch the graph, it may help to look at the key points.

Parent function	$(0, 1)$	$\left(\dfrac{\pi}{2},0\right)$	$(\pi,-1)$	$\left(\dfrac{3\pi}{2},0\right)$	$(2\pi,1)$
Shift right (add $\dfrac{\pi}{2}$ to the x-coordinate)	$\left(\dfrac{\pi}{2},1\right)$	$(\pi,0)$	$\left(\dfrac{3\pi}{2},-1\right)$	$(2\pi,0)$	$\left(\dfrac{5\pi}{2},1\right)$
Horizontal compression (divide the x-coordinate by 2)	$\left(\dfrac{\pi}{4},1\right)$	$\left(\dfrac{\pi}{2},0\right)$	$\left(\dfrac{3\pi}{4},-1\right)$	$(\pi,0)$	$\left(\dfrac{5\pi}{4},1\right)$
Vertical stretch (multiply the y-coordinate by 3)	$\left(\dfrac{\pi}{4},3\right)$	$\left(\dfrac{\pi}{2},0\right)$	$\left(\dfrac{3\pi}{4},-3\right)$	$(\pi,0)$	$\left(\dfrac{5\pi}{4},3\right)$
Reflect over x-axis (change sign of the y-coordinate)	$\left(\dfrac{\pi}{4},-3\right)$	$\left(\dfrac{\pi}{2},0\right)$	$\left(\dfrac{3\pi}{4},3\right)$	$(\pi,0)$	$\left(\dfrac{5\pi}{4},-3\right)$
Shift up (add 1 to the y-coordinate)	$\left(\dfrac{\pi}{4},-2\right)$	$\left(\dfrac{\pi}{2},1\right)$	$\left(\dfrac{3\pi}{4},4\right)$	$(\pi,1)$	$\left(\dfrac{5\pi}{4},-2\right)$

The graph of $y = -3\cos\left(2\left(\theta-\dfrac{\pi}{4}\right)\right)+1$ or $y = -3\cos\left(2\theta-\dfrac{\pi}{2}\right)+1$ should look like this:

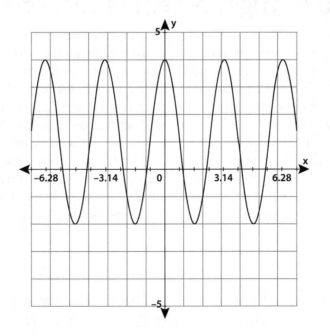

Use transformations to sketch the graph of each of the equations.

1. $y = -\cos\theta$

2. $y = 2\sin\theta$

3. $y = \cos(4\theta)$

4. $y = -3\cos\theta$

5. $y = 4\sin\theta + 1$

6. $y = \cos\left(x - \dfrac{\pi}{3}\right)$

7. $y = 4\cos\left(\theta + \dfrac{\pi}{3}\right)$

8. $y = \sin(\pi\theta) - 3$

9. $y = -\dfrac{1}{2}\sin(3\theta)$

10. $y = -2\sin\left(\theta - \dfrac{\pi}{4}\right)$

11. $y = \dfrac{1}{2}\sin\left(\theta + \dfrac{\pi}{6}\right)$

12. $y = -5\cos(3\theta) + 3$

13. $y = \sin\left(\theta - \dfrac{\pi}{3}\right) + 5$

14. $y = -3\sin\dfrac{\theta}{2}$

15. $y = \cos\left(\theta - \dfrac{\pi}{6}\right) + 4$

16. $y = \cos\dfrac{\theta}{4} - 3$

17. $y = -2\cos(\theta - 4) + 1$

18. $y = 4 - \dfrac{2}{3}\sin\theta$

19. $y = 4 + 5\cos\dfrac{\theta}{3}$

20. $y = 4 - 3\cos\left(2\theta - \dfrac{\pi}{3}\right)$

Graphs of other trigonometric functions

The sine and cosine graphs are continuous and periodic. They are smooth, connected curves that repeat the wavelike pattern over and over. In different equations, the length, or period, of the wave may change, its height, or amplitude, may change, and it may shift in different directions, but the basic wave form remains the same for all sine and cosine graphs.

All the other trigonometric functions have graphs that are discontinuous, but, like the sine and cosine, each repeats a pattern. They are discontinuous because each is defined as a quotient, and for each one there are values that make the denominator 0, and therefore make the function undefined.

The patterns that they repeat differ from the sine and cosine wave form. The tangent and cotangent, which are reciprocals of one another, have patterns that mirror one another, while the secant and cosecant, which are reciprocals of the cosine and sine, respectively, share a shape. You'll see that one graph appears to be a shifted form of the other, just as the cosine is a shifted version of the sine wave.

Tangent

The tangent function has a discontinuous graph, because the tangent is defined as the quotient $\dfrac{y}{x}$ of the coordinates of the point (x, y) at which the terminal side of the angle intersects the unit circle, or as the quotient of the sine and the cosine. Whenever the x-coordinate is 0, the cosine is 0, and the tangent will be undefined, so the graph will have a vertical asymptote at each of those points. Those discontinuities occur at multiples of $\frac{\pi}{2}$.

The tangent is periodic, however, repeating in a period of π units. In the space of π units between vertical asymptotes that fall at multiples of $\frac{\pi}{2}$, the same pattern is repeated. The parent graph has its y-intercept at the origin and x-intercepts at all multiples of π. Each wave goes to $-\infty$ on the left and ∞ on the right.

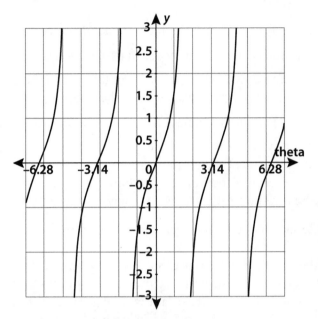

The key points to remember for the tangent graph are $\left(-\frac{\pi}{4}, -1\right)$, $(0, 0)$, and $\left(\frac{\pi}{4}, 1\right)$. The graph of the parent function is shown in the figure above.

Cotangent

Like the tangent, the cotangent is discontinuous, but its discontinuities fall wherever the sine function is 0, since the cotangent is the reciprocal of the tangent. The discontinuities of the cotangent

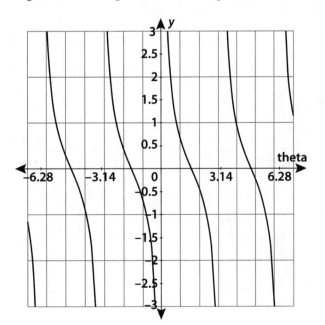

graph are shifted $\frac{\pi}{2}$ units to the left of those for the tangent because the tangent and cotangent are cofunctions, or complementary functions. The x-intercepts of the parent graph fall at odd multiples of $\frac{\pi}{2}$, and each wave goes to ∞ on the left and $-\infty$ on the right, as shown in the preceding figure.

The key points to remember for the cotangent graph are $\left(\frac{\pi}{4},1\right)$, $\left(\frac{\pi}{2},0\right)$, and $\left(\frac{3\pi}{4},-1\right)$.

Secant and cosecant

The secant and cosecant functions are the reciprocals of the cosine and sine functions, respectively, and, like the sine and cosine, differ by a shift of $\frac{\pi}{2}$. Each is made up of cup-shaped sections, alternating opening up and down, with each section tangent to the graph of its reciprocal.

The graphs have vertical asymptotes between the cup-shaped sections, at multiples of π for the cosecant function and at odd multiples of $\frac{\pi}{2}$ for the secant function. The vertical asymptotes of the cosecant function occur at the 0s of the sine function, and the vertical asymptotes of the secant function occur at the 0s of the cosine.

The sections of the secant function seem to balance on the peaks and troughs of the cosine graph. In the figure below, the cosine graph is shown in gray, with the secant graph in black. The discontinuities of the secant occur when the cosine is 0, at odd multiples of $\frac{\pi}{2}$, and the graph has vertical asymptotes at those values.

The graph of the secant function just touches the graph of the cosine at those points where both equal 1 or both equal –1, because the reciprocal of 1 is 1 and the reciprocal of –1 is –1. Where the cosine is positive but less than 1, the secant will be greater than 1, becoming larger and larger as the cosine gets close to 0. When the cosine is negative, between 0 and –1, the secant is negative, less than –1, and decreasing without bound as the cosine approaches 0.

The figure below shows the sine graph in gray and the cosecant graph in black, with the sections of the cosecant graph seeming to balance on the graph of the sine. The graph of the cosecant function has vertical asymptotes at multiples of π, where the sine function is 0.

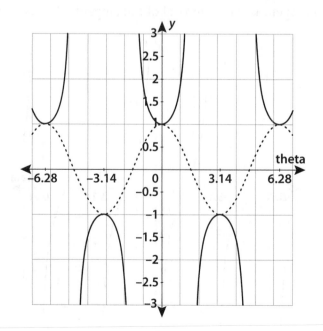

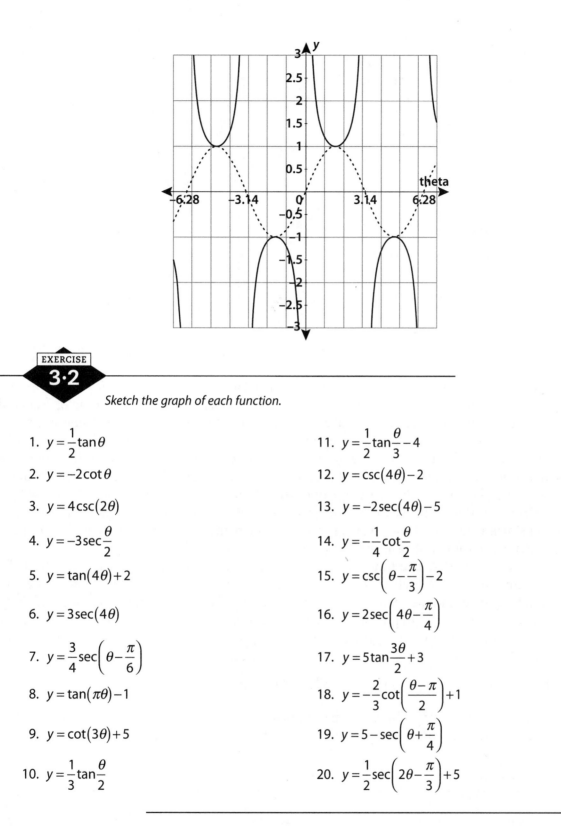

3·2

Sketch the graph of each function.

1. $y = \dfrac{1}{2}\tan\theta$

2. $y = -2\cot\theta$

3. $y = 4\csc(2\theta)$

4. $y = -3\sec\dfrac{\theta}{2}$

5. $y = \tan(4\theta) + 2$

6. $y = 3\sec(4\theta)$

7. $y = \dfrac{3}{4}\sec\left(\theta - \dfrac{\pi}{6}\right)$

8. $y = \tan(\pi\theta) - 1$

9. $y = \cot(3\theta) + 5$

10. $y = \dfrac{1}{3}\tan\dfrac{\theta}{2}$

11. $y = \dfrac{1}{2}\tan\dfrac{\theta}{3} - 4$

12. $y = \csc(4\theta) - 2$

13. $y = -2\sec(4\theta) - 5$

14. $y = -\dfrac{1}{4}\cot\dfrac{\theta}{2}$

15. $y = \csc\left(\theta - \dfrac{\pi}{3}\right) - 2$

16. $y = 2\sec\left(4\theta - \dfrac{\pi}{4}\right)$

17. $y = 5\tan\dfrac{3\theta}{2} + 3$

18. $y = -\dfrac{2}{3}\cot\left(\dfrac{\theta - \pi}{2}\right) + 1$

19. $y = 5 - \sec\left(\theta + \dfrac{\pi}{4}\right)$

20. $y = \dfrac{1}{2}\sec\left(2\theta - \dfrac{\pi}{3}\right) + 5$

Inverse trigonometric functions

The inverse of a function reverses whatever work the function has accomplished. If the function added, the inverse subtracts. If the function divided, the inverse multiplies. The inverse of the squaring function is the square root function. Each inverse sends every element of the range back to the element of the domain from which it came. The range of the function is the domain of the inverse, and the domain of the function is the range of the inverse.

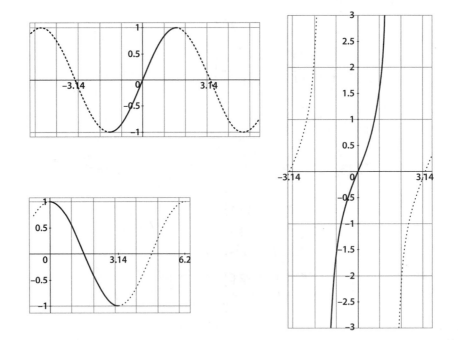

In order for a function to have an inverse function, the function must be one to one. This means that not only does every x-value have only one y-value, but every y-value comes from only one x-value. You may have learned about a vertical line test to tell if a graph represents a function. If any vertical line were to intersect the graph more than once, that would signal that the graph is not a function. To determine if a graph represents a one-to-one function, use a horizontal line test. If any horizontal line intersects the graph more than once, the function is not one to one.

The graphs of the three principal trigonometric functions, sin θ, cos θ, and tan θ, do not pass the horizontal line test; that is, they are not one-to-one functions. The periodic nature of the trig functions means that the same y-value is produced by many different x-values, and that in turn means that they would not have an inverse that is a function.

The hope of inverse trig functions is not lost, however. Each function can be restricted so that it is one to one. For each of the parent functions, choose first-quadrant values, where the function is positive, and the nearest continuous quadrant in which the function is negative. In the figure below, you see the graphs of $y = \sin \theta$, $y = \cos \theta$, and $y = \tan \theta$. On each graph, the restricted domain is shown by the heavier curve.

The sine function will be one to one if it is restricted to the interval $\left[-\dfrac{\pi}{2}, \dfrac{\pi}{2} \right]$. The cosine function is one to one on the interval $[0, \pi]$, and the tangent function on the interval $\left(-\dfrac{\pi}{2}, \dfrac{\pi}{2} \right)$.

Each of these restricted functions has an inverse, denoted as $\sin^{-1} x$, $\cos^{-1} x$, and $\tan^{-1} x$. The domain and range of each inverse function is shown next to its graph.

Inverse Function	Domain	Range	Graph
$\sin^{-1} x$	$[-1, 1]$	$\left[-\dfrac{\pi}{2}, \dfrac{\pi}{2} \right]$	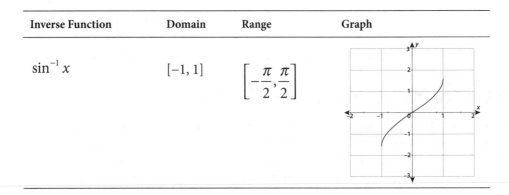

Inverse Function	Domain	Range	Graph
$\cos^{-1} x$	$[-1, 1]$	$[0, \pi]$	
$\tan^{-1} x$	$(-\infty, \infty)$	$\left(-\dfrac{\pi}{2}, \dfrac{\pi}{2}\right)$	

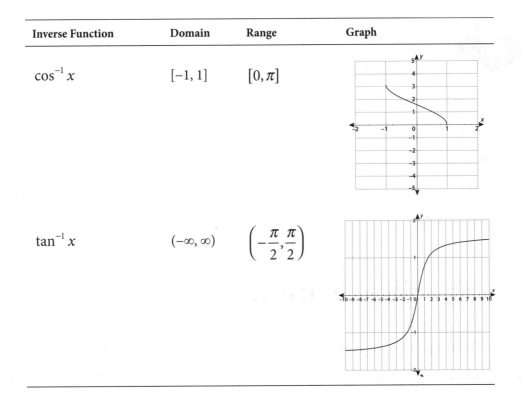

Graphs of the inverse functions

The same principles of translation, reflection, stretching, and compression that you used to sketch the graphs of variations on the trig functions can also be used to sketch variations of the inverse functions.

To graph $y = 4 - 3\cos^{-1}\dfrac{x}{2}$, identify the transformations. The parent function, $y = \cos^{-1} x$, is subjected to a horizontal stretch by a factor of 2, a vertical stretch by a factor of 3, a reflection over the x-axis, and a shift up by 4 units. The graph of $y = 4 - 3\cos^{-1}\dfrac{x}{2}$ is shown in the figure below.

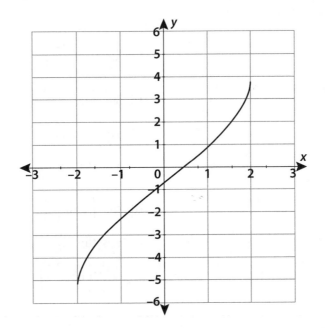

Sketch a graph of each function.

1. $y = \cos^{-1}(3x) + 4$

2. $y = -5\sin^{-1}(x-2)$

3. $y = 4\tan^{-1}x + 1$

4. $y = \dfrac{1}{2}\cos^{-1}\dfrac{x}{3} - 4$

5. $y = -\sin^{-1}(x+3) - 2$

6. $y = \dfrac{1}{2}\cos^{-1}(2x) - 3$

7. $y = 3\cos^{-1}(x+5)$

8. $y = -\dfrac{1}{2}\sin^{-1}x - 3$

9. $y = -2\sin^{-1}\dfrac{x}{4} + 1$

10. $y = \dfrac{1}{3}\sin^{-1}(x-5) + 4$

Evaluating inverse functions

Because the inverse functions have limited ranges, you need to think carefully when evaluating functions. It's tempting, for example, to say that $\sin^{-1}\left(\sin\dfrac{5\pi}{4}\right)$ would equal $\dfrac{5\pi}{4}$ because sin and $\sin^{-1}$ counteract each other. Unfortunately, that's not quite true. Working from the inside out, you can say that $\sin^{-1}\left(\sin\dfrac{5\pi}{4}\right) = \sin^{-1}\left(-\dfrac{\sqrt{2}}{2}\right)$, but $\sin^{-1}$ will never return $\dfrac{5\pi}{4}$. Instead, $\sin^{-1}\left(-\dfrac{\sqrt{2}}{2}\right) = -\dfrac{\pi}{4}$. Take things one step at a time and be aware of domains and ranges when evaluating.

Evaluate each expression. Be aware of the domains and ranges of the inverse functions.

1. $\sin\left(\sin^{-1}\dfrac{-\sqrt{3}}{2}\right)$

2. $\tan\left(\cos^{-1}\dfrac{1}{2}\right)$

3. $\cos(\tan^{-1}1)$

4. $\cos^{-1}\left(\cos\dfrac{4\pi}{3}\right)$

5. $\sin^{-1}\left(\tan\dfrac{\pi}{4}\right)$

6. $\tan^{-1}(\cos\pi)$

7. $\tan\left(\sin^{-1}\dfrac{\sqrt{2}}{2}\right)$

8. $\tan^{-1}\left(\tan\dfrac{7\pi}{4}\right)$

9. $\sin(\cos^{-1}1)$

10. $\sin^{-1}\left(\cos\dfrac{2\pi}{3}\right)$

11. $\tan\left(\cos^{-1}\dfrac{-1}{2}\right)$

12. $\sin(\tan^{-1}\sqrt{3})$

13. $\tan(\cos^{-1}1)$

14. $\sin^{-1}\left(\sin\dfrac{7\pi}{3}\right)$

15. $\sin^{-1}\left(\cos\dfrac{7\pi}{3}\right)$

16. $\cos^{-1}(\sin\pi)$

17. $\sin\left(\cos^{-1}\dfrac{\sqrt{2}}{2}\right)$

18. $\sin^{-1}\left(\tan\dfrac{7\pi}{4}\right)$

19. $\cos(\tan^{-1}1)$

20. $\cos^{-1}\left(\cos\dfrac{3\pi}{2}\right)$

Applications of sinusoidal functions

Sinusoidal functions, or functions based on the sine or cosine functions, occur in many natural phenomena. Sinusoidal functions are periodic; that is, they repeat a pattern over a fixed interval called the period of the function. Many situations involve repetitive motion that may fit this model. The motion of waves, both water waves and sound waves, fit a sinusoidal model, as do the vibrations that cause sound and the motion of pendulums. Even biological functions like heartbeats and environmental factors like average daily temperature repeat periodically.

Sinusoidal functions

Sinusoidal functions fit the model $f(t) = a\sin(b(t - c)) + d$. The variable is often t because the function generally describes motion over time. Each of the parameters a, b, c, and d affects the shape of the graph and corresponds to a characteristic of the motion described.

The parameter a is called the amplitude of the function, b is the frequency, c is the phase shift or horizontal shift, and d is the vertical shift, which describes the baseline of the motion. That baseline is the level at which the motion begins. Together with the phase shift, this baseline defines a starting point. The phase shift moves the start of the cycle left or right of the origin. The baseline and phase shift translate the basic wave to a new location.

From there, the object moves up (or in whatever is deemed the positive direction) a distance equal to the amplitude, back to the baseline, down a distance equal to the amplitude, and back to the baseline. This is one full cycle, and it is completed in a time interval called the period. The period is not directly visible in the equation, but the product of the frequency and the period is 2π, so the period is equal to $\dfrac{2\pi}{b}$. The frequency tells you how many full cycles are accomplished in a space of 2π, so dividing 2π by the frequency will tell you how long it takes to complete one full cycle.

In the basic function $f(t) = \sin t$, the amplitude is 1, the frequency is also 1, and the phase shift and vertical shift are both 0. The graph completes one full cycle in a space of 2π, and you can see a wave begin at the origin, rise to a high point of 1 at $\dfrac{\pi}{2}$, back to 0 at π, down to –1 at $\dfrac{3\pi}{2}$, and complete the cycle at 2π.

In the function $f(t) = 2\sin t$, because the amplitude is 2, the wave rises to +2 and drops to –2. The baseline, starting point, and ending point all remain the same. There are no shifts, and the frequency of 1 and period of 2π have not changed.

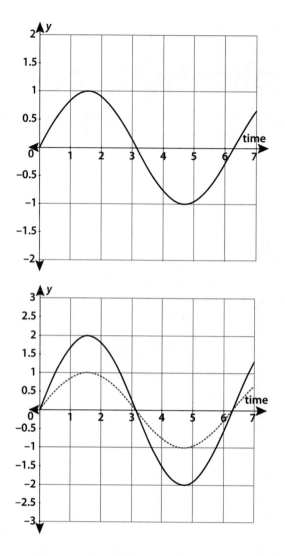

The function $f(t) = 2\sin t + 1$ has a vertical shift of +1, moving the baseline of the function up 1 unit. The horizontal line $y = 1$ now serves as the midline, as the x-axis did in prior examples. Because the amplitude is 2, the function rises 2 units above its midline, to a high point of 3 at $\frac{\pi}{2}$. It drops back to its midline—not the x-axis—at π and falls to a low point of –1, 2 units below its midline, at $\frac{3\pi}{2}$. By 2π, the graph returns to its midline.

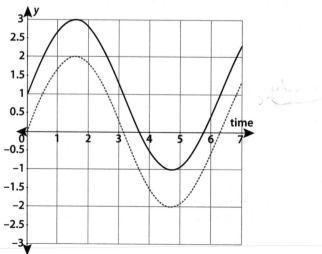

Adding a phase shift to the function moves the wave to the left or to the right. The function $f(t) = 2\sin\left(t - \dfrac{\pi}{4}\right) + 1$ is shifted $\dfrac{\pi}{4}$ units to the right. This moves key points to the right as well. The high point, which was at $\left(\dfrac{\pi}{2}, 3\right)$, moves to $\left(\dfrac{3\pi}{4}, 3\right)$, and the low point of $\left(\dfrac{3\pi}{2}, -1\right)$ moves to $\left(\dfrac{7\pi}{4}, -1\right)$.

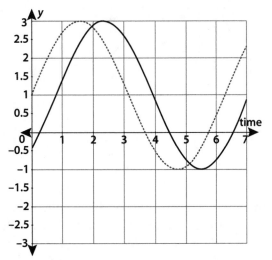

Increasing the frequency, and thereby shortening the period, forces you to complete the cycle faster and has the effect of compressing the wave horizontally. The function $f(t) = \sin(2t)$ completes two full cycles in 2π, so the cycle is complete by π.

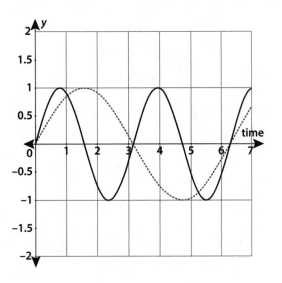

A frequency with a value less than 1 has the opposite effect: it stretches the wave horizontally, increasing the period. The function $f(t) = \sin\left(\dfrac{1}{2}t\right) = \sin\dfrac{t}{2}$ completes only half a wave in the space of 2π, taking 4π to complete a full cycle.

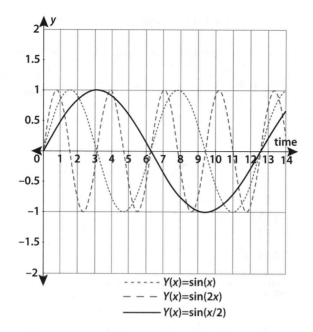

- - - - - $Y(x)=\sin(x)$
— — — $Y(x)=\sin(2x)$
——— $Y(x)=\sin(x/2)$

The final element to consider is the sign of the amplitude and the sign of the frequency. While both the amplitude and the frequency are taken as absolute values, the presence of a negative sign on either one indicates a reflection. A negative value of a indicates that the graph is reflected over the x-axis, and a negative value of b means a reflection over the y-axis.

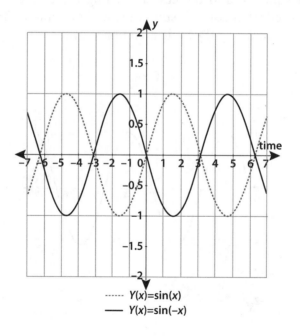

...... $Y(x)=\sin(x)$
—— $Y(x)=\sin(-x)$

A note on variations

Because of the periodic nature of the sinusoidal functions, it's often possible to have different equations that produce the same graph. Shift a sine wave $\dfrac{\pi}{2}$ units to the right and you have the same graph you'd produce by shifting it $\dfrac{3\pi}{2}$ to the left. Generally, you'll want to use the smaller shift.

Because the graph of $f(x) = \cos x$ is also the graph of $f(x) = \sin\left(x + \dfrac{\pi}{2}\right)$, you may also find that you can describe the same graph by a sine wave or a cosine wave. Unless instructed otherwise, you may choose whichever seems simpler.

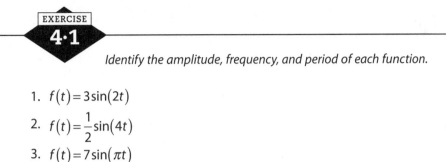

EXERCISE
4·1

Identify the amplitude, frequency, and period of each function.

1. $f(t) = 3\sin(2t)$

2. $f(t) = \dfrac{1}{2}\sin(4t)$

3. $f(t) = 7\sin(\pi t)$

4. $f(t) = \dfrac{\sin(6t)}{4}$

5. $f(t) = \dfrac{\pi}{4}\sin\dfrac{2t}{3}$

Identify the phase shift and any vertical shift.

6. $f(t) = \sin\left(t - \dfrac{\pi}{3}\right) + 5$

7. $f(t) = 6\sin\left(t + \dfrac{\pi}{4}\right) - 9$

8. $f(t) = \dfrac{1}{2}\sin\big(2(t + 5)\big) - \dfrac{3}{4}$

9. $f(t) = 4\sin\left(2\left(t + \dfrac{\pi}{6}\right)\right) - 3$

10. $f(t) = 2\sin(3t - \pi) + 1$

Write a function that describes the graph. Use the sine model.

11.

12.

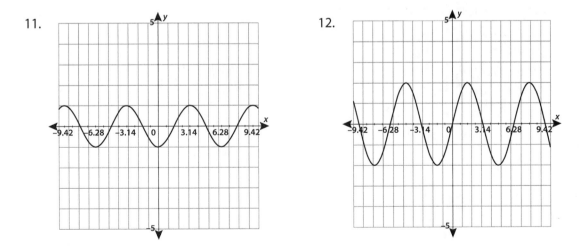

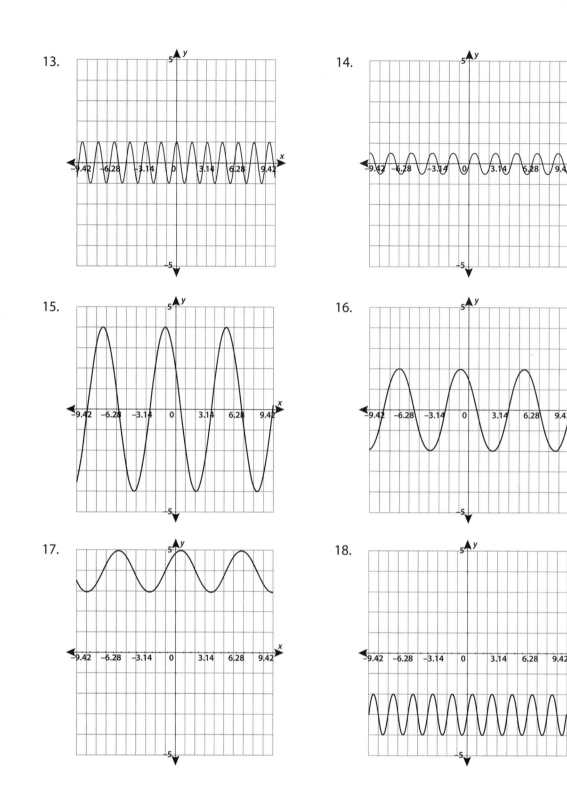

13.

14.

15.

16.

17.

18.

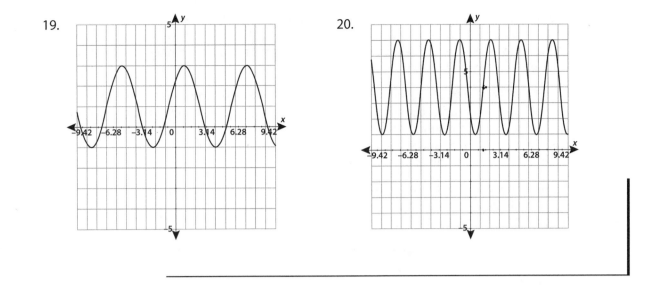

19. 20.

Circular motion

When an object moves around a circle, both its horizontal and its vertical position relative to the center of the circle vary in a periodic fashion. If the radius of the circle is r, the horizontal position of the object varies between r units left of the center and r units right of the center. The vertical position varies between r units below the center and r units above.

Imagine a point moving around a circle of radius 2, centered at the origin, and suppose the point begins its movement from (2, 0). As it moves around the circle in a counterclockwise direction, the y-coordinate of its location gradually increases from 0 to 2, falls back to 0 and down to −2 and climbs back to 0. The vertical motion of the point can be described by a sinusoidal function, if you can identify the amplitude, frequency and period, phase shift, and midline.

The point moves between a low of −2 and a high of +2, so the amplitude is 2 and the midline is $y = 0$. To identify the frequency and period, you'll need to know something about how fast the point is moving, so suppose it makes a full trip around the circle in 6 minutes. The period is 6 minutes, and the frequency is $\frac{2\pi}{6} = \frac{\pi}{3}$. The function that describes the vertical motion of the point is $f(t) = 2\sin\left(\frac{\pi}{3}t\right)$.

EXERCISE
4·2

In questions 1–10, write a sinusoidal function that describes the motion in each problem as a function of time.

1. An object moves counterclockwise around a circle of radius 5, centered at the origin. It completes the trip around the circle in 2 minutes. Write a sinusoidal function that describes the vertical motion of the object.

2. An object moves clockwise around a circle of radius 4, centered at the origin. It completes the trip around the circle in 8 minutes. Write a sinusoidal function that describes the vertical motion of the object.

3. An object moves counterclockwise around a circle of radius 5, centered at (0, 3). It completes the trip around the circle in 4 minutes. Write a sinusoidal function that describes the vertical motion of the object.

4. A Ferris wheel is 160 feet in diameter and is mounted with its center 90 feet above the ground. You board the Ferris wheel from a platform at the wheel's lowest point. It takes 5 minutes for the Ferris wheel to make one revolution. Find a sinusoidal model that gives your height above the ground.

5. The original Ferris wheel, built for the 1893 World's Fair in Chicago, had a diameter of 250 feet and completed a full turn in 9 minutes. The wheel was destroyed in the early 1900s, but it appears that passengers loaded at the bottom of the wheel from a loading platform that was about 15 feet above the ground. Find a sinusoidal function that describes the height of a rider over the course of the ride.

6. The Ferris wheel at the Navy Pier in Chicago has a diameter of 140 feet and completes a trip in 7 minutes. At the top of the ride, you are 150 feet above the ground. Find a sinusoidal function that describes your height over the course of the ride.

7. The London Eye, originally called the Millennium Wheel, has a circumference of 424 meters and completes a rotation in 30 minutes. If passengers load just 0.1 meter above ground level, find a sinusoidal function that describes the height of a passenger riding the Eye.

8. The drum of a washing machine rotates at 1,000 revolutions per minute during its spin cycle. If the drum has a radius of 8 inches, find a sinusoidal function that models the motion of a sock stuck to the edge of the drum.

9. The King Arthur Carousel in Disneyland has a diameter of 22 meters and completes approximately 8 revolutions in 2 minutes. Find a sinusoidal function that models the position of a passenger.

10. Popular in the 1960s, 45s, or vinyl recordings with a single song on each side, played at 45 revolutions per minute. The records had a diameter of 7 inches. Find a sinusoidal function to describe the position of a speck of dust on the outer edge of the record.

For questions 11–20, the height of a passenger on a Ferris wheel is modeled by the sinusoidal function

$$(ht) = 45\sin\left(\frac{\pi}{4}(t-1)\right) + 5,$$ *where h is the height in feet and t is the time in minutes, with t = 0 being the moment at which you board the wheel.*

11. What is the diameter of the Ferris wheel?

12. How far above the ground are you at the moment you board the Ferris wheel?

13. What is the maximum height you reach while riding the Ferris wheel?

14. What is the lowest point you reach while riding?

15. How long does it take to go once around the wheel?

16. How long after boarding do you reach the highest point?

17. How long after boarding do you reach the lowest point?

18. How high are you after 1 minute?

19. How high are you after 5 minutes?

20. When are you 98 feet high?

Springs and pendulums

If you place a mass on the end of a hanging spring and pull down to stretch the spring, the spring will snap back up as soon as you release it. In fact, the spring will compress so that the weight moves up above its starting point. The distance it contracts above the starting point is equal to the distance you pulled it down from its starting point. The mass on the end of the spring will continue to bounce up and down, and if you chart its position, you'll find that it fits a sinusoidal model.

The motion of a pendulum also fits this model, called simple harmonic motion. The pendulum begins hanging vertically and is displaced to one side. Then it swings back to the middle and then to the other side a distance equal to the first displacement. Again the motion can be described with a sinusoidal function.

In each of these situations, the amplitude of the function is equal to the original displacement. If you stretch the spring 2 inches, it will compress until the mass is 2 inches above the resting point. The amplitude will be 2. A full cycle is considered to be the movement from the resting position to the extreme position on one side, back through the rest position to the other extreme and back to rest. The time it takes to complete a full cycle is the period. The frequency is 2π divided by the period. Vertical shifts might be caused by the positioning of the spring (or the method of recording the position) and horizontal or phase shifts by adjustments to the timing.

A spring with a mass on the end is hung so that the mass is 4 feet above the floor. The mass is drawn downward 6 inches and held there. On a signal, the mass is released and timing is begun. The mass completes a full cycle in 0.75 second. Find a sinusoidal function that describes the position of the mass.

The resting position is 4 feet above the floor, and the displacement is 6 inches, or 0.5 foot, so the amplitude is $\dfrac{1}{2}$. The mass oscillates between 3.5 feet and 4.5 feet above the floor, so the midline is $y = 4$. The function has a vertical shift of 4 and an amplitude of $\dfrac{1}{2}$, so you can begin with $f(t) = \dfrac{1}{2}\sin\big(b(t-c)\big) + 4$.

It takes 0.75 second to complete the cycle, so the period is 0.75, or $\dfrac{3}{4}$, second, and the frequency is $\dfrac{2\pi}{0.75} = \dfrac{2\pi}{3/4} = \dfrac{8\pi}{3}$. You can put that piece of information into the function to get $f(t) = \dfrac{1}{2}\sin\left(\dfrac{8\pi}{3}(t-c)\right) + 4$. The timing begins, so $t = 0$, when the mass is at its lower extreme point, 3.5 feet above the floor. The point $(0, 3.5)$ should be on the graph. You need to find a value for c that will shift the graph sideways until one of the minimum points is at the vertical axis. The sine wave hits its minimum $\dfrac{3}{4}$ of the way through the cycle, and in this situation, each cycle is $\dfrac{3}{4}$ of a second long, so you need to shift the graph to the left for a value of $c = \dfrac{3}{4} \cdot \dfrac{3}{4} = \dfrac{9}{16}$. The function that defines this motion is $f(t) = \dfrac{1}{2}\sin\left(\dfrac{8\pi}{3}\left(t - \dfrac{9}{16}\right)\right) + 4$ or $f(t) = \dfrac{1}{2}\sin\left(\dfrac{8\pi}{3}t - \dfrac{3\pi}{2}\right) + 4$.

Solve the following.

1. A mass suspended from the ceiling on a spring is at rest at time $t = 0$ and bounces through a complete cycle in 1 second. If the lowest position of the mass is 4.5 feet above the floor and the highest position is 7.5 feet above the floor, find a sinusoidal function that describes the motion.

2. Find the position of the mass in question 1 at time $t = 0.5$ second.

3. Find the position of the mass in question 1 at time $t = 1.25$ seconds.

4. Find the first time when the mass in question 1 is 4.5 feet off the floor.

5. A mass suspended from the ceiling on a spring is at rest at time $t = 0$ and bounces through a complete cycle in $\dfrac{2}{3}$ second. If the lowest position of the mass is 2 feet above the floor and the highest position is 5 feet above the floor, find a sinusoidal function that describes the motion.

6. Find the position of the mass in question 5 at time $t = 2$ seconds.

7. Find the position of the mass in question 5 at time $t = 3$ seconds.

8. Find the first time when the mass in question 5 is 4 feet off the floor.

9. A pendulum swings 5° to either side of vertical, completing a full cycle in 3 seconds. If the pendulum is in the vertical position, or the zero position, when timing begins, find a sinusoidal function that describes the motion of the pendulum.

10. What is the position of the pendulum in question 9 at time $t = 10$ seconds?

11. What is the position of the pendulum in question 9 at time $t = 5$ seconds?

12. If the pendulum described in question 9 were in the extreme positive position at the moment timing began ($t = 0$), what sinusoidal function would describe its motion?

13. The motion of a pendulum is described by the function $f(t) = 8\sin\left(\dfrac{\pi}{2}t - \dfrac{\pi}{4}\right)$. Sketch a graph of the function.

14. What is the position of the pendulum described in question 13 at the moment when $t = 0$ second?

15. What is the position of the pendulum described in question 13 at the moment when $t = 1$ second?

16. When is the position of the pendulum in question 13 equal to 8?

17. What is the period of the pendulum in question 13?

18. The motion of a mass on a spring suspended from the ceiling is described by the function $f(t) = 2\sin(2\pi t) + 5$, where t is the time in seconds and f is the distance from the floor in feet. Sketch a graph of the function.

19. What is the position of the mass described in question 18 at the moment when $t = 2.5$ seconds?

20. How long does it take for the mass in question 18 to complete a full cycle? Where is its resting point?

Rhythms in nature

Many of the rising and falling movements in nature can be modeled by sinusoidal functions. The ebb and flow of tides fit the model, as do the changing hours of daylight over the course of a year and the rise and fall of the average temperature as the seasons change. While the model is unlikely to be a perfect fit to the observed phenomena, it represents the changing values well enough to allow you to estimate some answers to questions.

If the high tide and low tide are recorded 12 hours apart, a full cycle, from low tide to high tide and back to low tide, will take a period of 24 hours. The frequency is $\frac{2\pi}{24} = \frac{\pi}{12}$. Low tide is recorded as 1 foot and high tide as 8 feet, which means the amplitude is $\frac{8-1}{2} = 3.5$ and the midline is $y = 4.5$. You can begin to think about the equation as

$$f(t) = 3.5\sin\left(\frac{\pi}{12}(t-c)\right) + 4.5$$

The remaining parameter is the phase shift. If the time $t = 0$ corresponds to low tide, the shift would be a quarter cycle, or 6 hours, to the right:

$$f(t) = 3.5\sin\left(\frac{\pi}{12}(t-6)\right) + 4.5$$

If $t = 0$ corresponds to high tide, the shift would be 6 hours to the left:

$$f(t) = 3.5\sin\left(\frac{\pi}{12}(t+6)\right) + 4.5$$

If $t = 0$ corresponds to some other point in the cycle, you'll need more information to determine the shift.

Your body temperature rises and falls over the course of a day, and the parameters of the cycle differ with age and other factors. The hormones that affect your desire to sleep fluctuate over the course of a year, changing with the number of hours of daylight. Respiration, heart rate, and even the pain of arthritis follow roughly sinusoidal rhythms.

Body temperature will fluctuate almost 1°F over the course of a day. If you have a "normal" body temperature of 98.6°F, you will actually vary between a low of about 98.1°F toward the end of your cycle to a high of approximately 99.1°F in the late afternoon or early evening. If your lowest body temperature is recorded at 4 A.M. and your highest at 4 P.M., your body temperature can be described by a sinusoidal function with an amplitude of half a degree Fahrenheit, a midline of $y = 98.6°F$, and a period of 24 hours. The frequency is therefore $\frac{2\pi}{24} = \frac{\pi}{12}$. If you take midnight as time $t = 0$, the horizontal or phase shift is 10 hours to the right. The equation that describes your body temperature is $f(t) = 0.5\sin\left(\frac{\pi}{12}(t-10)\right) + 98.6$. If you take your temperature at noon, or $t = 12$, your "normal" temperature would be

$$f(12) = 0.5\sin\left(\frac{\pi}{12}(12-10)\right) + 98.6$$

$$= 0.5\sin\left(\frac{\pi}{6}\right) + 98.6$$

$$= 0.5(0.5) + 98.6$$

$$= 0.25 + 98.6$$

$$= 98.85$$

To determine when you actually have a temperature of 98.6°F, solve

$$f(t) = 0.5\sin\left(\frac{\pi}{12}(t-10)\right) + 98.6$$

$$98.6 = 0.5\sin\left(\frac{\pi}{12}(t-10)\right) + 98.6$$

$$0 = 0.5\sin\left(\frac{\pi}{12}(t-10)\right)$$

$$0 = \sin\left(\frac{\pi}{12}(t-10)\right)$$

The sine will be equal to 0 when $\frac{\pi}{12}(t-10)$ is equal to 0 or a multiple of π:

$$\frac{\pi}{12}(t-10) = n\pi$$

$$t - 10 = \frac{12n\,\cancel{\pi}}{\cancel{\pi}}$$

$$t = 12n + 10$$

If $n = 0$, $t = 10$, which means that your body temperature is 98.6°F at 10 A.M., as your body temperature rises from the early morning low. Your temperature is also 98.6°F 12 hours later, when $n = 1$ and $t = 22$, but at 10 P.M. your temperature is slowly going down.

When medications are administered, dosages are calculated and timed to maintain a level in the blood stream that is high enough to have a positive effect, called the therapeutic level, but low enough to minimize negative effects, below the toxic level. When a dose of the drug is given, the level in the blood stream rises to a level between the therapeutic level and the toxic level. As the body metabolizes the drug, levels in the blood stream fall, until a new dose is given, and the level begins to rise again. The amount and timing of each dose must be calculated to keep the amount in the blood stream between the therapeutic level and the toxic level.

Aspirin is sometimes used to reduce the fever that accompanies the common cold or other illness. A patient with a temperature of 39.0°C was given a 1 gram dose of aspirin. The reduction in temperature began in half an hour. After 3 hours, the temperature was 37.3°C, and after 6 hours, 38.0°C. The fluctuation in temperature can be described by the sinusoidal function

$$f(t) = \sin\left(\frac{\pi}{4}(t+2)\right) + 38$$

The period of this function is $2\pi \div \dfrac{\pi}{4} = 8$ hours, suggesting that the doses should be spaced less than 8 hours apart to prevent the fever from returning to the 39.0°C level. Patients are generally advised to take aspirin at 4 hour intervals. At time $t = 4$, the patient's temperature is approximately

$$f(4) = \sin\left(\frac{\pi}{4}(4+2)\right) + 38$$

$$= \sin\left(\frac{3\pi}{2}\right) + 38$$

$$= -1 + 38 = 37°C$$

This is the point in the cycle when the temperature is at its lowest and administering another dose at that point would assure that the temperature remains low.

EXERCISE
4·4

Solve the following.

1. If the tides at a particular beach are cyclical with a low tide of 3 feet occurring at midnight ($t = 0$) and a high tide of 11 feet occurring at noon, find a sinusoidal model for these tides.

2. At Cold Spring Harbor on Long Island Sound, high tides of approximately 8 feet were recorded near midnight. At approximately 6 A.M., low tides of −1 feet were noted. Find a sinusoidal model for the tides at Cold Spring Harbor.

3. The following table shows the number of hours of daylight in New York City on the 15th of each month over the course of a year. Find a sinusoidal function that models the data.

Date	Jan.	Feb.	Mar.	Apr.	May	Jun.	Jul.	Aug.	Sept.	Oct.	Nov.	Dec.
t	0	1	2	3	4	5	6	7	8	9	10	11
Hours of light	9.5	10.6	11.7	13.1	14.2	14.8	14.6	13.6	12.3	11.0	9.8	9.2

4. The following table shows the number of hours of daylight in Helsinki, Finland, on the 15th of each month over the course of a year. Find a sinusoidal function that models the data.

Date	Jan.	Feb.	Mar.	Apr.	May	Jun.	Jul.	Aug.	Sept.	Oct.	Nov.	Dec.
t	0	1	2	3	4	5	6	7	8	9	10	11
Hours of light	6.4	9.0	11.6	14.4	16.9	18.4	17.7	15.4	12.6	9.9	7.2	5.6

5. The following table shows average monthly temperatures in Las Vegas, Nevada. Find a sinusoidal function that describes the fluctuation in average low temperature in Las Vegas.

Date	Jan.	Feb.	Mar.	Apr.	May	Jun.	Jul.	Aug.	Sept.	Oct.	Nov.	Dec.
Average high temperature	57	63	69	78	88	99	104	102	94	81	66	57
Average low temperature	37	41	47	54	63	72	78	77	69	57	44	37

6. Use the preceding table to find a sinusoidal function that describes the fluctuation in average high temperature in Las Vegas.

7. The International Space Station orbits the earth in a nearly circular orbit, but the orbit path is not parallel to the equator. Instead the station crosses back and forth between the northern and southern hemispheres. In the course of a 90 minute orbit, the station is as far north as latitude 60° N and as far south as 60° S. Find a sinusoidal equation that gives the latitude of the International Space Station as a function of time.

8. Use the equation found in question 7 to find the latitude of the station after 1 hour of the 90 minute orbit.

9. Use the equation found in question 7 to estimate when the station is at a latitude of 55° N, the approximate latitude of Moscow.

10. On earth, the distance between lines of latitude is about 69 miles. Modify the equation found in question 7 to express the distance of the International Space Station from the equator in miles as a function of time.

11. Based on selected data recorded between 1970 and 2008, it appears that the annual rainfall in Los Angeles, California might be modeled by the sinusoidal function $f(t) = 18\sin(3t) + 20$, where t is the time in years since 1970 and $f(t)$ is the annual rainfall in inches in year t. Using this model, estimate the approximate annual rainfall in Los Angeles in 2004.

12. The electricity supplied to most homes in the United States is referred to as alternating current. It takes its name from the fact that the flow of electrons changes direction, alternating 60 times per second. If the amperage of alternating current varies between 5 amps and −5 amps, find a sinusoidal function that models the current.

13. The voltage supplied by a typical electrical outlet in the United States is modeled by a sinusoidal function that varies between −165 and +165 volts. If the frequency of the fluctuation is 60 cycles per second, find the equation of the sinusoidal function that models the voltage over time.

Identities and equations

In trigonometry, a great deal of time is spent learning and working with identities. Remember that an identity is an equation that is true for all values of the variable involved. In ordinary algebraic equations, demonstrating that a particular equation is an identity is generally just a matter of simplifying each side. Removing parentheses and combining like terms usually will quickly reduce both sides of the equation to the same expression. In trigonometry, because the different trig functions are interrelated, it will often take some substitutions as well as some algebra before you can demonstrate that an equation is an identity.

Because an identity is a statement that is always true, the two sides of the equation are interchangeable and one can be substituted for the other whenever convenient. You'll memorize some key identities and use them to make substitutions into other equations, either to demonstrate that those equations are also identities or to simplify an equation so that it can be solved. Equations that might be difficult or impossible to solve otherwise can be transformed, by substitutions of identities, into equivalent equations that can easily be solved.

Fundamental identities

There are many trigonometric identities, but a few are particularly important for simplifying trigonometric equations. These essential equivalences derive easily from the basic definitions of the trig functions. These identities are key to making the substitutions that allow you to simplify and solve trigonometric equations.

There are four groups of fundamental identities: reciprocal, quotient, cofunction, and Pythagorean identities.

Reciprocal identities

The first group is a collection of identities commonly referred to as the reciprocal identities. Working from the basic definitions of the trig functions, it is simple to show that each of the trigonometric functions is a reciprocal of another:

$$\sin x = \frac{1}{\csc x} \qquad \cos x = \frac{1}{\sec x} \qquad \tan x = \frac{1}{\cot x}$$

$$csx = \frac{1}{\sin x} \qquad \sec x = \frac{1}{\cos x} \qquad \cot x = \frac{1}{\tan x}$$

The expression $\frac{2}{\csc \theta} - \sin \theta$ becomes easier to simplify if $\sin x = \frac{1}{\csc \theta}$ is replaced with $\sin x = \frac{1}{\sin \theta}$. With that substitution,

$$\frac{2}{\csc\theta} - \sin\theta = 2\left(\frac{1}{\csc\theta}\right) - \sin\theta$$
$$= 2\sin\theta - \sin\theta$$
$$= \sin\theta$$

The product of any nonzero number and its reciprocal is always 1. Because these identities are reciprocal relationships, it's also true that the reciprocal functions have a product of 1:

$$\sin\theta\,\csc\theta = 1 \qquad \cos\theta\,\sec\theta = 1 \qquad \tan\theta\,\cot\theta = 1$$

Multiplying through an equation by the reciprocal of a function in the equation can often simplify the equation. Solving $\sec\theta = \cos\theta$ might seem difficult at first, but multiplying both sides by $\cos\theta$ turns the equation into something simpler:

$$\sec\theta = \cos\theta$$
$$\cos\theta\,\sec\theta = \cos^2\theta$$
$$1 = \cos^2\theta$$
$$\cos\theta = \pm 1$$

Because you know the unit circle, you know that $\cos\theta$ is equal to 1 or −1 when θ is equal to a multiple of π.

Quotient identities

The next group of identities is called the quotient identities. Like the reciprocal identities, these can be shown to be true by working from the definitions of the trig functions. It's possible to show that each function is the quotient of two other functions. For example, $\dfrac{\sin\theta}{\cos\theta} = \dfrac{y}{x} = \tan\theta$. The most commonly used of these quotient identities are

$$\tan x = \frac{\sin x}{\cos x} \qquad \cot x = \frac{\cos x}{\sin x}$$

The less frequently used quotient identities are

$$\sin\theta = \frac{\tan\theta}{\sec\theta} \qquad \cos\theta = \frac{\cot\theta}{\csc\theta}$$

$$\csc\theta = \frac{\cot\theta}{\cos\theta} \qquad \sec\theta = \frac{\tan\theta}{\sin\theta}$$

On first glance, you may not think you can simplify the expression $\tan\theta + \sec\theta$, but if you make substitutions, you can rewrite the expression:

$$\tan\theta + \sec\theta = \frac{\sin\theta}{\cos\theta} + \frac{1}{\cos\theta}$$
$$= \frac{\sin\theta + 1}{\cos\theta}$$

Cofunction identities

The cofunction, or complementary function, identities get their names because they refer to a function of one angle being equal to a different function of the complement of the angle. Sine and cosine, tangent and cotangent, and secant and cosecant are complementary functions:

$$\sin x = \cos(90° - x) \qquad \cos x = \sin(90° - x)$$
$$\sec x = \csc(90° - x) \qquad \csc x = \sec(90° - x)$$
$$\tan x = \cot(90° - x) \qquad \cot x = \tan(90° - x)$$

You've probably noticed this relationship when you memorized common values. For example, $\sin\dfrac{\pi}{3} = \cos\dfrac{\pi}{6}$ because $\dfrac{\pi}{3}$ and $\dfrac{\pi}{6}$ are complementary.

Pythagorean identities

The Pythagorean identities take their names from the Pythagorean theorem by which they're derived. The fundamental Pythagorean identity is

$$\sin^2 x + \cos^2 x = 1$$
$$1 + \cot^2 x = \csc^2 x$$
$$\tan^2 x + 1 = \sec^2 x$$

In any right triangle, with legs x and y and hypotenuse h, the Pythagorean theorem says $x^2 + y^2 = h^2$. If that relationship is divided by h^2, the result, $\dfrac{x^2}{h^2} + \dfrac{y^2}{h^2} = \dfrac{h^2}{h^2}$ or $\left(\dfrac{x}{h}\right)^2 + \left(\dfrac{y}{h}\right)^2 = 1$, is equivalent to the Pythagorean identity $\begin{aligned}\sin^2 x + \cos^2 x &= 1 \\ \tan^2 x + 1 &= \sec^2 x\end{aligned}$. Probably the most commonly used identity, this one may be more helpful to you when rearranged as

$$\sin^2 x + \cos^2 x = 1$$
$$\sin^2 \theta = 1 - \cos^2 \theta$$

or

$$\cos^2 \theta = 1 - \sin^2 \theta$$
$$\tan^2 x + 1 = \sec^2 x$$

In that form, you can easily replace $\begin{aligned}\sin^2 x + \cos^2 x &= 1 \\ 1 + \sin^2 \theta &= \csc^2 x \\ \tan^2 x + 1 &= \sec^2 x\end{aligned}$ or $\begin{aligned}\sin^2 x + \cos^2 \theta &= 1 \\ 1 + \cot^2 x &= \csc^2 x \\ \tan^2 x + 1 &= \sec^2 x\end{aligned}$ with an expression in terms of the other function. The expression $\cos^2 \theta + 2\sin^2 \theta$ can be simplified by substituting:

$$\begin{aligned}\cos^2 \theta + 2\sin^2 \theta &= 1 - \sin^2 \theta + 2\sin^2 \theta \\ &= 1 + \sin^2 \theta\end{aligned}$$

or

$$\begin{aligned}\cos^2 \theta + 2\sin^2 \theta &= \cos^2 \theta + 2\left(1 - \cos^2 \theta\right) \\ &= \cos^2 \theta + 2 - 2\cos^2 \theta \\ &= 2 - \cos^2 \theta\end{aligned}$$

There are two other Pythagorean identities, each derived by dividing the fundamental Pythagorean identity by one of its terms. Divide the fundamental Pythagorean identity by $\sin^2 \theta$ to get

$$\frac{\sin^2 \theta}{\sin^2 \theta} + \frac{\cos^2 \theta}{\sin^2 \theta} = \frac{1}{\sin^2 \theta}$$

or

$$1 + \cot^2 \theta = \csc^2 \theta$$

Divide the fundamental Pythagorean identity by $\cos^2 x$ to get

$$\frac{\sin^2 \theta}{\cos^2 \theta} + \frac{\cos^2 \theta}{\cos^2 \theta} = \frac{1}{\cos^2 \theta}$$

or

$$\tan^2 \theta + 1 = \sec^2 \theta$$

Each version can be useful in different circumstances. To simplify the expression $\tan^2 \theta \csc^2 \theta - \tan^2 \theta$, substitute for $\csc^2 \theta$:

$$\begin{aligned} \tan^2 \theta \csc^2 \theta - \tan^2 \theta &= \tan^2 \theta \left(1 + \cot^2 \theta\right) - \tan^2 \theta \\ &= \tan^2 \theta + \tan^2 \theta \cot^2 \theta - \tan^2 \theta \\ &= 1 \end{aligned}$$

Alternatively, you could substitute for $\tan^2 \theta$:

$$\begin{aligned} \tan^2 \theta \csc^2 \theta - \tan^2 \theta &= \left(\sec^2 \theta - 1\right)\csc^2 \theta - \left(\sec^2 \theta - 1\right) \\ &= \sec^2 \theta \csc^2 \theta - \csc^2 \theta - \sec^2 \theta + 1 \\ &= \sec^2 \theta \csc^2 \theta - \sec^2 \theta - \csc^2 \theta + 1 \\ &= \sec^2 \theta \left(\csc^2 \theta - 1\right) - \csc^2 \theta + 1 \\ &= \sec^2 \theta \left(\cot^2 \theta\right) - \csc^2 \theta + 1 \\ &= \frac{1}{\cos^2 \theta} \frac{\cos^2 \theta}{\sin^2 \theta} - \csc^2 \theta + 1 \\ &= \frac{1}{\sin^2 \theta} - \csc^2 \theta + 1 \\ &= \csc^2 \theta - \csc^2 \theta + 1 \\ &= 1 \end{aligned}$$

Verifying identities

To verify an identity, you need to demonstrate that the two sides of the equation are identical. To do this, first decide which side of the equation seems simpler. Leave this side untouched, as your goal. If you start making changes on both sides, you can easily lose track of what you're trying to accomplish and find yourself going in circles.

On the side you've decided to change, use known identities to substitute for pieces of the expression. You might use a reciprocal identity or one of the Pythagorean identities to replace a part of the given equation. Then use algebraic techniques to simplify until the more complicated side matches the goal. You may multiply and cancel, combine like terms, or even factor the expression.

When the identity you're trying to prove contains more than one trig function, it's usually helpful to make substitutions that will reduce the number of functions involved. For that reason, it's often a wise idea to put as much of the equation as possible in terms of the sine and cosine.

Verify: $\sin\theta + \cot\theta\cos\theta = \csc\theta$.

The right side, $\csc\theta$, seems simpler, so keep that as the goal. To reduce the number of functions involved, replace $\cot\theta$ by the quotient identity $\dfrac{\cos\theta}{\sin\theta}$:

$$\sin\theta + \cot\theta\cos\theta = \csc\theta$$

$$\sin\theta + \frac{\cos\theta}{\sin\theta}\cos\theta = \csc\theta$$

$$\sin\theta + \frac{\cos^2\theta}{\sin\theta} = \csc\theta$$

If you remember that your goal $\csc\theta = \dfrac{1}{\sin\theta}$, you won't be alarmed by the appearance of a fraction. Find a common denominator and add the terms on the left side:

$$\sin\theta + \frac{\cos^2\theta}{\sin\theta} = \csc\theta$$

$$\frac{\sin^2\theta}{\sin\theta} + \frac{\cos^2\theta}{\sin\theta} = \csc\theta$$

$$\frac{\sin^2\theta + \cos^2\theta}{\sin\theta} = \csc\theta$$

Use the Pythagorean identity to replace the numerator with 1 and then replace $\dfrac{1}{\sin\theta}$ with $\csc\theta$:

$$\frac{1}{\sin\theta} = \csc\theta$$

$$\csc\theta = \csc\theta$$

EXERCISE

5·1

Verify each identity.

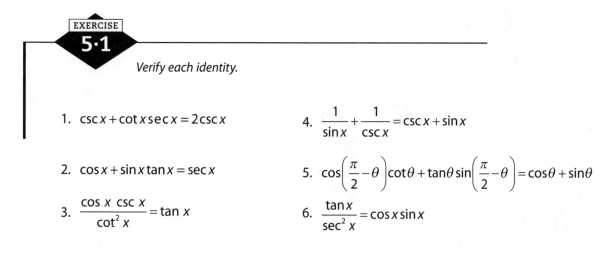

1. $\csc x + \cot x\sec x = 2\csc x$

2. $\cos x + \sin x\tan x = \sec x$

3. $\dfrac{\cos x\,\csc x}{\cot^2 x} = \tan x$

4. $\dfrac{1}{\sin x} + \dfrac{1}{\csc x} = \csc x + \sin x$

5. $\cos\left(\dfrac{\pi}{2} - \theta\right)\cot\theta + \tan\theta\sin\left(\dfrac{\pi}{2} - \theta\right) = \cos\theta + \sin\theta$

6. $\dfrac{\tan x}{\sec^2 x} = \cos x\sin x$

7. $\tan\left(\dfrac{\pi}{2}-\theta\right)\left(1-\cos^2\theta\right)\sec\theta = \sin\theta$

8. $\dfrac{\tan x\left(1-\sin^2 x\right)}{\sin^2 x} = \cot x$

9. $\cos\left(\dfrac{\pi}{2}-\theta\right)\left(\sin\theta+\cot\theta\cos\theta\right)=1$

10. $\dfrac{\sin x -1}{\csc x}\left(\csc x+1\right)=-\cos^2 x$

11. $\dfrac{\csc^2\theta\tan\theta-1}{\csc\theta}=\sec\theta-\sin\theta$

12. $\sin\theta=\sin\left(\dfrac{\pi}{2}-\theta\right)\cot\left(\dfrac{\pi}{2}-\theta\right)$

13. $\sin\theta+\cos\theta\cot\theta=\csc\theta$

14. $\csc\theta\tan\theta-\sin\theta=\dfrac{\tan\theta-\sin^2\theta}{\sin\theta}$

15. $\sec\theta\tan\theta-\cot\theta=\dfrac{\tan^2\theta-\cos\theta}{\sin\theta}$

16. $\sec^2\theta\left(\cos^2\theta-1\right)=-\tan^2\theta$

17. $\sec x = \csc(90° - x)$

18. $\tan^2\theta\sin\theta+\sin\theta=\dfrac{\tan\theta}{\cos\theta}$

19. $\cos^2\theta-\csc\theta=\dfrac{\sin\theta\cos\theta-\sec\theta}{\sec\theta\sin\theta}$

20. $\cos x = \dfrac{1}{\sec x}$

Solving trigonometric equations

When you start to solve an equation involving trigonometric functions, you may face a number of different complications. The periodic nature of the trig functions means that you'll be looking for multiple solutions, even if you're only solving over a limited domain. You'll need to isolate the trigonometric function in the equation first, and that may be complicated if the equation contains more than one function. The equation may be quadratic in form, requiring factoring or, occasionally, even the use of the quadratic formula.

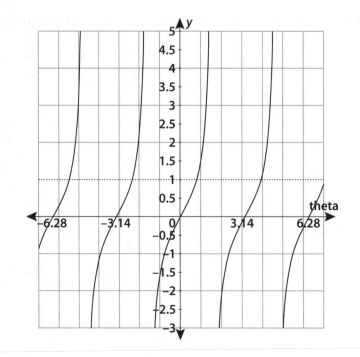

Solving a trigonometric equation can often be made simpler by following these steps:

- If the equation involves more than one trig function, use identities to substitute and simplify, getting down to one function if you can. Whenever possible, try to put the equation in terms of the sine or cosine, since these are the functions you likely know best.
- Let a single variable represent the remaining trig function. For example, replace all occurrences of $\cos x$ with t.
- Solve the equation for this new placeholder variable.
- Reinsert the trig function and determine the value of the argument that will produce the desired value. If, for example, you find that $t = 1$ and t was taking the place of $\cos \theta$, you need to determine what values of θ will make $\cos \theta = 1$.
- Remember that trigonometric functions are periodic. Equations commonly have multiple solutions. Be sure to give all the values of the variable that satisfy the equation. To specify all solutions, use the period of the function to summarize the repetition. For example, $\tan \theta = 1$ for $\theta = \dfrac{\pi}{4} \pm n\pi$. The above figure shows the graph of $y = \tan \theta$ and the graph of $y = 1$.

To find all solutions of the equation $3 - 3\sin x - 2\cos^2 x = 0$ in the interval $[0, 2\pi)$, it might be helpful to look at the graph if you have access to a graphing utility. The figure below shows the graph of $3 - 3\sin x - 2\cos^2 x = 0$ over the interval $[0, 2\pi)$. You're looking for the x-intercepts.

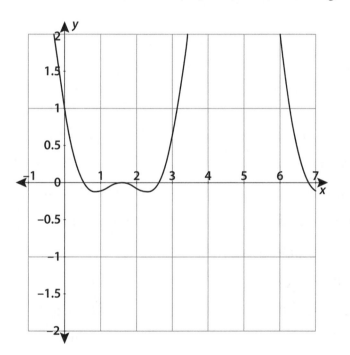

The equation contains both $\sin \theta$ and $\cos \theta$, so the first step is to rewrite the equation in terms of a single function. If you don't have access to a graphing utility, getting the equation in terms of one function may simplify it enough that you can sketch the graph by hand. In any case, it will make the equation easier to solve. Use the Pythagorean identity to replace $\cos^2 x$ with $1 - \sin^2 x$. Then

$$3 - 3\sin x - 2\cos^2 x = 0$$
$$3 - 3\sin x - 2\left(1 - \sin^2 x\right) = 0$$
$$3 - 3\sin x - 2 + 2\sin^2 x = 0$$
$$1 - 3\sin x + 2\sin^2 x = 0$$
$$2\sin^2 x - 3\sin x + 1 = 0$$

The equation has a quadratic form, and it will be easier to deal with that if you streamline it a little bit. Let $t = \sin x$ and $x = \dfrac{\pi}{6}, \dfrac{5\pi}{6}, \dfrac{\pi}{2}$ becomes $2t^2 - 3t + 1 = 0$. Factor and solve:

$$2t^2 - 3t + 1 = 0$$
$$(2t - 1)(t - 1) = 0$$
$$2t - 1 = 0 \qquad t - 1 = 0$$
$$2t = 1 \qquad\quad t = 1$$
$$t = \dfrac{1}{2}$$

Now you need to undo the streamlining and get back to what you're actually looking for. Replace $t = \sin x$:

$$\sin x = \dfrac{1}{2} \text{ when } x = \dfrac{\pi}{6} \text{ or } \dfrac{5\pi}{6}$$

and

$$\sin x = 1 \text{ when } x = \dfrac{\pi}{2}$$

So the solutions are $x = \dfrac{\pi}{6}, \dfrac{5\pi}{6}, \dfrac{\pi}{2}$.

EXERCISE
5·2

Solve each equation over the domain $[-2\pi, 2\pi]$.

1. $4\sin^2 x = 3$

2. $2\tan x \cos x - \tan x = 0$

3. $3 + 3\sin x = 2\cos^2 x$

4. $2\cos^2 x + 3\cos x + 1 = 0$

5. $\tan^3 x - 3\tan x = 4 - \sec^2 x$

6. $4\cos\theta = 3\sec\theta$

7. $6\sec^2\theta - \sec\theta = 12$

8. $2\sin^2\theta + 12\cos^2\theta = 2 - 6\cos\theta$

9. $\cot^2\theta + 2\csc^2\theta = 5$

10. $5\sin^2\theta + 2\cos^2\theta - \dfrac{22}{8} = 0$

Solve each equation over the real numbers.

11. $\cot^2 x + \left(\sqrt{3} - 1\right)\cot x = \sqrt{3}$

12. $\tan x \csc x - \tan x \sec x = 0$

13. $\csc x - \cot^2 x = 1$

14. $4 - 4\cos^2 x - 2\sin x = \sqrt{2}\left(1 - 2\sin x\right)$

15. $2\sin x \cos x - 1 = \sqrt{2}\left(\sin x - \cos x\right)$

16. $2\sin^2\theta - \sin\theta - 1 = 0$

17. $2\cos^2\theta - 5\cos\theta + 1 = 0$

18. $3\tan^2\theta \sin\theta - \sin\theta = 0$

19. $\sec\theta - 1 = 2\sin\theta \sec\theta - 2\sin\theta$

20. $\cos^2\theta - \sin^2\theta = 0$

Sum and difference identities

Why do you need sum and difference identities? A brief examination of common values will tell you that the trig functions are not additive. For example,

$$\sin\dfrac{\pi}{6} + \sin\dfrac{\pi}{3} \neq \sin\left(\dfrac{\pi}{6} + \dfrac{\pi}{3}\right)$$

because $\sin\dfrac{\pi}{6}=\dfrac{1}{2}$ and $\sin\dfrac{\pi}{3}=\dfrac{\sqrt{3}}{2}$ so $\sin\dfrac{\pi}{6}+\sin\dfrac{\pi}{3}=\dfrac{1}{2}+\dfrac{\sqrt{3}}{2}=\dfrac{1+\sqrt{3}}{2}$, which is greater than 1,

but $\sin\left(\dfrac{\pi}{6}+\dfrac{\pi}{3}\right)=\sin\dfrac{\pi}{2}=1$. It is helpful, therefore, to have identities for the trig functions of sums and differences:

$$\sin(\alpha+\beta)=\sin\alpha\cos\beta+\cos\alpha\sin\beta \qquad \sin(\alpha-\beta)=\sin\alpha\cos\beta-\cos\alpha\sin\beta$$

$$\cos(\alpha+\beta)=\cos\alpha\cos\beta-\sin\alpha\sin\beta \qquad \cos(\alpha-\beta)=\cos\alpha\cos\beta+\sin\alpha\sin\beta$$

$$\tan(\alpha+\beta)=\dfrac{\tan\alpha+\tan\beta}{1-\tan\alpha\tan\beta} \qquad \tan(\alpha-\beta)=\dfrac{\tan\alpha-\tan\beta}{1+\tan\alpha\tan\beta}$$

Notice that the difference between the sum and difference identity for each formula is only the change of signs. For the sine identities, the sign in the formula matches the sign in the argument. The sign of a sum is a sum, and the sign of a difference is a difference. The sine identities have matching signs, but the cosine identities do not. For the tangent identities, remember that $\tan\theta=\dfrac{\sin\theta}{\cos\theta}$. The identities for the tangent of a sum or difference come from the quotient of the identities for the sine and cosine of a sum or of a difference, so the sign in the numerator will match the argument, but the sign in the denominator will not.

The sum and difference identities can be used in simplifying identities or simplifying equations before solving, but they're also useful for finding the exact value of trig functions of angles that can be expressed as the sum or difference of angles whose values you've memorized. The key is finding the combination of angles that add or subtract to the angle you need. For example, $\dfrac{\pi}{3}$ and $\dfrac{\pi}{4}$ subtract to $\dfrac{\pi}{12}$ and add to $\dfrac{7\pi}{12}$. To find $\tan\dfrac{7\pi}{12}$, rewrite it as $\tan\left(\dfrac{\pi}{3}+\dfrac{\pi}{4}\right)$ and apply the identity

$$\tan\dfrac{7\pi}{12}=\tan\left(\dfrac{\pi}{3}+\dfrac{\pi}{4}\right)$$

$$=\dfrac{\tan\dfrac{\pi}{3}+\tan\dfrac{\pi}{4}}{1-\tan\dfrac{\pi}{3}\tan\dfrac{\pi}{4}}$$

Evaluate each function

$$\tan\dfrac{7\pi}{12}=\dfrac{\sqrt{3}+1}{1-\sqrt{3}\cdot 1}$$

Simplify and rationalize the denominator:

$$\tan\dfrac{7\pi}{12}=\dfrac{1+\sqrt{3}}{1-\sqrt{3}}\cdot\dfrac{1+\sqrt{3}}{1+\sqrt{3}}$$

$$=\dfrac{\left(1+\sqrt{3}\right)^{2}}{1-3}$$

$$=-\dfrac{4+2\sqrt{3}}{2}$$

$$=-2-\sqrt{3}$$

Verify each identity.

1. $\sin(\alpha + \beta) + \sin(\alpha - \beta) = 2\sin\alpha\cos\beta$

2. $\cos(\alpha - \beta) - \cos(\alpha + \beta) = 2\sin\alpha\sin\beta$

3. $\dfrac{\sin(\alpha - \beta)}{\sin(\alpha + \beta)} = \dfrac{\cot\beta - \cot\alpha}{\cot\beta + \cot\alpha}$

4. $\sin(\alpha + \beta)\sin(\alpha - \beta) = \sin^2\alpha - \sin^2\beta$

5. $\sin(\alpha + \beta)\sin(\alpha - \beta) = \cos^2\beta - \cos^2\alpha$

6. $\dfrac{\sin(\alpha + \beta) + \sin(\alpha - \beta)}{\cos(\alpha + \beta) + \cos(\alpha - \beta)} = \tan\alpha$

7. Use the difference identities to verify that $\sin\left(\dfrac{\pi}{2} - x - y\right) = \cos(x + y)$.

8. Use the difference identities to verify the cofunction identity $\tan\left(\dfrac{\pi}{2} - \theta\right) = \cot\theta$.

9. Use the difference identities to verify the cofunction identity $\sin\left(\dfrac{\pi}{2} - \theta\right) = \cos\theta$.

10. Use the difference identities to verify the cofunction identity $\csc\left(\dfrac{\pi}{2} - \theta\right) = \sec\theta$.

Use the sum and difference identities to find the value of each expression.

11. $\sin\dfrac{\pi}{12} = \sin\left(\dfrac{\pi}{3} - \dfrac{\pi}{4}\right)$

12. $\cos\dfrac{7\pi}{12}$

13. $\tan\dfrac{17\pi}{12}$

14. $\sin\dfrac{5\pi}{12}$

15. $\cos\dfrac{13\pi}{12}$

16. $\tan\dfrac{5\pi}{12}$

17. $\tan\dfrac{13\pi}{12}$

18. $\sin\dfrac{7\pi}{12}$

19. $\tan\dfrac{\pi}{12}$

20. $\sin\dfrac{17\pi}{12}$

Solve each equation over the domain $[0, 2\pi]$.

21. $\tan\left(\theta + \dfrac{\pi}{4}\right) = 6\tan\theta$

22. $\cos\left(\theta + \dfrac{\pi}{6}\right) - \sin\left(\theta + \dfrac{\pi}{3}\right) = \dfrac{1}{2}$

23. $\cos\alpha\cos(\alpha - \beta) + \sin\alpha\sin(\alpha - \beta) = 0$

24. $\sec\left(\theta + \dfrac{5\pi}{3}\right) + \sec\left(\theta - \dfrac{5\pi}{3}\right) = 2\sec\theta$

25. $\sin(\alpha + \beta) = \sin(\alpha - \beta)$

Double-angle and half-angle identities

If the sum identities are applied to two angles of equal measure, the results are called the double-angle identities. Like the sum and difference identities, the double-angle identities can be used both to verify identities and to simplify equations so they can be solved. They can, in theory, be used to find exact values of the trig functions of angles that are double known values, but since most of those are known values, that application is not common.

From the identity for the cosine of a double angle, however, you can derive the half-angle identities, and those can be useful both in identities and equations and in finding the exact values of the trig functions of angles that are half of the common angles.

Double-angle identities

If you begin with the sum identities and substitute α for β, you can derive identities for the sine, cosine, and tangent of 2α:

$$\sin(2\alpha) = \sin(\alpha + \alpha) = \sin\alpha\cos\alpha + \cos\alpha\sin\alpha = 2\sin\alpha\cos\alpha$$

$$\cos(2\alpha) = \cos(\alpha + \alpha) = \cos\alpha\cos\alpha - \sin\alpha\sin\alpha = \cos^2\alpha - \sin^2\alpha$$

$$\tan(2\alpha) = \tan(\alpha + \alpha) = \frac{\tan\alpha + \tan\alpha}{1 - \tan\alpha\tan\alpha} = \frac{2\tan\alpha}{1 - \tan^2\alpha}$$

It's useful to remember that there are three versions of the $\cos(2\alpha)$ identity. The original, above, involves both the sine and cosine functions, but using the Pythagorean identities to substitute lets you create a version involving only the sine and a version involving only the cosine.

The sine-only version is

$$\begin{aligned}
\cos(2\alpha) &= \cos^2\alpha - \sin^2\alpha \\
&= \left(1 - \sin^2\alpha\right) - \sin^2\alpha \\
&= 1 - 2\sin^2\alpha
\end{aligned}$$

The cosine-only version is

$$\begin{aligned}
\cos(2\alpha) &= \cos^2\alpha - \sin^2\alpha \\
&= \cos^2\alpha - \left(1 - \cos^2\alpha\right) \\
&= 2\cos^2\alpha - 1
\end{aligned}$$

In different situations, the different versions allow convenient substitutions. To simplify the expression $\dfrac{1 + \sin\theta}{\cos(2\theta) + \sin^2\theta}$, substitute $1 - 2\sin^2\theta$ for $\cos(2\theta)$:

$$\begin{aligned}
\frac{1 + \sin\theta}{\cos(2\theta) + \sin^2\theta} &= \frac{1 + \sin\theta}{\left(1 - 2\sin^2\theta\right) + \sin^2\theta} \\
&= \frac{1 + \sin\theta}{1 - \sin^2\theta} \\
&= \frac{1 + \sin\theta}{(1 - \sin\theta)(1 + \sin\theta)} \\
&= \frac{1}{1 - \sin\theta}
\end{aligned}$$

To simplify the expression $\sec\theta(\cos(2\theta)+1)$, replace $\cos(2\theta)$ with $2\cos^2\theta - 1$:

$$\sec\theta(\cos(2\theta)+1) = \sec\theta(2\cos^2\theta - 1 + 1)$$
$$= 2\sec\theta\cos^2\theta$$
$$= \frac{2}{\cos\theta}\cos^2\theta$$
$$= 2\cos\theta$$

Half-angle identities

To derive the half-angle identities, you need to begin with the identity for the cosine of a double angle. You'll do a little bit of renaming of angles and a little bit of algebra to arrive at the half-angle formula.

If you begin with the sine-only version of the cosine of a double-angle formula, $\cos(2\alpha) = 1 - 2\sin^2\alpha$, and let $\theta = 2\alpha$ and $\alpha = \dfrac{\theta}{2}$, then $\cos\theta = 1 - 2\sin^2\dfrac{\theta}{2}$. Solve for $\sin^2\dfrac{\theta}{2}$ to get $\sin^2\dfrac{\theta}{2} = \dfrac{1-\cos\theta}{2}$ and then take the square root of both sides:

$$\sin\frac{\theta}{2} = \pm\sqrt{\frac{1-\cos\theta}{2}}$$

Whether you use the positive or the negative version will be determined by the quadrant in which $\dfrac{\theta}{2}$ falls. If $\dfrac{\theta}{2}$ falls in the first or second quadrant, the sine will be positive. If it falls in quadrant III or IV, the sine will be negative.

If you use the half-angle formula to find $\sin\dfrac{5\pi}{8}$ by taking $\sin\left(\dfrac{1}{2}\cdot\dfrac{5\pi}{4}\right)$, you need to realize that $\dfrac{5\pi}{8}$ has a terminal side in quadrant II, so the sine will be positive. Because you know that the sine will be positive, you'll calculate the value as

$$\sin\frac{5\pi}{8} = \sin\left(\frac{1}{2}\cdot\frac{5\pi}{4}\right)$$
$$= \sqrt{\frac{1-\cos\dfrac{5\pi}{4}}{2}}$$
$$= \sqrt{\frac{1-\left(-\dfrac{\sqrt{2}}{2}\right)}{2}}$$
$$= \sqrt{\frac{2+\sqrt{2}}{4}}$$

You can find a decimal approximation for this value on a calculator, if you wish, or simply leave it in radical form.

If you begin instead with the cosine-only version, $\cos(2\alpha) = 2\cos^2\alpha - 1$, make the same substitutions of $\theta = 2\alpha$ and $\alpha = \dfrac{\theta}{2}$, and solve for $\cos\dfrac{\theta}{2}$, you get

$$\cos\frac{\theta}{2} = \pm\sqrt{\frac{1+\cos\theta}{2}}$$

If $\frac{\theta}{2}$ falls in the first or fourth quadrant, the cosine will be positive. If $\frac{\theta}{2}$ falls in quadrant II or III, the cosine is negative. To find $\cos\frac{5\pi}{8}$ using the half-angle formula, remember that the terminal side of the angle is in quadrant II, so the cosine will be negative:

$$\cos\frac{5\pi}{8} = \cos\left(\frac{1}{2}\cdot\frac{5\pi}{4}\right)$$

$$= -\sqrt{\frac{1+\cos\dfrac{5\pi}{4}}{2}}$$

$$= -\sqrt{\frac{1+\left(-\dfrac{\sqrt{2}}{2}\right)}{2}}$$

$$= -\sqrt{\frac{2-\sqrt{2}}{4}}$$

The identity for $\tan\frac{\theta}{2}$ can be found by using the quotient identity:

$$\tan\frac{\theta}{2} = \frac{\sin\dfrac{\theta}{2}}{\cos\dfrac{\theta}{2}}$$

$$= \frac{\pm\sqrt{\dfrac{1-\cos\theta}{2}}}{\pm\sqrt{\dfrac{1+\cos\theta}{2}}}$$

$$= \pm\sqrt{\frac{1-\cos\theta}{1+\cos\theta}}$$

To find $\tan\frac{5\pi}{8}$, recognize that the tangent will be negative for a second-quadrant angle. Then calculate

$$\tan\frac{5\pi}{8} = \tan\left(\frac{1}{2}\cdot\frac{5\pi}{4}\right)$$

$$= -\sqrt{\frac{1-\cos\dfrac{5\pi}{4}}{1+\cos\dfrac{5\pi}{4}}}$$

$$= -\sqrt{\frac{1-\left(-\dfrac{\sqrt{2}}{2}\right)}{1+\left(-\dfrac{\sqrt{2}}{2}\right)}}$$

$$= -\sqrt{\frac{2+\sqrt{2}}{2-\sqrt{2}}}$$

$$= -\frac{\sqrt{2+\sqrt{2}}}{\sqrt{2-\sqrt{2}}}$$

$$= -\frac{\sqrt{2+\sqrt{2}} \cdot \sqrt{2-\sqrt{2}}}{2-\sqrt{2}}$$

$$= -\frac{\sqrt{4-2}}{2-\sqrt{2}}$$

$$= -\frac{\sqrt{2}}{2-\sqrt{2}} \cdot \frac{2+\sqrt{2}}{2+\sqrt{2}}$$

$$= -\frac{2\sqrt{2}+2}{4-2}$$

$$= -\left(\sqrt{2}+1\right)$$

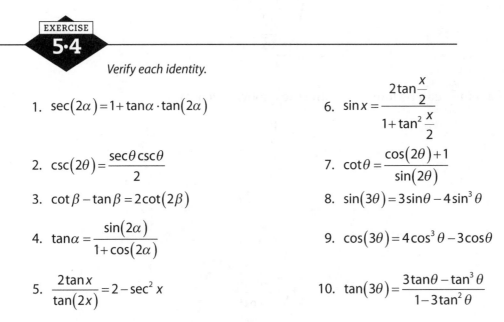

EXERCISE
5·4

Verify each identity.

1. $\sec(2\alpha) = 1 + \tan\alpha \cdot \tan(2\alpha)$

2. $\csc(2\theta) = \dfrac{\sec\theta\,\csc\theta}{2}$

3. $\cot\beta - \tan\beta = 2\cot(2\beta)$

4. $\tan\alpha = \dfrac{\sin(2\alpha)}{1+\cos(2\alpha)}$

5. $\dfrac{2\tan x}{\tan(2x)} = 2 - \sec^2 x$

6. $\sin x = \dfrac{2\tan\dfrac{x}{2}}{1+\tan^2\dfrac{x}{2}}$

7. $\cot\theta = \dfrac{\cos(2\theta)+1}{\sin(2\theta)}$

8. $\sin(3\theta) = 3\sin\theta - 4\sin^3\theta$

9. $\cos(3\theta) = 4\cos^3\theta - 3\cos\theta$

10. $\tan(3\theta) = \dfrac{3\tan\theta - \tan^3\theta}{1 - 3\tan^2\theta}$

Use the half-angle identities to find the value of each expression.

11. $\sin\dfrac{\pi}{12}$

12. $\cos\dfrac{\pi}{12}$

13. $\tan\dfrac{\pi}{12}$

14. $\sin\dfrac{5\pi}{12}$

15. $\cos\dfrac{7\pi}{12}$

Solve each equation over the real numbers.

16. $2\sin^2(2\theta) = 1$

17. $\cos(2\theta) = -\cos\theta$

18. $\cos\theta = \sin(2\theta)$

19. $2\csc\theta - \tan\theta\,\csc^2\theta = 0$

20. $\sin\dfrac{\theta}{2} = \cos\theta$

Product-sum and power-reducing identities

Combinations and variations on the sum, difference, double-angle, and half-angle identities allow you to simplify many trigonometric expressions. Some combinations occur frequently enough that they warrant their own names.

Product-sum identities

The product-sum identities use the sum and difference identities to provide equivalents for some common products:

$$\sin\alpha \sin\beta = \frac{\cos(\alpha - \beta) - \cos(\alpha + \beta)}{2}$$

$$\cos\alpha \cos\beta = \frac{\cos(\alpha + \beta) + \cos(\alpha - \beta)}{2}$$

$$\sin\alpha \cos\beta = \frac{\sin(\alpha + \beta) + \sin(\alpha - \beta)}{2}$$

$$\cos\alpha \sin\beta = \frac{\sin(\alpha + \beta) - \sin(\alpha - \beta)}{2}$$

Power-reducing identities

The power-reducing identities use the half-angle identities (which are in turn derived from the double-angle identities) to express squares of the common trig functions:

$$\sin^2\theta = \frac{1 - \cos(2\theta)}{2}$$

$$\cos^2\theta = \frac{1 + \cos(2\theta)}{2}$$

$$\tan^2\theta = \frac{1 - \cos(2\theta)}{1 + \cos(2\theta)}$$

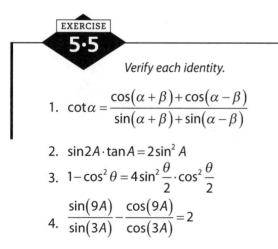

EXERCISE
5·5

Verify each identity.

1. $\cot\alpha = \dfrac{\cos(\alpha + \beta) + \cos(\alpha - \beta)}{\sin(\alpha + \beta) + \sin(\alpha - \beta)}$

2. $\sin 2A \cdot \tan A = 2\sin^2 A$

3. $1 - \cos^2\theta = 4\sin^2\dfrac{\theta}{2} \cdot \cos^2\dfrac{\theta}{2}$

4. $\dfrac{\sin(9A)}{\sin(3A)} - \dfrac{\cos(9A)}{\cos(3A)} = 2$

5. $2\cos\alpha\tan\beta = \sin\alpha + \cos\alpha\left(2\tan\beta - \tan\alpha\right)$

6. $4\sin\alpha\sin\beta\cos\alpha\cos\beta = \sin^2\left(\alpha + \beta\right) - \sin^2\left(\alpha - \beta\right)$

7. $\tan^2\theta\cos\left(2\theta\right) + \cos\left(2\theta\right) = 2 - \sec^2\theta$

8. $2\sin\theta\cos\theta = \tan\theta + \tan\theta\cos\left(2\theta\right)$

9. $2\sin^2\theta\cos^2\theta = 1 - \sin^2\theta - \cos\left(2\theta\right) + \sin^2\theta\cos\left(2\theta\right)$

10. $\sin^3\left(2\theta\right) = \sin\theta\cos\theta\left(1 - \cos\left(4\theta\right)\right)$

Law of sines and law of cosines

·6·

The trigonometric ratios that began your study of trigonometry allow you to find unknown sides in right triangles if you have the length of one side and the measure of one acute angle. You can use right triangle trigonometry to find the acute angles of a right triangle if you know two of the sides. Up to this point, you were only able to find that missing information in right triangles, but the usefulness of the trig functions can be extended to other triangles, non-right triangles, with the help of two rules called the law of sines and the law of cosines.

The law of sines

In geometry, you learned that the longest side of a triangle was opposite the largest angle, and the shortest side opposite the smallest angle, but you may also have learned that the lengths of the sides were not proportional to the size of the angles. The law of sines fills in the missing piece by telling you that the lengths of the sides are proportional to the sines of the angles.

If $\triangle ABC$ is a triangle (not necessarily a right triangle) with side a opposite $\angle A$, side b opposite $\angle B$, and side c opposite $\angle C$, as shown in the figure below, then

$$\frac{a}{\sin A} = \frac{b}{\sin B} = \frac{c}{\sin C}$$

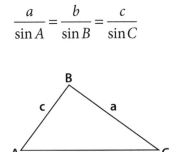

Finding sides with the law of sines

If you know the measures of two angles of a triangle and the length of one side, you can use a proportion from the law of sines to solve for a missing side. You will need the measurement of the angle opposite the known side and the measure of the angle opposite the side you're trying to find, but if you know any two angles of the triangle, you can find the third by subtracting from 180°.

71

Suppose that, in $\triangle ABC$, $\angle A$ measures 29° and $\angle B$ measures 85°. You know that $AB = 3$ centimeters, and you want to find AC. Because you know two of the angles, you can find the third. $\angle C$ measures $180° - (29° + 85°) = 66°$. The side labeled as a is the side opposite $\angle A$, or BC, and b is side AC and c is side AB. The law of sines becomes

$$\frac{BC}{\sin 29°} = \frac{AC}{\sin 85°} = \frac{AB}{\sin 66°}$$

You know $AB = 3$ centimeters and you want to find AC, so use the last two ratios:

$$\frac{AC}{\sin 85°} = \frac{3}{\sin 66°}$$

Cross multiply and solve for AC:

$$\frac{AC}{\sin 85°} = \frac{3}{\sin 66°}$$
$$AC \cdot \sin 66° = 3 \sin 85°$$
$$AC = \frac{3 \sin 85°}{\sin 66°} = \frac{3(0.9962)}{0.9135} = 3.27$$

AC is approximately 3.27 centimeters.

EXERCISE 6·1

Use the given information to solve for the missing side to the nearest hundredth.

1. In $\triangle ABC$, $\angle A$ measures 74° and $\angle B$ measures 41°. If $BC = 58$ inches, find AC.

2. In $\triangle XYZ$, $\angle X$ measures 35° and $\angle Y$ measures 88°. If $XZ = 28$ meters, find XY.

3. In $\triangle RST$, $\angle R$ measures 18° and $\angle S$ measures 44°. If $ST = 6$ feet, find RS.

4. In $\triangle PQR$, $\angle P$ measures 25° and $\angle Q$ measures 118°. If $PQ = 158$ yards, find PR.

5. In $\triangle FGH$, $\angle F$ measures 76° and $\angle G$ measures 53°. If $FG = 583$ yards, find GH.

6. In $\triangle PQR$, $\angle P$ measures 26° and $\angle Q$ measures 52°. If $PQ = 3{,}268$ inches, find QR.

7. In $\triangle ABC$, $\angle A$ measures 106° and $\angle B$ measures 32°. If $BC = 0.76$ centimeters, find AB.

8. In $\triangle RST$, $\angle R$ measures 60° and $\angle S$ measures 43°. If $RT = 4{,}236$ feet, find ST.

9. In $\triangle XYZ$, $\angle X$ measures 15.5° and $\angle Y$ measures 66.5°. If $XZ = 71.75$ inches, find XY.

10. In $\triangle MNP$, $\angle M$ measures 138°52′ and $\angle N$ measures 16°27′. If $MN = 44.44$ centimeters, find MP.

11. In $\triangle ABC$, $\angle A$ measures 83° and $\angle B$ measures 17°. If $BC = 59$ inches, find AC.

12. In $\triangle DEF$, $\angle D$ measures 102° and $\angle E$ measures 22°. If $EF = 28$ feet, find DF.

13. In $\triangle GHI$, $\angle G$ measures 19° and $\angle H$ measures 75°. If $HI = 506$ centimeters, find GI.

14. In $\triangle JKL$, $\angle J$ measures 27° and $\angle K$ measures 48°. If $KL = 75$ meters, find JL.

15. In $\triangle MNO$, $\angle M$ measures $41°$ and $\angle N$ measures $38°$. If $NO = 34$ yards, find MO.

16. In $\triangle PQR$, $\angle P$ measures $93°$ and $\angle Q$ measures $29°$. If $QR = 13$ inches, find PR.

17. In $\triangle RST$, $\angle R$ measures $36°$ and $\angle S$ measures $49°$. If $ST = 112$ meters, find RT.

18. In $\triangle XYZ$, $\angle X$ measures $77°$ and $\angle Y$ measures $21°$. If $YZ = 12$ millimeters, find XZ.

19. In $\triangle ABC$, $\angle A$ measures $102°$ and $\angle B$ measures $18°$. If $BC = 92$ miles, find AC.

20. In $\triangle XYZ$, $\angle X$ measures $115°$ and $\angle Y$ measures $7°$. If $YZ = 49$ kilometers, find XZ.

21. If $\triangle ABC$ is an isosceles triangle, with vertex angle of $12°$ and a base of 14 centimeters, find the lengths of the congruent sides.

22. If the base angles of an isosceles triangle measure $40°$ and the legs are 8 inches each, find the length of the base.

23. If $\triangle XYZ$ is actually a right triangle with an acute angle of $36°$ and a shorter leg of 8 centimeters, use the law of sines to find the longer leg.

24. Use right triangle trigonometry, rather than the law of sines, to find the longer leg of the right triangle described in question 23.

25. If $\angle A$ and $\angle C$ are the acute angles of right triangle $\triangle ABC$, and the values of those angles are known (or easily found), and the length of side a is known, explain why the law of sines equation $\dfrac{a}{\sin A} = \dfrac{c}{\sin C}$ and the right triangle trigonometry equation $\tan C = \dfrac{c}{a}$ produce the same value for c.

Finding angles with the law of sines

To find a missing angle, you must know two sides and one angle. One of the sides must be opposite the angle you know and the other must be opposite the angle you're trying to find. When you know two angles, you can calculate the third angle, but knowing two sides doesn't let you find the third side, so you must be given the specific information you need, or you won't be able to use the law of sines.

In $\triangle ABC$, $AB = 12$ centimeters and $AC = 18$ centimeters. If $\angle B$ measures $77°$, find the measure of $\angle C$:

$$\frac{a}{\sin A} = \frac{b}{\sin B} = \frac{c}{\sin C}$$

You know that the side opposite $\angle C$ measures 12 centimeters and the side opposite $\angle B$ measures 18 centimeters, so use the last two ratios from the law of sines:

$$\frac{18}{\sin B} = \frac{12}{\sin C}$$

The measure of $\angle B$ is $77°$, so you'll be able to find that sine. You'll need to solve for the sine of $\angle C$ and then use the inverse sine key on your calculator to find the measure of $\angle C$:

$$\frac{18}{\sin 77°} = \frac{12}{\sin C}$$
$$18 \sin C = 12 \sin 77°$$

$$\sin C = \frac{12 \sin 77°}{18} \approx 0.6496$$

$$m\angle C = \sin^{-1}(0.6496) \approx 40.5°$$

The law of sines will only let you find a side that lies opposite a known angle, but once you've found a second angle in the triangle, you can subtract the total of the two known angles from 180° to find the third angle.

EXERCISE
6·2

Use the given information to solve for the missing angle to the nearest hundredth of a degree.

1. In $\triangle ABC$, AB = 342 yards and AC = 263 yards. If $\angle C$ measures 46°, find the measure of $\angle B$.

2. In $\triangle RST$, ST = 0.47 centimeter and RT = 0.29 centimeter. If $\angle R$ measures 89°, find the measure of $\angle S$.

3. In $\triangle PQR$, PQ = 7 meters and QR = 56 meters. If $\angle P$ measures 107°, find the measure of $\angle R$.

4. In $\triangle MNP$, MP = 12 feet and NP = 6 feet. If $\angle N$ measures 178°, find the measure of $\angle M$.

5. In $\triangle XYZ$, XZ = 67.5 inches and YZ = 53 inches. If $\angle Y$ measures 89°, find the measure of $\angle Z$.

6. In $\triangle VWX$, VW = 4.77 centimeters and WX = 4.24 centimeters. If $\angle X$ measures 58°, find the measure of $\angle V$.

7. In $\triangle DEF$, DE = 914 feet and DF = 726 feet. If $\angle F$ measures 133°, find the measure of $\angle D$.

8. In $\triangle ABC$, AB = 6,874 meters and AC = 7,593 meters. If $\angle B$ measures 58°, find the measure of $\angle A$.

9. In $\triangle CAT$, CA = 9,321 yards and AT = 12,273 yards. If $\angle C$ measures 127.5°, find the measure of $\angle T$.

10. In $\triangle DOG$, DO = 438 centimeters and OG = 335 centimeters. If $\angle G$ measures 115°, find the measure of $\angle D$.

11. In $\triangle ABC$, AB = 290 inches and AC = 316 inches. If $\angle C$ measures 29°, find the measure of $\angle B$.

12. In $\triangle CAT$, CA = 111 feet and CT = 119 feet. If $\angle A$ measures 85°, find the measure of $\angle T$.

13. In $\triangle DOG$, DO = 89 yards and DG = 103 yards. If $\angle O$ measures 117°, find the measure of $\angle G$.

14. In $\triangle LET$, LE = 1,193 meters and LT = 1,250 meters. If $\angle T$ measures 149°, find the measure of $\angle E$.

15. In $\triangle TAR$, TA = 791 centimeters and TR = 814 centimeters. If $\angle R$ measures 157°, find the measure of $\angle A$.

16. In $\triangle RST$, RS = 293 kilometers and RT = 375 kilometers. If $\angle S$ measures 87°, find the measure of $\angle T$.

17. In $\triangle PQR$, $PQ = 842$ miles and $PR = 901$ miles. If $\angle R$ measures $32°$, find the measure of $\angle Q$.

18. In $\triangle RST$, $RS = 638$ feet and $RT = 712$ feet. If $\angle T$ measures $139°$, find the measure of $\angle S$.

19. In $\triangle ABC$, $AB = 11.83$ inches and $AC = 15.97$ inches. If $\angle B$ measures $94°$, find the measure of $\angle C$.

20. In $\triangle XYZ$, $XY = 118.5$ centimeters and $XZ = 132.75$ centimeters. If $\angle Z$ measures $125°$, find the measure of $\angle Y$.

The ambiguous case of the law of sines

The one difficulty of the law of sines is that you may encounter situations in which there are two triangles that fit your given information. This is called the ambiguous case. (There is also the possibility that no triangle will satisfy your requirements, but that case is easier to spot.)

Recognizing the ambiguous case

In geometry, you learned how to prove that a pair of triangles is congruent. You learned SSS, SAS, ASA, and AAS as the abbreviations for valid ways to prove that triangles are congruent, and you learned that SSA was not valid. That information can help you to recognize the ambiguous case when you're working with the law of sines.

SSS, SAS, ASA, and AAS work as ways to prove triangles congruent because once you set the lengths of the three sides, or of two sides and the angle that lies between them, or two angles and a side, there is only one triangle that can be drawn that has those pieces. If you know that those pieces of one triangle match those pieces of another, the triangles will be copies of one another, so they'll be congruent.

Translating that information over to trigonometry, if your given information is ASA, two angles and the side included between them, or AAS, two angles and a side, you can use the law of sines without any concern. (If your given information is SSS, three sides, or SAS, two sides and the angle included between them, you'll need the law of cosines, which we'll look at a little later.)

When you're using the law of sines to find an angle, your given information is SSA—two sides and an angle, but not the angle included between the sides—and you're not guaranteed a unique triangle. You're in the ambiguous case. If you call the known angle $\angle A$, then you will have two solutions when $\angle A$ is acute and side a is shorter than side b. You'll have no solution if $\angle A$ is acute and side a is less than $b\sin A$. Because $\sin A < 1$, $b\sin A < b$, so you can order the possibilities:

$\angle A$ is acute	$b\sin A > a$	No triangle
$\angle A$ is acute	$b\sin A = a$	One right triangle
$\angle A$ is acute	$b\sin A < a < b$	Two triangles
$\angle A$ is acute	$b < a$	One triangle
$\angle A$ is obtuse		One triangle

If you know that $\angle R$ measures $50°$ and that the triangle containing $\angle R$ has a side adjacent to $\angle R$, called RS, that measures 18 centimeters and a side opposite $\angle R$, called ST, that measures 25 centimeters, how many possible triangles $\triangle RST$ can be formed?

Start by looking at the angle. $\angle R$ is acute, so you need to look at the sides. The product of RS, the side adjacent to $\angle R$, and $\sin R$ is $18\sin 50° = 18(0.7660) \approx 13.7888$. That's less than the side opposite the angle, so there is a triangle. The opposite side is larger than the adjacent side, which tells you to expect one solution.

How many triangles $\triangle XYZ$ are possible if $\angle X$ measures $50°$, $XY = 22$ inches, and $YZ = 14$ inches? $\angle X$ is acute, so calculate $XY \sin X = 22 \sin 50° = 22(0.7660) = 16.852$. This is larger than the opposite side of 14 inches, so there is no solution.

How many triangles $\triangle ABC$ are possible if $\angle A$ measures $20°$, $AB = 20$ feet, and $BC = 8$ feet? $\angle A$ is acute, so first check to see if any solution is possible. Because the result of $AB \sin A = 20 \sin 20° = 6.8404$ is less than BC, there is some solution. But, since BC, the opposite side is less than AB, the adjacent side, there may be two solutions.

Solve $\dfrac{8}{\sin 20°} = \dfrac{20}{\sin C}$ to find that $\sin C = \dfrac{20 \sin 20°}{8} \approx 0.8551$. Your calculator will say that $\sin^{-1} 0.8551 \approx 58.77°$, so one possible triangle is one with angles of $20°$, $58.77°$, and $101.23°$. But an obtuse angle, $180° - 58.77° = 121.23°$, also has a sine of approximately 0.8551, so a second triangle is possible with angles of $20°$, $121.23°$, and $38.77°$.

EXERCISE
6·3

Determine the number of possible triangles that contain the sides and angle given.

1. $a = 29$, $b = 31$, $\angle A = 65°$

2. $b = 42$, $c = 45$, $\angle B = 81°$

3. $a = 8$, $c = 4$, $\angle C = 14°$

4. $b = 91$, $c = 62$, $\angle B = 101°$

5. $a = 63$, $b = 50$, $\angle A = 47°$

6. $b = 8$, $c = 9$, $\angle B = 53°$

7. $a = 18$, $c = 7$, $\angle C = 22°$

8. $b = 4$, $c = 7$, $\angle B = 94°$

9. $a = 15$, $b = 3$, $\angle A = 11°$

10. $b = 22$, $c = 6$, $\angle C = 35°$

11. $a = 17$, $b = 29$, $\angle A = 35°$

12. $b = 75$, $c = 68$, $\angle C = 48°$

13. $a = 11$, $b = 6$, $\angle B = 110°$

14. $a = 37$, $c = 45$, $\angle A = 30°$

15. $b = 82$, $c = 52$, $\angle B = 65°$

16. $a = 50$, $b = 94$, $\angle A = 84°$

17. $a = 48$, $b = 51$, $\angle B = 92°$

18. $b = 22$, $c = 18$, $\angle B = 115°$

19. $b = 19$, $c = 25$, $\angle C = 130°$

20. $a = 11$, $b = 28$, $\angle A = 80°$

Coping with the ambiguous case

The no-solution situation of the ambiguous case takes care of itself. If you check before solving the problem and find that $\angle A$ is acute and side a is less than $b \sin A$, you'll know there's no solution. If you don't check and start trying to solve, you'll get a value for $\sin B$ that is greater than 1 or less than -1—impossible!

You need to be alert for the case that may have two solutions, however. You'll set up and start solving the same way as any other case, but when you get to finding the size of the angle, you'll have to look for the other possible triangle. One triangle will have the given $\angle A$, the acute $\angle B$ you'll get from using the $\sin^{-1}$ key on your calculator, and an $\angle C$ that is equal to $180° - (m\angle A + m\angle B)$. But the $\sin B$ you found in your calculation also belongs to an obtuse $\angle B$, specifically to $180°$—the angle your calculator returns. The second possible triangle contains $\angle A$, the obtuse version of $\angle B$, and an $\angle C$ that completes the 180°.

How many triangles $\triangle ABC$ are possible if $\angle A$ measures 20°, $AB = 20$ feet, and $BC = 8$ feet? Solve $\dfrac{8}{\sin 20°} = \dfrac{20}{\sin C}$ to find that $\sin C = \dfrac{20\sin 20°}{8} \approx 0.8551$. Your calculator will say that $\sin^{-1} 0.8551 \approx 58.77°$, so one possible triangle is one with angles of 20°, 58.77°, and 101.23°. But an obtuse angle, $180° - 58.77° = 121.23°$, also has a sine of approximately 0.8551, so a second triangle is possible with angles of 20°, 121.23°, and 38.77°.

EXERCISE
6·4

Find the requested angle of the triangle to the nearest hundredth of a degree. If more than one triangle is possible, find both. If no triangle is possible, indicate that.

1. In $\triangle ABC$, $AB = 51$, $BC = 58$, and $\angle C = 54°$. Find $\angle A$.

2. In $\triangle XYZ$, $XY = 11$, $YZ = 5.4$, and $\angle Z = 154°$. Find $\angle X$.

3. In $\triangle RST$, $RS = 492$, $ST = 672$, and $\angle T = 55°$. Find $\angle R$.

4. In $\triangle CAT$, $CA = 8$, $AT = 4$, and $\angle T = 28°$. Find $\angle C$.

5. In $\triangle DOG$, $DO = 93$, $OG = 74$, and $\angle G = 52°$. Find $\angle D$.

6. In $\triangle HAT$, $HA = 268$, $AT = 524$, and $\angle T = 144°$. Find $\angle H$.

7. In $\triangle JET$, $JE = 5$, $ET = 3$, and $\angle T = 123°$. Find $\angle J$.

8. In $\triangle LOG$, $LO = 439$, $OG = 346$, and $\angle G = 66°$. Find $\angle L$.

9. In $\triangle BAT$, $BA = 85$, $AT = 57$, and $\angle T = 14°$. Find $\angle B$.

10. In $\triangle FGH$, $FG = 30$, $GH = 36$, and $\angle H = 28°$. Find $\angle F$.

11. In $\triangle ABC$, $AB = 84$, $BC = 119$, and $\angle C = 35°$. Find $\angle A$.

12. In $\triangle XYZ$, $XY = 13$, $YZ = 21$, and $\angle Z = 56°$. Find $\angle X$.

13. In $\triangle RST$, $RS = 27$, $ST = 16$, and $\angle T = 154°$. Find $\angle R$.

14. In $\triangle CAT$, $CA = 64$, $AT = 42$, and $\angle T = 49°$. Find $\angle C$.

15. In $\triangle DOG$, $DO = 102$, $OG = 97$, and $\angle G = 74°$. Find $\angle D$.

16. In $\triangle ELM$, $EL = 94$, $LM = 58$, and $\angle M = 46°$. Find $\angle E$.

17. In $\triangle OAK$, $OA = 81$, $AK = 54$, and $\angle K = 50°$. Find $\angle O$.

18. In $\triangle TOE$, $TO = 17$, $OE = 16$, and $\angle E = 154°$. Find $\angle T$.

19. In $\triangle ARM$, $AR = 44$, $RM = 43$, and $\angle M = 68°$. Find $\angle A$.

20. In $\triangle LEG$, $LE = 29$, $EG = 21$, and $\angle G = 121°$. Find $\angle L$.

The law of cosines

The law of cosines may remind you a bit of the Pythagorean theorem, and there's a reason for that. It's derived by dividing the triangle into two right triangles by drawing an altitude.

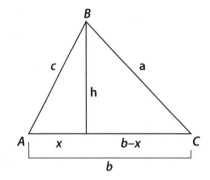

The altitude creates two right triangles. Applying the Pythagorean theorem to each of those right triangles, you get

$$c^2 = h^2 + x^2$$
$$a^2 = h^2 + (b - x)^2$$

Solve the second equation for h^2:

$$h^2 = a^2 - (b - x)^2$$

Substitute for h^2 in the first equation and simplify:

$$
\begin{aligned}
c^2 &= a^2 - (b - x)^2 + x^2 \\
&= a^2 - (b^2 - 2bx + x^2) + x^2 \\
&= a^2 - b^2 + 2bx - x^2 + x^2 \\
&= a^2 - b^2 + 2bx
\end{aligned}
$$

Write the ratio for $\cos C$ and use it to express x in terms of a, b, and $\cos C$:

$$
\begin{aligned}
\cos C &= \frac{b - x}{a} \\
a \cos C &= b - x \\
x &= b - a \cos C
\end{aligned}
$$

Replace x and simplify:

$$
\begin{aligned}
c^2 &= a^2 - b^2 + 2b(b - a \cos C) \\
&= a^2 - b^2 + 2b^2 - 2ab \cos C \\
&= a^2 + b^2 - 2ab \cos C
\end{aligned}
$$

Finding sides with the law of cosines

To find a side with the law of cosines, you'll need to know the angle opposite the unknown side. (While it's theoretically possible to find a side other than the one opposite the known angle, it would require a lot of nasty algebra.) Substitute the two known sides for a and b and the known angle for $\angle C$. Evaluate the expression to find the value of c^2 and take the square root of both sides.

In $\triangle ABC$, $\angle C$ measures $34°$. If side a is 14 centimeters and side b is 19 centimeters, find the length of side c.

Use the law of cosines with $a = 14$, $b = 18$, and $\angle C = 34°$:

$$c^2 = a^2 + b^2 - 2ab\cos C$$
$$= 14^2 + 18^2 - 2(14)(18)\cos 34°$$

Simplify, observing the order of operations carefully:

$$c^2 = 196 + 324 - 504(0.8290)$$
$$= 196 + 324 - 417.8349$$
$$= 102.1651$$

Find the square root:

$$c \approx 10.11$$

EXERCISE
6·5

Find the requested side of the triangle to the nearest hundredth by using the law of cosines.

1. In $\triangle ABC$, $\angle C$ measures $42°$. If side BC is 4 centimeters and side AC is 8 centimeters, find the length of side AB.

2. In $\triangle XYZ$, $\angle Y$ measures $78°$. If side XY is 37 inches and side YZ is 42 inches, find the length of side XZ.

3. In $\triangle RST$, $\angle T$ measures $163°$. If side ST is 81 feet and side RT is 90 feet, find the length of side RS.

4. In $\triangle JET$, $\angle J$ measures $48°$. If side JE is 9 yards and side JT is 11 yards, find the length of side ET.

5. In $\triangle TAP$, $\angle A$ measures $29°$. If side TA is 32 meters and side AP is 45 meters, find the length of side TP.

6. In $\triangle CAT$, $\angle C$ measures $66°$. If side CA is 11 kilometers and side CT is 19 kilometers, find the length of side AT.

7. In $\triangle DOG$, $\angle D$ measures $92°$. If side DO is 189 inches and side DG is 201 inches, find the length of side OG.

8. In $\triangle DEF$, $\angle E$ measures $59°$. If side DE is 19 centimeters and side EF is 25 centimeters, find the length of side DF.

9. In $\triangle RST$, $\angle R$ measures $73°$. If side RS is 69 feet and side RT is 77 feet, find the length of side ST.

10. In $\triangle MNO$, $\angle N$ measures 119°. If side MN is 14 meters and side NO is 18 meters, find the length of side MO.

11. In $\triangle XYZ$, $\angle Y$ measures 37°. If side XY is 83 feet and side YZ is 67 feet, find the length of side XZ.

12. In $\triangle ABC$, $\angle B$ measures 50°. If side AB is 29 inches and side BC is 32 inches, find the length of side AC.

13. In $\triangle CAT$, $\angle A$ measures 72°. If side CA is 58 centimeters and side AT is 56 centimeters, find the length of side CT.

14. In $\triangle RST$, $\angle S$ measures 93°. If side RS is 40 yards and side ST is 39 yards, find the length of side RT.

15. In $\triangle LEG$, $\angle E$ measures 105°. If side LE is 128 meters and side EG is 111 meters, find the length of side LG.

16. In $\triangle DOG$, $\angle O$ measures 56°. If side DO is 485 feet and side OG is 496 feet, find the length of side DG.

17. In $\triangle ARM$, $\angle R$ measures 120°. If side AR is 394 kilometers and side RM is 377 kilometers, find the length of side AM.

18. In $\triangle HAT$, $\angle A$ measures 55°. If side HA is 86 inches and side AT is 79 inches, find the length of side HT.

19. In $\triangle NFL$, $\angle F$ measures 12°. If side NF is 49 centimeters and side FL is 53 centimeters, find the length of side NL.

20. In $\triangle NBA$, $\angle B$ measures 87°. If side NB is 443 feet and side BA is 501 feet, find the length of side NB.

Finding angles with the law of cosines

To find an angle using the law of cosines, you'll need to know all three sides of the triangle. You'll also need to be on the alert to avoid a common error. Replace c with the side opposite the angle you're trying to find. Substitute the other two known sides for a and b. Evaluate the squares, combine a^2 and b^2, but don't try to subtract $2ab$ from $a^2 + b^2$. The $2ab$ is the coefficient of $\cos C$, and that multiplication takes precedence over any addition or subtraction. Instead, subtract $a^2 + b^2$ from c^2 and divide by $-2ab$ to find $\cos C$. Then use the $\cos^{-1}$ key on your calculator to find the measure of $\angle C$.

Find the measures of the angles of a triangle with sides of 9 inches, 11 inches, and 15 inches. Use the law of cosines with $a = 9$, $b = 11$, and $c = 15$:

$$c^2 = a^2 + b^2 - 2ab\cos C$$

$$15^2 = 9^2 + 11^2 - 2(9)(11)\cos C$$

$$225 = 81 + 121 - 198\cos C$$

$$225 = 202 - 198\cos C$$

Solve for $\cos C$:

$$23 = -198\cos C$$

$$-\frac{23}{198} = \cos C$$

$$\cos C = -0.1162$$

Find the angle that has a cosine of −0.1162:

$$\angle C = \cos^{-1}(-0.1162) \approx 96.67°$$

Find a second angle by repeating the law of cosines with $b^2 = a^2 + c^2 - 2ac\cos B$ or by using the law of sines with $\dfrac{b}{\sin B} = \dfrac{c}{\sin C}$:

$$\frac{b}{\sin B} = \frac{c}{\sin C}$$

$$\frac{11}{\sin B} = \frac{15}{\sin 96.67°}$$

$$15\sin B = 11\sin 96.67°$$

$$\sin B = \frac{11\sin 96.67°}{15}$$

$$\sin B = \frac{11(0.9932)}{15} = 0.7284$$

$$\angle B = \sin^{-1}(0.7284) = 46.75°$$

The third angle is $180° - (96.67° + 46.75°) = 180° - 143.42 = 36.58°$.

EXERCISE

6·6

Find the requested angle of the triangle to the nearest hundredth of a degree by using the law of cosines.

1. In $\triangle ABC$, $AB = 57$ centimeters, $BC = 37$ centimeters, and $AC = 46$ centimeters. Find the measure of $\angle B$.

2. In $\triangle PQR$, $PQ = 3{,}467$ feet, $QR = 2{,}783$ feet, and $PR = 1{,}769$ feet. Find the measure of $\angle P$.

3. In $\triangle XYZ$, $XY = 454$ yards, $YZ = 537$ yards, and $XZ = 416.5$ yards. Find the measure of $\angle Z$.

4. In $\triangle DEF$, $DE = 9{,}553$ meters, $EF = 5{,}786$ meters, and $DF = 5{,}887$ meters. Find the measure of $\angle F$.

5. In $\triangle RST$, $RS = 13$ inches, $ST = 16$ inches, and $RT = 25$ inches. Find the measure of $\angle T$.

6. In $\triangle CAT$, $CA = 28$ centimeters, $AT = 66$ centimeters, and $CT = 73$ centimeters. Find the measure of $\angle A$.

7. In $\triangle DOG$, $DO = 684$ feet, $OG = 932$ feet, and $DG = 841.5$ feet. Find the measure of $\angle D$.

8. In $\triangle MOP$, $MO = 53$ yards, $OP = 47$ yards, and $MP = 39$ yards. Find the measure of $\angle P$.

9. In $\triangle JET$, $JE = 29$ inches, $ET = 22$ inches, and $JT = 27$ inches. Find the measure of $\angle E$.

10. In $\triangle HOT$, $HO = 118$ feet, $OT = 91$ feet, and $HT = 101$ feet. Find the measure of $\angle H$.

11. In $\triangle MOP$, $MO = 54$ meters, $OP = 45$ meters, and $MP = 84$ meters. Find the measure of $\angle M$.

12. In $\triangle KIT$, $KI = 42$ centimeters, $IT = 32$ centimeters, and $KT = 62$ centimeters. Find the measure of $\angle T$.

13. In $\triangle LIP$, $LI = 74$ inches, $IP = 97$ inches, and $LP = 100$ inches. Find the measure of $\angle P$.

14. In $\triangle RED$, $RE = 96$ feet, $ED = 102$ feet, and $RD = 150$ feet. Find the measure of $\angle D$.

15. In $\triangle ART$, $AR = 86$ miles, $RT = 93$ miles, and $AT = 145$ miles. Find the measure of $\angle R$.

16. In $\triangle ZIP$, $ZI = 933$ kilometers, $IP = 875$ kilometers, and $ZP = 777$ kilometers. Find the measure of $\angle Z$.

17. In $\triangle BAT$, $BA = 12$ feet, $AT = 15$ feet, and $BT = 7$ feet. Find the measure of $\angle B$.

18. In $\triangle NAP$, $NA = 36$ centimeters, $AP = 49$ centimeters, and $NP = 63$ centimeters. Find the measure of $\angle N$.

19. In $\triangle YOU$, $YO = 338$ meters, $OU = 394$ meters, and $YU = 209$ meters. Find the measure of $\angle Y$.

20. In $\triangle HER$, $HE = 392$ yards, $ER = 286$ yards, and $HR = 476$ yards. Find the measure of $\angle R$.

Solving triangles

The instruction to "solve the triangle" means to find the measurements of all angles and the lengths of all sides not already known. Accomplishing that will require that you use the law of sines or the law of cosines, possibly both, and perhaps right triangle trigonometry. Which law you use will be determined by what information you are given or have already found.

EXERCISE
6·7

Solve each problem by the most efficient method. Round to the nearest hundredth. Use the law of sines or the law of cosines, as appropriate. If more than one solution is possible, give both solutions.

1. In $\triangle ABC$, $\angle A$ measures $74°$, $\angle B$ measures $49°$, and side BC is 14 centimeters long. Solve the triangle.

2. Solve $\triangle RST$ if $RS = 4$ feet, $ST = 7$ feet, and $\angle T$ measures $107°$.

3. Triangle XYZ has sides of lengths 15, 22, and 35. Find the measures of the angles of the triangle.

4. Find the lengths of the diagonals of a parallelogram whose sides are 32 centimeters and 48 centimeters, if the acute angle between the sides is $47°$.

5. The beginning of a forest fire is spotted by two rangers in observation towers 3,800 meters apart. The line segment connecting the two towers is the base of a triangle, with the line of sight from each tower to the fire forming the other two sides. If the angle between the base and one line of sight is 83° and the angle between the base and the other line of sight is 74°, find the distance from each tower to the fire.

6. Giant helium balloons in the shape of cartoon characters are a favorite feature of a Thanksgiving Day parade. The balloons are controlled by handlers on the ground by means of wires attached to the balloon. Two handlers with wires connected to the same point on the balloon have let out 50 feet and 75 feet of wire, respectively. If the wires make an angle of 97° at the point of attachment to the balloon, how far apart are the handlers?

7. A researcher needs to estimate the length of a crater caused by a meteorite striking the ground. After choosing a point from which she can see both ends of the crater, she measures the distance to each end of the crater and the angle between these two sightings. If the distances to the ends of the crater are 2,290 meters and 1,458 meters and the angle between them is 71°, find the length of the crater.

8. The angle of elevation from the foot of one building to the roof of a taller building nearby is 48°. The angle of depression from the top of the taller building to the top of the shorter one is 29°. If the shorter building is 65 feet tall, find the distance between the buildings.

9. From a bench on the shoreline of a lake, a boat is spotted at a bearing of N 53° E. The same boat is spotted from a second bench directly east of the first at N 41° W. If the perpendicular distance from the boat to the shoreline is 60 meters, how far apart are the two benches?

10. The airline distance from Chicago to New York is 750 miles. The distance from Chicago to Boston is 920 miles. The distance from Boston to New York is 210 miles. Find the angle between the two routes to New York.

Polar coordinate system

In the Cartesian, or rectangular, coordinate system, points in the plane are located by an ordered pair of coordinates. The first coordinate indicates movement left or right of the origin, and the second, motion up or down. The polar coordinate system also uses an ordered pair of coordinates to locate a point in the plane, but the movement from the origin, or pole, is indicated by an angle of rotation and a distance.

Polar coordinates

The polar grid is a set of concentric circles, centered about the pole, with radii that increase by a fixed unit, to allow you to count distances from the pole. The concentric circles are crisscrossed by spokes that are spaced at fixed degree or radian intervals, to allow you to measure angles. Movement begins from the pole, similar to the origin in rectangular coordinates. Rotation begins from polar axis, which corresponds to the positive x-axis of rectangular coordinates or the traditional initial side for an angle in standard position.

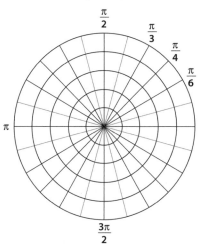

In the polar coordinate system, a point is located by a radius, or distance from the pole, and an angle, representing a rotation, which you can think of as an angle in standard form. The ordered pair that denotes a point is given in the form (r, θ), where r is the radius, or distance from the pole, and θ is the angle.

To plot the point $\left(3, \dfrac{\pi}{4}\right)$, count out to the third ring and then around the circle to the spoke that represents $\dfrac{\pi}{4}$. You may find it easier to first locate the $\dfrac{\pi}{4}$ spoke and then follow it out to the third ring. The ordered pair $\left(8, -\dfrac{\pi}{2}\right)$ tells you to plot a point on the eighth circle but to move $\dfrac{\pi}{2}$ units clockwise, or in the negative

85

direction. While a negative radius may seem odd, it can be accomplished in polar coordinates. To plot $\left(-4, \frac{7\pi}{6}\right)$, imagine you are standing at the pole. Turn until you are facing the spoke that represents $\frac{7\pi}{6}$ and walk backward four rings. If you think this seems to take you to the point $\left(4, \frac{\pi}{6}\right)$, you're absolutely correct. In the polar coordinate system, it's quite possible to name the same point with different coordinates.

EXERCISE

7·1

Plot each point on the polar grid. Each ordered pair has the form (r, θ).

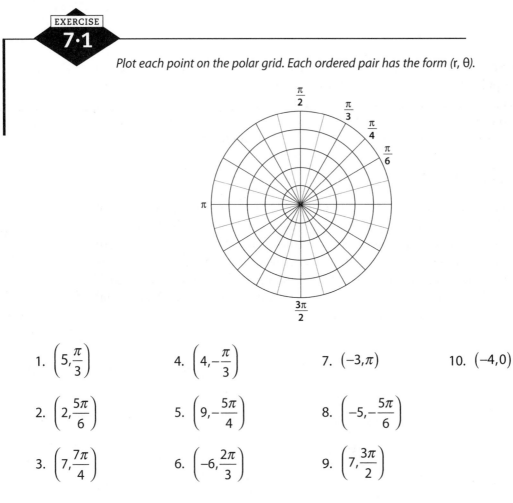

1. $\left(5, \frac{\pi}{3}\right)$ 4. $\left(4, -\frac{\pi}{3}\right)$ 7. $(-3, \pi)$ 10. $(-4, 0)$

2. $\left(2, \frac{5\pi}{6}\right)$ 5. $\left(9, -\frac{5\pi}{4}\right)$ 8. $\left(-5, -\frac{5\pi}{6}\right)$

3. $\left(7, \frac{7\pi}{4}\right)$ 6. $\left(-6, \frac{2\pi}{3}\right)$ 9. $\left(7, \frac{3\pi}{2}\right)$

Give the polar coordinates for each point.

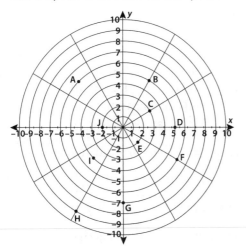

11. A	16. F
12. B	17. G
13. C	18. H
14. D	19. I
15. E	20. J

Multiple representations

One of the key features of polar coordinates is that a single point may be represented by more than one set of coordinates. In fact, each point in the plane has infinitely many sets of coordinates. Because rotation can be counterclockwise or clockwise, a point like $\left(4, \frac{\pi}{3}\right)$ can also be represented as $\left(4, -\frac{5\pi}{3}\right)$. Because it's possible to have angles greater than 2π, each of those representations is one of infinitely many of the form $\left(4, \frac{\pi}{3} \pm 2n\pi\right)$ or $\left(4, -\frac{5\pi}{3} \pm 2n\pi\right)$. So $\left(4, \frac{\pi}{3}\right)$ is also $\left(4, \frac{7\pi}{3}\right)$ and $\left(4, -\frac{11\pi}{3}\right)$ and $\left(4, \frac{37\pi}{3}\right)$ and many others. The same point can also be represented using a negative radius with an angle offset by half a rotation. So the point $\left(4, \frac{\pi}{3}\right)$ can also be represented by $\left(-4, \frac{4\pi}{3}\right)$ or $\left(-4, -\frac{2\pi}{3}\right)$. That adds to the list of possibilities of all representations of the form $\left(-4, \frac{4\pi}{3} \pm 2n\pi\right)$ and $\left(-4, -\frac{2\pi}{3} \pm 2n\pi\right)$.

EXERCISE
7·2

For each point given, find ordered pairs that name the same point and meet the conditions:

a. $r > 0, 0 \leq \theta < 2\pi$ c. $r > 0, \theta > 2\pi$ e. $r < 0, -2\pi \leq \theta < 0$

b. $r > 0, -2\pi \leq \theta < 0$ d. $r < 0, 0 \leq \theta < 2\pi$

1. $\left(5, \frac{\pi}{3}\right)$ 6. $\left(-6, \frac{2\pi}{3}\right)$

2. $\left(2, \frac{5\pi}{6}\right)$ 7. $(-3, \pi)$

3. $\left(7, \frac{7\pi}{4}\right)$ 8. $\left(-5, -\frac{5\pi}{6}\right)$

4. $\left(4, -\frac{\pi}{3}\right)$ 9. $\left(7, \frac{3\pi}{2}\right)$

5. $\left(9, -\frac{5\pi}{4}\right)$ 10. $(-4, 0)$

Name each point using a positive r and a negative θ.

11.

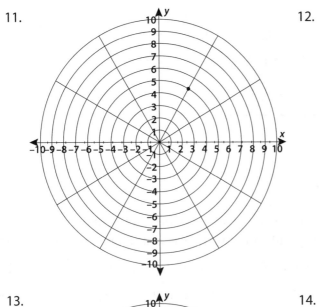

12.

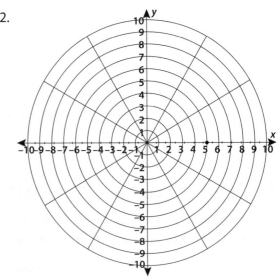

13.

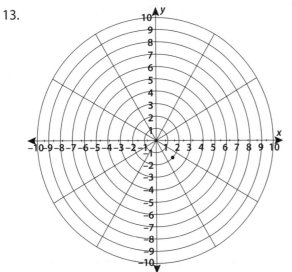

14.

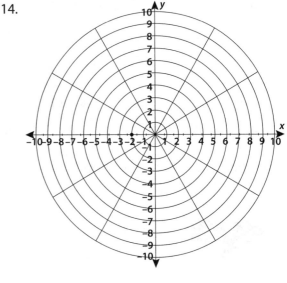

Name each point using a negative r and a positive θ.

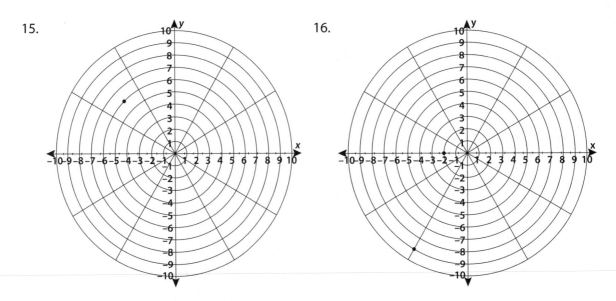

15.

16.

17.

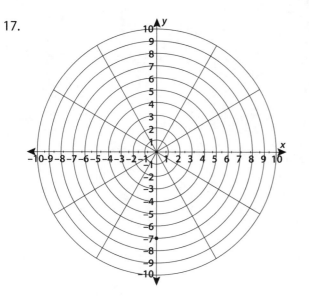

Name each point using a negative r and a negative θ.

18.

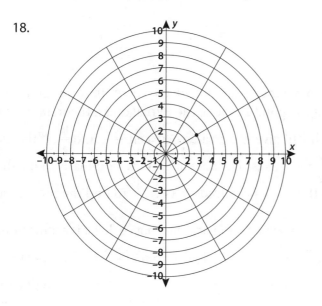

19.

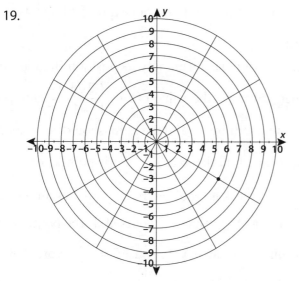

20.

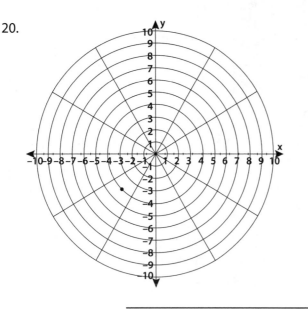

Converting coordinates

To convert from rectangular coordinates to polar coordinates, given a point in rectangular coordinates (x, y), first note in which quadrant the point lies. Use the Pythagorean theorem to calculate $r = \sqrt{x^2 + y^2}$. Then find $\tan^{-1} \dfrac{y}{x}$, which will give you a value between $-\dfrac{\pi}{2}$ and $\dfrac{\pi}{2}$. If the point lies in quadrant I or IV, the value $\tan^{-1} \dfrac{y}{x}$ returns is the value of θ. If the point falls in quadrant II or III, however, you'll need to add π to the value produced by $\tan^{-1} \dfrac{y}{x}$ to find the proper value of θ.

To convert the rectangular point $(4, -4)$ to polar coordinates, first notice that it is a fourth-quadrant point. Then find $r = \sqrt{4^2 + (-4)^2} = \sqrt{32} = 4\sqrt{2}$ and calculate $\tan^{-1}\left(\dfrac{-4}{4}\right) = \tan^{-1}(-1) = -\dfrac{\pi}{4}$. Because the point is in quadrant IV, you can use the value of $\tan^{-1} \dfrac{y}{x}$ as θ, so the point can be named as $\left(4\sqrt{2}, -\dfrac{\pi}{4}\right)$. Of course, if you want to use a positive θ, you can express this as $\left(4\sqrt{2}, \dfrac{7\pi}{4}\right)$ and other representations are possible as well.

To convert the rectangular point $\left(-3, 3\sqrt{3}\right)$ to polar form, note its position in quadrant II. Find $r = \sqrt{(-3)^2 + \left(3\sqrt{3}\right)^2} = \sqrt{9 + 27} = 6$. Then calculate the value of $\tan^{-1}\left(\dfrac{3\sqrt{3}}{-3}\right) = \tan^{-1}\left(-\sqrt{3}\right) = -\dfrac{\pi}{3}$, but remember this value would put you in quadrant IV and the point should be in quadrant II. Adjust by adding π to the value $\tan^{-1} \dfrac{y}{x}$ gave and find that θ is $\dfrac{2\pi}{3}$, so the point is $\left(6, \dfrac{2\pi}{3}\right)$.

For points that fall on the y-axis, a little extra work is required. If the point lies on the y-axis, $\tan^{-1} \dfrac{y}{x}$ will be undefined, and you'll have to supply the value of θ yourself. If the point is on the positive y-axis, use $\theta = \dfrac{\pi}{2}$, and if the point is on the negative y-axis, use $\theta = -\dfrac{\pi}{2}$. Note that those are the values for θ when using a positive value for r. The rectangular point $(0, 5)$ is the polar point $\left(5,\dfrac{\pi}{2}\right)$ and the rectangular point $(0,-3)$ is $\left(3,-\dfrac{\pi}{2}\right)$. Of course, many other representations are possible for each point.

To convert from polar coordinates to rectangular coordinates, use right triangle trigonometry. Given the polar point (r, θ), find $x = r\cos\theta$ and $y = r\sin\theta$. So the polar point $\left(8,\dfrac{3\pi}{4}\right)$ has an x-coordinate of $8\cos\dfrac{3\pi}{4} = 8\left(-\dfrac{\sqrt{2}}{2}\right) = -4\sqrt{2}$ and a y-coordinate of $8\sin\dfrac{3\pi}{4} = 8\left(\dfrac{\sqrt{2}}{2}\right) = 4\sqrt{2}$. The polar point $\left(8,\dfrac{3\pi}{4}\right)$ is equivalent to the rectangular point $\left(-4\sqrt{2}, 4\sqrt{2}\right)$.

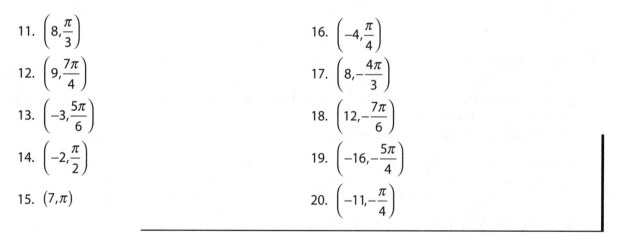

EXERCISE 7·3

Convert each point from rectangular coordinates to polar coordinates.

1. $(3,4)$

2. $(-5,12)$

3. $(-6,0)$

4. $\left(-4,-4\sqrt{3}\right)$

5. $(0,-1)$

6. $\left(7,-7\sqrt{3}\right)$

7. $(4,-4)$

8. $\left(6\sqrt{3},-6\right)$

9. $(-3,-3)$

10. $\left(9\sqrt{6},-9\sqrt{2}\right)$

Convert each point from polar coordinates to rectangular coordinates.

11. $\left(8,\dfrac{\pi}{3}\right)$

12. $\left(9,\dfrac{7\pi}{4}\right)$

13. $\left(-3,\dfrac{5\pi}{6}\right)$

14. $\left(-2,\dfrac{\pi}{2}\right)$

15. $(7,\pi)$

16. $\left(-4,\dfrac{\pi}{4}\right)$

17. $\left(8,-\dfrac{4\pi}{3}\right)$

18. $\left(12,-\dfrac{7\pi}{6}\right)$

19. $\left(-16,-\dfrac{5\pi}{4}\right)$

20. $\left(-11,-\dfrac{\pi}{4}\right)$

Polar equations

Equations in polar form generally express r in terms of θ and often define distinctive curves that would be difficult to represent in rectangular coordinates. In addition to the shape of the curve, you should pay attention to the direction in which it is traced out.

To sketch a graph, build a table of values and plot points, using values of θ in order and connecting as you go along. Because values of r may be negative, the graph may trace in unexpected ways. It can even trace over itself, because the periodic nature of the trig functions can give multiple representations of the same point. Remember that most polar graphs are curves, so avoid straight-line connections.

Lines, circles, and spirals

A line passing through the pole can be represented simply by $\theta = c$, where c is a constant. The line $\theta = \dfrac{2\pi}{3}$ passes through the pole. Other equations that produce lines include the vertical line $r = \dfrac{a}{\cos\theta}$ and the horizontal line $r = \dfrac{a}{\sin\theta}$. The general form of the equation of a line is $r = \dfrac{b\cos\phi}{\sin(\theta - \phi)}$, where b is the y-intercept of the line in rectangular form, and $\phi = \tan^{-1}m$, where m is the slope of the line. The line $y = \sqrt{3}x - 2$ becomes

$$
\begin{aligned}
r &= \frac{-2\cos\dfrac{\pi}{3}}{\sin\left(\theta - \dfrac{\pi}{3}\right)} \\[2ex]
&= \frac{-2\left(\dfrac{1}{2}\right)}{\sin\theta\cos\dfrac{\pi}{3} - \cos\theta\sin\dfrac{\pi}{3}} \\[2ex]
&= \frac{-1}{\dfrac{1}{2}\sin\theta - \dfrac{\sqrt{3}}{2}\cos\theta} \\[2ex]
&= \frac{-2}{\sin\theta - \sqrt{3}\cos\theta}
\end{aligned}
$$

The equation $r = c$, for some constant c, defines a circle of radius c centered at the pole. The equations $r = 2a\sin\theta$ and $r = 2a\cos\theta$ represent circles of radius a tangent to the pole. The graph of $r = 2a\cos\theta$ is symmetric about the horizontal axis, while the graph of $r = 2a\sin\theta$ is symmetric with respect to the vertical axis. In general, the equation of a circle of radius c is $r^2 - 2rd\cos(\theta - \phi) + d^2 = c^2$, where d is the distance from the pole to the center, (h,k), and $\phi = \tan^{-1}\dfrac{k}{h}$. The circle centered at $\left(2\sqrt{3}, -2\right)$ with radius 3 has the rectangular equation $\left(x - 2\sqrt{3}\right)^2 + \left(y + 2\right)^2 = 9$. The distance of the center from the origin is $d = \sqrt{\left(2\sqrt{3}\right)^2 + (-2)^2} = 4$, and $\phi = \tan^{-1}\left(\dfrac{-2}{2\sqrt{3}}\right) = -\dfrac{\pi}{6}$. In polar form, this would become

$$
r^2 - 2r \cdot 4\cos\left(\theta - -\frac{\pi}{6}\right) + 4^2 = 3^2
$$

or

$$
r^2 - 8r\cos\left(\theta + \frac{\pi}{6}\right) + 7 = 0
$$

Common equations of spirals are $r = a\theta$, the Archimedean spiral, and $r = e^{a\theta}$, the logarithmic spiral.

Limaçons and cardioids

Classic polar graphs include the limaçons, named for snails, and the heart-shaped cardioids. Limaçons have equations of the form $r = a \pm b\cos\theta$ or $r = a \pm b\sin\theta$. If $a < b$, the limaçon will have an inner loop, but if $a > b$, there will be no inner loop. If a and b are equal, the special case of the limaçon is the cardioid, with equations of the form $r = a \pm a\cos\theta$ or $r = a \pm a\sin\theta$. Equations based on the cosine will have graphs symmetric about the horizontal axis, while those involving the sine will be symmetric about the vertical axis.

Roses

Polar roses, which actually look more like daisies, have equations of the form $r = a\cos(b\theta)$ or $r = a\sin(b\theta)$. The value of a gives the length of the petal, while b controls the number of petals. If b is an odd number, there will be b petals, but if b is even, there will be $2b$ petals. In fact, there are always $2b$ petals, but when b is odd, petals trace on top of one another, so only half the petals are seen, while for even values of b, all the petals are visible.

Conics

Conic sections with focus at the pole have equations of the form $r = \dfrac{ep}{1 \pm e\cos\theta}$ or $r = \dfrac{ep}{1 \pm e\sin\theta}$, where p is the distance from the pole to the directrix and e is the eccentricity of the conic. The eccentricity of an ellipse is $0 < e < 1$, the eccentricity of a hyperbola is $e > 1$, and the parabola has $e = 1$. The equation

$$r = \frac{3}{2 + \cos\theta} = \frac{0.5(3)}{1 + 0.5\cos\theta}$$

describes an ellipse, while

$$r = \frac{9}{2 + 3\cos\theta} = \frac{1.5(3)}{1 + 1.5\cos\theta}$$

is a hyperbola, and

$$r = \frac{3}{1 + \cos\theta}$$

is a parabola.

EXERCISE 7·4

Sketch a graph of each equation.

1. $r = 3 + 5\cos\theta$

2. $r = 1 - \sin\theta$

3. $r = 4\cos(3\theta)$

4. $r = \dfrac{3}{\cos\theta}$

5. $r = 10\sin\theta$

6. $r = 3 + 3\cos\theta$

7. $r = 5\sin(4\theta)$

8. $r = 4 - 2\sin\theta$

9. $r = \dfrac{-2\sqrt{2}}{\sin\left(\theta - \dfrac{\pi}{4}\right)}$

10. $r = \dfrac{4}{2 - \cos\theta}$

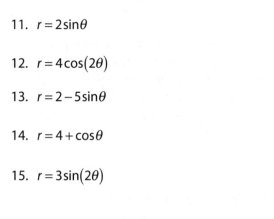

11. $r = 2\sin\theta$

12. $r = 4\cos(2\theta)$

13. $r = 2 - 5\sin\theta$

14. $r = 4 + \cos\theta$

15. $r = 3\sin(2\theta)$

16. $r = \dfrac{-2}{\sin\theta}$

17. $r = 2 - 4\sin\theta$

18. $r = \dfrac{3}{5 + \sin\theta}$

19. $r = 5 + 2\cos\theta$

20. $r = \dfrac{6}{\cos\left(\theta + \dfrac{\pi}{6}\right)}$

Converting equations

The same conversions that you used to change points from rectangular coordinates to polar coordinates or polar coordinates to rectangular coordinates can be used to change equations from one form to another.

To convert an equation from rectangular form to polar form, replace x with $r\cos\theta$ and y with $r\sin\theta$ and simplify. The equation $x^2 + y^2 = 9$ becomes

$$(r\cos\theta)^2 + (r\sin\theta)^2 = 9$$
$$r^2 \cos^2\theta + r^2 \sin^2\theta = 9$$
$$r^2 \left(\cos^2\theta + \sin^2\theta\right) = 9$$

Because $\cos^2\theta + \sin^2\theta = 1$, the equation becomes $r^2 = 9$ or simply $r = 3$.

To convert the rectangular equation $x = y^2 - 4$ to polar form, make the substitutions of $r\cos\theta$ and $r\sin\theta$ for x and y:

$$x = y^2 - 4$$
$$r\cos\theta = (r\sin\theta)^2 - 4$$

Make a reasonable attempt to simplify the equation, but don't go to great lengths:

$$r\cos\theta = (r\sin\theta)^2 - 4$$
$$= r^2 \sin^2\theta - 4$$
$$= r^2 \left(1 - \cos^2\theta\right) - 4$$
$$= r^2 - r^2 \cos^2\theta - 4$$

Bring all non-zero terms to one side and the equation is $r^2 - r^2 \cos^2\theta - r\cos\theta - 4 = 0$.

To convert an equation from polar form to rectangular form, use the substitutions $r = \sqrt{x^2 + y^2}$ and $\theta = \tan^{-1} \dfrac{y}{x}$. The equation $r = 3 + 4\cos\theta$ becomes

$$\sqrt{x^2 + y^2} = 3 + 4\cos\left(\tan^{-1}\frac{y}{x}\right)$$

$$\sqrt{x^2 + y^2} = 3 + \frac{4x}{\sqrt{x^2 + y^2}}$$

$$x^2 + y^2 = 3\sqrt{x^2 + y^2} + 4x$$

$$x^2 - 4x + y^2 = 3\sqrt{x^2 + y^2}$$

$$\left(x^2 - 4x + y^2\right)^2 = 9\left(x^2 + y^2\right)$$

$$x^4 - 8x^3 + 2x^2 y^2 + 16x^2 - 8xy^2 + y^4 = 9x^2 + 9y^2$$

$$x^4 - 8x^3 + 2x^2 y^2 + 7x^2 - 8xy^2 - 9y^2 + y^4 = 0$$

Clearly, the polar form of the equation is easier to manage.

EXERCISE 7·5

Convert to polar form.

1. $y = 3x - 4$

2. $(x - 1)^2 + y^2 = 25$

3. $y = x^2 - 4$

4. $4x^2 + 9y^2 = 36$

5. $16y^2 - 4x^2 = 64$

6. $x = 7$

7. $y = x^2 - 1$

8. $(x - 2)^2 + (y + 1)^2 = 16$

9. $x = y^2 + 4$

10. $y = -5$

Convert to rectangular form.

11. $\theta = \dfrac{\pi}{3}$

12. $r = 12\cos\theta$

13. $r = \dfrac{3}{\sin\theta}$

14. $r = 1 - \sin\theta$

15. $r = \dfrac{21}{2 + 3\sin\theta}$

16. $r = 2 - 3\cos\theta$

17. $r = \dfrac{4}{\cos\theta}$

18. $r = \dfrac{5}{3 + 2\sin\theta}$

19. $r = 8$

20. $r = 8\cos\theta$

Complex numbers

In the set of real numbers, the equation $x^2 + 1 = 0$ has no solution, an unsatisfying fact. No one likes to face a problem and have to say that it can't be solved. Sometimes there's no other choice, but in the case of quadratic equations, mathematicians were able to define a new set of numbers that literally solved the problem.

Defining an imaginary unit $i = \sqrt{-1}$ not only provides a solution for that equation but also generates a system of imaginary numbers of the form ai for all real numbers a. These pure imaginary numbers include numbers like $2i$, which squares to -4, and $-9i$, which squares to -81.

When you begin to combine these imaginary numbers with the real numbers, you form a new set of numbers, called the complex numbers, which includes the reals and the imaginaries and all the combinations. The complex numbers are all numbers of the form $a + bi$, where a is a real number and bi is an imaginary number. The real numbers have the form $a + 0i$, and the imaginaries have the form $0 + bi$. Examples of complex numbers include $3 - 7i$ and $\frac{1}{2} + \sqrt{2}i$.

Graphing complex numbers

When you graph in the Cartesian coordinate plane, each point in the plane corresponds to an ordered pair of real numbers. There is no place in that system for complex numbers. If you keep the rectangular coordinate system, but redefine the axes so that the horizontal axis represents the real numbers and the vertical axis represents the imaginary numbers, then each point in the plane (a, b) corresponds to a complex number.

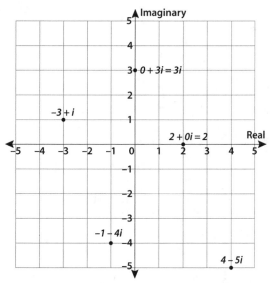

97

The complex number $4-5i$ corresponds to the point $(4,-5)$, and the point $(-3,1)$ represents the complex number $-3+i$. All numbers of the form $a+0i$ lie on the horizontal axis, and all numbers of the form $0+bi$ lie on the vertical axis.

For any complex number $a+bi$, there is a point in the plane (a,b). The reflection of that point across the x-axis is the point $(a,-b)$, which corresponds to the number $a-bi$. The point (a,b) and its reflection $(a,-b)$ represent the numbers $a+bi$ and $a-bi$, which are called complex conjugates. The conjugate of $3+7i$ is $3-7i$, and the points that correspond to these numbers, $(3,7)$ and $(3,-7)$, are reflections of one another in the x-axis.

The pure imaginaries lie on the vertical axis, are represented by points of the form $(0,b)$, and have the form $0+bi$ or simply bi. The conjugate of a pure imaginary number bi is $-bi$. The reflection of $(0,b)$ is $(0,-b)$. The imaginary number $5i$ has a conjugate of $-5i$. Notice that the reals lie on the x-axis and correspond to points of the form $(a,0)$. Since they lie on the axis, they are unchanged by reflection, so a real number—depending on your point of view—has no conjugate or is its own conjugate.

When a complex number has been plotted as a point in the plane, it is possible to calculate the distance of that point from the origin. That distance is called the modulus of the complex number. The point that represents the complex number $a+bi$ has coordinates (a,b). The distance between the origin and the point (a,b) is $\sqrt{(a-0)^2+(b-0)^2}=\sqrt{a^2+b^2}$. The modulus of $a+bi$ is

$$|a+bi|=\sqrt{a^2+b^2}$$

The modulus of the complex number $-4+3i$ is

$$|-4+3i|=\sqrt{(-4)^2+3^2}=\sqrt{16+9}=5$$

Notice that the modulus of $-4-3i$, the conjugate of $-4+3i$, is also

$$|-4-3i|=\sqrt{(-4)^2+(-3)^2}=\sqrt{16+9}=5$$

EXERCISE 8·1

Graph each complex number.

1. $5+2i$ 2. $-5-3i$ 3. $4-5i$ 4. $3i$ 5. $2-i$

Identify each of the points in the following figure by a complex number in $a+bi$ form.

6. C 7. M 8. P 9. L 10. X

Find the conjugate of each complex number.

11. $2 - 7i$ 12. $-1 + i$ 13. $\sqrt{3} - 2\sqrt{3}i$ 14. $-5 - 8i$ 15. $-\dfrac{1}{2} + 5i$

Find the modulus of each complex number.

16. $5 + 12i$ 18. $\sqrt{3} + i$ 20. $-2 - i$ 22. $-3 + 4i$ 24. $-i$

17. $-6 - 8i$ 19. $5 + 5i$ 21. $10 + 5i$ 23. $12 + 9i$ 25. -4

Arithmetic of complex numbers

The arithmetic operations on complex numbers are similar to other operations from algebra. In basic algebra, you learned to add and subtract by combining like terms. When adding and subtracting complex numbers, you'll combine the real parts with real parts and imaginary parts with imaginary parts.

If you remember that the imaginary unit i is defined as the square root of -1, you'll see that the rules for multiplication and division are similar to those you learned for working with radicals. To multiply $5\sqrt{2} \cdot 4\sqrt{2}$, you multiply $5 \cdot 4 \cdot \sqrt{2} \cdot \sqrt{2} = 20\sqrt{4} = 20 \cdot 2 = 40$, multiplying the numbers outside the radicals together and the numbers under the radical together. Because you knew the square root of 4, you could replace it with its value and eliminate the radical. When you multiply imaginary numbers, you'll multiply the coefficients together and multiply the is, replacing i^2 with -1. Just as you don't actually divide by a radical, but rather rationalize the denominator, you'll use similar techniques with complex numbers.

Addition and subtraction

Adding or subtracting complex numbers is similar to combining like terms when adding or subtracting binomials. The real parts are added and the imaginary parts are added. Attention should be paid to signs when subtracting. Remember that the minus sign affects the entire number that follows it:

$$(a + bi) + (c + di) = (a + c) + (b + d)i$$

$$(a + bi) - (c + di) = (a - c) + (b - d)i$$

Adding $3 + 5i$ to $6 - 9i$ gives you $(3 + 6) + (5 - 9)i = 9 - 4i$, because you add the real parts, $3 + 6$, and then the imaginary parts, $5i + -9i$. Subtracting $7 - 4i$ from $5 + 2i$ produces

$$\begin{aligned}
(5 + 2i) - (7 - 4i) &= 5 + 2i - 7 + 4i \\
&= (5 - 7) + (2 + 4)i \\
&= -2 + 6i
\end{aligned}$$

Multiplication and powers

Because the complex numbers include the real numbers and the imaginary numbers as subsets, there are a variety of cases to consider when talking about multiplication. You already know how to multiply a real number by a real number, but you'll need to think about a real times a pure imaginary, the product of two pure imaginaries, a real number times a complex number, an imaginary number times a complex number, and a complex number times a complex number. Multiplying a real number times an imaginary number is a simple matter. Multiply the numbers and let the i tag along: $a \cdot bi = (ab)i$, so $3 \cdot 5i = 15i$. Multiplying an imaginary by another imaginary is almost as simple but requires you to remember the definition of the imaginary unit. To multiply $-6i \cdot \frac{1}{2}i$, multiply $-6 \cdot \frac{1}{2}$ and $i \cdot i$. That gives you the product $-6i \cdot \frac{1}{2}i = -3i^2$, but because $i = \sqrt{-1}$, $i^2 = -1$. That means the product is actually $-6i \cdot \frac{1}{2}i = -3i^2 = -3(-1) = 3$. In general terms, $ai \cdot bi = (ab)i^2 = -ab$.

A word about powers of i is in order here. Powers of the imaginary unit cycle through four values: $i = \sqrt{-1}$, $i^2 = -1$, $i^3 = i^2 \cdot i = -1 \cdot i = -i$, and $i^4 = i^2 \cdot i^2 = (-1)(-1) = 1$. For powers beyond that, you'll find the power will simplify down to one of these; for example, $i^7 = i^3 \cdot i^4 = i^3 \cdot 1 = i^3$. To simplify higher powers quickly, divide the exponent by 4 and keep the remainder. The power $i^{325} = i^1$ because $325 \div 4 = 81$ with a remainder of 1.

Multiplication of a real number times a complex number requires distributing the real factor and simplifying: $c(a + bi) = ca + (cb)i$. The product $5(3 - 2i) = 15 - 10i$.

Multiplying by an imaginary number is accomplished in a similar manner, but it's important to remember that $i^2 = -1$:

$$ci(a + bi) = (ca)i + (cb)i^2$$
$$= (ca)i - cb$$
$$= -cb + (ca)i$$

The product

$$8i(3 - 4i) = 24i - 32i^2$$
$$= 24i - 32(-1)$$
$$= 32 + 24i$$

To multiply two complex numbers, use the FOIL (first, outer, inner, last) rule, as you would for binomials, but remember that $i^2 = -1$:

$$(a + bi)(c + di) = ac + (ad)i + (bc)i + (bd)i^2$$
$$= (ac - bd) + (ad + bc)i$$

So

$$(3 + 5i)(2 - 7i) = 6 - 21i + 10i - 35i^2$$
$$= (6 + 35) + (-21 + 10)i$$
$$= 41 - 11i$$

Division

Dividing a complex number by a real number doesn't require any special tools. Divide both the real and the imaginary part of the number by the real divisor: $\frac{a + bi}{c} = \frac{a}{c} + \frac{b}{c}i$. The quotient $\frac{12 - 8i}{2} = 6 - 4i$.

There is no true division by imaginary or complex numbers, but because $i = \sqrt{-1}$, the techniques of rationalizing denominators are used to simplify quotients. Remember the imaginary unit is effectively a radical expression.

Dividing by a pure imaginary number requires rationalizing the denominator by multiplying the numerator and denominator by i and replacing i^2 with -1:

$$\frac{a+bi}{ci} \cdot \frac{i}{i} = \frac{ai + bi^2}{ci^2} = \frac{-b + ai}{-c} = \frac{b}{c} - \frac{a}{c}i$$

The quotient $\dfrac{5+3i}{2i} \cdot \dfrac{i}{i} = \dfrac{5i-3}{-2} = 1.5 - 2.5i$.

To rationalize a denominator that is a complex number rather than a pure imaginary, you'll need to multiply by the conjugate of the denominator. The numbers $a+bi$ and $a-bi$ are complex conjugates. If you multiply a complex number and its conjugate, for example, $(2+5i)$ and $(2-5i)$, the product will be a real number:

$$(2+5i)(2-5i) = 4 - 10i + 10i - 25i^2$$
$$= 4 - 25(-1)$$
$$= 4 + 25$$
$$= 29$$

Because the product of a complex number $a+bi$ and its conjugate $a-bi$ will always be a real number $a^2 + b^2$, quotients with a complex number in the denominator can be simplified by multiplying the numerator and denominator by the conjugate of the denominator:

$$\frac{a+bi}{c+di} \cdot \frac{c-di}{c-di} = \frac{(ac+bd) + (bc-ad)i}{c^2 + d^2}$$

The quotient $\dfrac{5-5i}{2-6i} \cdot \dfrac{2+6i}{2+6i} = \dfrac{10 + 30i - 10i + 30}{4 + 36} = \dfrac{40 + 20i}{40} = 1 + \dfrac{1}{2}i$.

EXERCISE

8·2

Perform each operation and give your answer in simplest form.

1. $(2+9i) + 6i$

2. $(3-7i) + (2+5i)$

3. $(11-2i) - (9+8i)$

4. $4 - (-3-5i)$

5. $-7(3-4i)$

6. $5i(9-2i)$

7. $-7i(12-9i) + 5i(3-2i)$

8. $2(6-4i) - 5i(3-8i)$

9. i^{14}

10. i^{39}

11. $(-3i)^5$

12. $(4-7i)(6+2i)$

13. $(-6-4i)(2-7i)$

14. $(5+3i)(5-3i)$

15. $\dfrac{21-30i}{6}$

16. $\dfrac{27-18i}{3}$

17. $\dfrac{2-7i}{5i}$

18. $\dfrac{4-9i}{2+3i}$

19. $\dfrac{2+i}{2-i}$

20. $2i\left(\dfrac{5+3i}{2-i}\right) - (4+3i)\left(\dfrac{6-5i}{2+i}\right)$

Rectangular and trigonometric form

It's possible to establish a correspondence between the complex numbers and the points in the plane by mapping each complex number $a + bi$ to the point (a,b). Because you know how to convert those rectangular coordinates to trigonometric coordinate equivalents, it's possible to represent complex numbers in a trigonometric form, similar to trigonometric coordinates. The rectangular coordinates convert to trigonometric coordinates of the form (r, θ). Remember when you find θ to make adjustments if your point falls in the second or third quadrant. So you can see $a + bi$ form as a point (a,b) that converts to a point (r, θ), which in turn represents $r \cos \theta + i \cdot r \sin \theta$ or $r(\cos \theta + i \sin \theta)$. The trigonometric form $r(\cos \theta + i \sin \theta)$ is sometimes abbreviated $r \operatorname{cis} \theta$.

Rectangular form of complex number	Rectangular coordinates	Polar coordinates	Trigonometric form of complex number
$a + bi$	(a,b)	(r, θ)	$r(\cos \theta + i \sin \theta)$
$4\sqrt{3} - 4i$	$(4\sqrt{3}, -4)$	$\left(\sqrt{\left(4\sqrt{3}\right)^2 + (-4)^2}, \tan^{-1}\left(\dfrac{-4}{4\sqrt{3}}\right) \right)$	$8\left(\cos \dfrac{-\pi}{6} + i \sin \dfrac{-\pi}{6} \right)$
		$= \left(8, -\dfrac{\pi}{6} \right) = \left(8, \dfrac{11\pi}{6} \right)$	$= 8\left(\cos \dfrac{11\pi}{6} + i \sin \dfrac{11\pi}{6} \right)$
$-6 + 6i$	$(-6, 6)$	$\left(\sqrt{(-6)^2 + 6^2}, \tan^{-1}\left(\dfrac{6}{-6}\right)^* \right)$	$6\sqrt{2}\left(\cos \dfrac{3\pi}{4} + i \sin \dfrac{3\pi}{4} \right)$
		* adjusted for quadrant	
		$= \left(\sqrt{72}, -\dfrac{\pi}{4} + \pi \right) = \left(6\sqrt{2}, \dfrac{3\pi}{4} \right)$	

EXERCISE 8·3

Convert to trigonometric form.

1. $(5,5)$

2. $\left(-7\sqrt{3}, 7\right)$

3. $\left(-12, -12\sqrt{3}\right)$

4. $\left(3\sqrt{5}, -3\sqrt{15}\right)$

5. $(-8, -8)$

6. $(-3, 4)$

7. $(0, -5)$

8. $(12, -6)$

9. $(3, 6)$

10. $(-9, 0)$

Convert to rectangular form.

11. $4\left(\cos \dfrac{\pi}{3} + i \sin \dfrac{\pi}{3} \right)$

12. $4\sqrt{3}\left(\cos \dfrac{\pi}{6} + i \sin \dfrac{\pi}{6} \right)$

13. $12\left(\cos \dfrac{3\pi}{4} + i \sin \dfrac{3\pi}{4} \right)$

14. $15\left(\cos \dfrac{5\pi}{3} + i \sin \dfrac{5\pi}{3} \right)$

15. $9(\cos 7\pi + i\sin 7\pi)$

16. $8\left(\cos\dfrac{7\pi}{4} + i\sin\dfrac{7\pi}{4}\right)$

17. $8\left(\cos\dfrac{13\pi}{4} + i\sin\dfrac{13\pi}{4}\right)$

18. $2(\cos\pi + i\sin\pi)$

19. $5\left(\cos\dfrac{7\pi}{2} + i\sin\dfrac{7\pi}{2}\right)$

20. $11\left(\cos\dfrac{\pi}{2} + i\sin\dfrac{\pi}{2}\right)$

Multiplication and division

One of the advantages of representing complex numbers in trigonometric form is that it provides a simple method of multiplying and dividing complex numbers. To multiply complex numbers in rectangular form, you must foil and simplify. To divide complex numbers in rectangular form, you need to rationalize the denominator. Both can be done, but can be tedious.

The basic multiplication of two complex numbers in trigonometric form would be tedious if you did the obvious steps every time:

$$r_1(\cos\theta_1 + i\sin\theta_1) \cdot r_2(\cos\theta_2 + i\sin\theta_2) = r_1 \cdot r_2 \left[\cos\theta_1\cos\theta_2 + i\sin\theta_2\cos\theta_1 + i\sin\theta_1\cos\theta_2 - \sin\theta_1\sin\theta_2\right]$$
$$= r_1 \cdot r_2 \left[\cos\theta_1\cos\theta_2 - \sin\theta_1\sin\theta_2 + i(\sin\theta_2\cos\theta_1 + \sin\theta_1\cos\theta_2)\right]$$

But with that rearrangement and the application of identities, you have

$$r_1(\cos\theta_1 + i\sin\theta_1) \cdot r_2(\cos\theta_2 + i\sin\theta_2) = r_1 \cdot r_2 \left[\cos(\theta_1 + \theta_2) + i\sin(\theta_1 + \theta_2)\right]$$

That means that you have a shortcut for multiplying complex numbers in trigonometric form: multiply the rs and add the θs. To multiply $\dfrac{3}{2} + \dfrac{3\sqrt{3}}{2}i$ by $-2\sqrt{3} - 2i$ would require you to foil:

$$\left(\frac{3}{2} + \frac{3\sqrt{3}}{2}i\right)\left(-2\sqrt{3} - 2i\right) = -3\sqrt{3} - 3i - 9i + 3\sqrt{3}$$
$$= -12i$$

If those same numbers are expressed in trigonometric form,

$$\frac{3}{2} + \frac{3\sqrt{3}}{2}i = 3\left(\cos\frac{\pi}{3} + i\sin\frac{\pi}{3}\right) \text{ and } -2\sqrt{3} - 2i = -4\left(\cos\frac{\pi}{6} + i\sin\frac{\pi}{6}\right)$$

you can multiply $3(-4)$ and add $\dfrac{\pi}{3} + \dfrac{\pi}{6}$:

$$3\left(\cos\frac{\pi}{3} + i\sin\frac{\pi}{3}\right) \cdot -4\left(\cos\frac{\pi}{6} + i\sin\frac{\pi}{6}\right) = -12\left(\cos\frac{\pi}{2} + i\sin\frac{\pi}{2}\right)$$
$$= -12i$$

A similar argument shows that

$$\frac{r_1(\cos\theta_1 + i\sin\theta_1)}{r_2(\cos\theta_2 + i\sin\theta_2)} = \frac{r_1}{r_2}\left[\cos(\theta_1 - \theta_2) + i\sin(\theta_1 - \theta_2)\right]$$

The quotient

$$\frac{24\left(\cos\dfrac{5\pi}{6}-i\sin\dfrac{5\pi}{6}\right)}{8\left(\cos\dfrac{3\pi}{2}+i\sin\dfrac{3\pi}{2}\right)}=\frac{24}{8}\left[\cos\left(\frac{5\pi}{6}-\frac{3\pi}{2}\right)+i\sin\left(\frac{5\pi}{6}-\frac{3\pi}{2}\right)\right]$$

$$=3\left(\cos\frac{-4\pi}{3}+i\sin\frac{-4\pi}{3}\right)$$

Remember the two shortcuts for multiplication and division of complex numbers in trigonometric form:

♦ To multiply two numbers in trigonometric form, multiply the *r*s and add the θs.
♦ To divide, divide the *r*s and subtract the θs.

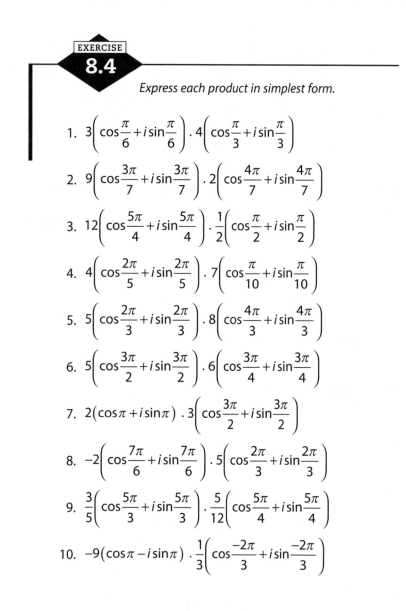

EXERCISE
8.4

Express each product in simplest form.

1. $3\left(\cos\dfrac{\pi}{6}+i\sin\dfrac{\pi}{6}\right)\cdot 4\left(\cos\dfrac{\pi}{3}+i\sin\dfrac{\pi}{3}\right)$

2. $9\left(\cos\dfrac{3\pi}{7}+i\sin\dfrac{3\pi}{7}\right)\cdot 2\left(\cos\dfrac{4\pi}{7}+i\sin\dfrac{4\pi}{7}\right)$

3. $12\left(\cos\dfrac{5\pi}{4}+i\sin\dfrac{5\pi}{4}\right)\cdot\dfrac{1}{2}\left(\cos\dfrac{\pi}{2}+i\sin\dfrac{\pi}{2}\right)$

4. $4\left(\cos\dfrac{2\pi}{5}+i\sin\dfrac{2\pi}{5}\right)\cdot 7\left(\cos\dfrac{\pi}{10}+i\sin\dfrac{\pi}{10}\right)$

5. $5\left(\cos\dfrac{2\pi}{3}+i\sin\dfrac{2\pi}{3}\right)\cdot 8\left(\cos\dfrac{4\pi}{3}+i\sin\dfrac{4\pi}{3}\right)$

6. $5\left(\cos\dfrac{3\pi}{2}+i\sin\dfrac{3\pi}{2}\right)\cdot 6\left(\cos\dfrac{3\pi}{4}+i\sin\dfrac{3\pi}{4}\right)$

7. $2\left(\cos\pi+i\sin\pi\right)\cdot 3\left(\cos\dfrac{3\pi}{2}+i\sin\dfrac{3\pi}{2}\right)$

8. $-2\left(\cos\dfrac{7\pi}{6}+i\sin\dfrac{7\pi}{6}\right)\cdot 5\left(\cos\dfrac{2\pi}{3}+i\sin\dfrac{2\pi}{3}\right)$

9. $\dfrac{3}{5}\left(\cos\dfrac{5\pi}{3}+i\sin\dfrac{5\pi}{3}\right)\cdot\dfrac{5}{12}\left(\cos\dfrac{5\pi}{4}+i\sin\dfrac{5\pi}{4}\right)$

10. $-9\left(\cos\pi-i\sin\pi\right)\cdot\dfrac{1}{3}\left(\cos\dfrac{-2\pi}{3}+i\sin\dfrac{-2\pi}{3}\right)$

Express each quotient in simplest form.

11. $\dfrac{16\left(\cos\dfrac{4\pi}{3}+i\sin\dfrac{4\pi}{3}\right)}{8\left(\cos\dfrac{\pi}{6}+i\sin\dfrac{\pi}{6}\right)}$

16. $\dfrac{7\left(\cos\dfrac{\pi}{5}+i\sin\dfrac{\pi}{5}\right)}{14\left(\cos\dfrac{\pi}{8}+i\sin\dfrac{\pi}{8}\right)}$

12. $\dfrac{12\left(\cos\dfrac{11\pi}{12}+i\sin\dfrac{11\pi}{12}\right)}{-6\left(\cos\dfrac{7\pi}{6}+i\sin\dfrac{7\pi}{6}\right)}$

17. $\dfrac{8\sqrt{6}\left(\cos\pi+i\sin\pi\right)}{2\sqrt{3}\left(\cos\dfrac{3\pi}{2}+i\sin\dfrac{3\pi}{2}\right)}$

18. $\dfrac{28\left(\cos\pi+i\sin\pi\right)}{-7\left(\cos\dfrac{-\pi}{3}+i\sin\dfrac{-\pi}{3}\right)}$

13. $\dfrac{2\sqrt{2}\left(\cos\dfrac{\pi}{4}+i\sin\dfrac{\pi}{4}\right)}{\sqrt{2}\left(\cos\dfrac{5\pi}{6}+i\sin\dfrac{5\pi}{6}\right)}$

19. $\dfrac{9\left(\cos\pi+i\sin\pi\right)}{3\left(\cos\dfrac{\pi}{4}+i\sin\dfrac{\pi}{4}\right)}$

14. $\dfrac{8\sqrt{15}\left(\cos\dfrac{11\pi}{2}+i\sin\dfrac{11\pi}{2}\right)}{2\sqrt{3}\left(\cos\dfrac{5\pi}{6}+i\sin\dfrac{5\pi}{6}\right)}$

20. $\dfrac{256\left(\cos 3\pi+i\sin 3\pi\right)}{64\left(\cos 7\pi+i\sin 7\pi\right)}$

15. $\dfrac{2\sqrt{3}\left(\cos\dfrac{3\pi}{2}+i\sin\dfrac{3\pi}{2}\right)}{4\left(\cos\dfrac{3\pi}{4}+i\sin\dfrac{3\pi}{4}\right)}$

Powers and roots

Because powers are repeated multiplication, the technique for multiplying complex numbers in trigonometric form can be extended to find powers of complex numbers. With a little help from multiple representations, the rule can also be used to find roots of complex numbers in trigonometric form.

Powers

If you apply the multiplication rule to square a complex number in trigonometric form, you get

$$\begin{aligned}
\left[r(\cos\theta+i\sin\theta)\right]^2 &= r[\cos\theta+i\sin\theta]\cdot r[\cos\theta+i\sin\theta]\\
&= r^2\left[\cos^2\theta+2i\cos\theta\sin\theta-\sin^2\theta\right]\\
&= r^2\left[\cos^2\theta-\sin^2\theta+2i\cos\theta\sin\theta\right]\\
&= r^2\left[\cos 2\theta+i\sin 2\theta\right]
\end{aligned}$$

This result tells you that to raise a complex number to the second power, you raise r to the second power and double θ. You can generalize that rule for any power n:

$$\left[r(\cos\theta+i\sin\theta)\right]^n = r^n\left[\cos(n\theta)+i\sin(n\theta)\right]$$

To raise a complex number in trigonometric form to the nth power, raise r to the nth power and multiply θ by n:

$$\left[2\left(\cos\frac{2\pi}{3}+i\sin\frac{2\pi}{3}\right)\right]^6 = 2^6\left[\cos\left(6\cdot\frac{2\pi}{3}\right)+i\sin\left(6\cdot\frac{2\pi}{3}\right)\right]$$

$$= 64[\cos 4\pi + i\sin 4\pi]$$

$$= 64[1+0i]=64$$

Roots

The strategy for finding the roots of complex numbers in trigonometric form is based on the rule for powers and the ability to represent roots as fractional exponents. You know that $\sqrt{x}=x^{1/2}$, $\sqrt[3]{x}=x^{1/3}$, and, in general, $\sqrt[n]{x}=x^{1/n}$. The basic rule for powers of complex numbers in trigonometric form would say that

$$\sqrt[n]{r(\cos\theta+i\sin\theta)} = [r(\cos\theta+i\sin\theta)]^{1/n}$$

$$= r^{1/n}\left[\cos\frac{\theta}{n}+i\sin\frac{\theta}{n}\right]$$

The problem is that, over the complex numbers, every number should have n nth roots—two square roots, three cube roots, five fifth roots, and so on—but this rule only seems to produce one root. Where will you find the others? The answer comes from the fact that each complex number has infinitely many representations in trigonometric coordinates.

To find all n nth roots of a complex number, start with n representations of the number, formed by adding 2π to the value of θ. For example, to find the three cube roots of $8\left(\cos\frac{\pi}{3}+i\sin\frac{\pi}{3}\right)$, begin with

$$8\left(\cos\frac{\pi}{3}+i\sin\frac{\pi}{3}\right)$$

and

$$8\left(\cos\frac{\pi}{3}+2\pi+i\sin\frac{\pi}{3}+2\pi\right)=8\left(\cos\frac{7\pi}{3}+i\sin\frac{7\pi}{3}\right)$$

and

$$8\left(\cos\frac{\pi}{3}+4\pi+i\sin\frac{\pi}{3}+4\pi\right)=8\left(\cos\frac{13\pi}{3}+i\sin\frac{13\pi}{3}\right)$$

To find the fifth roots of $32\left(\cos\frac{\pi}{4}+i\sin\frac{\pi}{4}\right)$, use

$$32\left(\cos\frac{\pi}{4}+i\sin\frac{\pi}{4}\right)$$

$$32\left(\cos\frac{9\pi}{4}+i\sin\frac{9\pi}{4}\right)$$

$$32\left(\cos\frac{17\pi}{4}+i\sin\frac{17\pi}{4}\right)$$

$$32\left(\cos\frac{25\pi}{4}+i\sin\frac{25\pi}{4}\right)$$

and

$$32\left(\cos\frac{33\pi}{4}+i\sin\frac{33\pi}{4}\right)$$

Then apply the basic rule to each representation of the number. To find the three cube roots of $8\left(\cos\dfrac{\pi}{3}+i\sin\dfrac{\pi}{3}\right)$, take the cube root of r (or evaluate $r^{1/3}$) and multiply θ by $\dfrac{1}{3}$ (or divide by 3). Repeat for each of the three representations of the number:

$$\sqrt[3]{8}\left[\cos\frac{\pi/3}{3}+i\sin\frac{\pi/3}{3}\right]=2\left[\cos\frac{\pi}{9}+i\sin\frac{\pi}{9}\right]$$
$$\sqrt[3]{8}\left[\cos\frac{\pi/3+2\pi}{3}+i\sin\frac{\pi/3+2\pi}{3}\right]=2\left[\cos\frac{7\pi}{9}+i\sin\frac{7\pi}{9}\right]$$
$$\sqrt[3]{8}\left[\cos\frac{\pi/3+4\pi}{3}+i\sin\frac{\pi/3+4\pi}{3}\right]=2\left[\cos\frac{13\pi}{9}+i\sin\frac{13\pi}{9}\right]$$

The three cube roots of $8\left(\cos\dfrac{\pi}{3}+i\sin\dfrac{\pi}{3}\right)$ are $2\left[\cos\dfrac{\pi}{9}+i\sin\dfrac{\pi}{9}\right]$, $2\left[\cos\dfrac{7\pi}{9}+i\sin\dfrac{7\pi}{9}\right]$, and $2\left[\cos\dfrac{13\pi}{9}+i\sin\dfrac{13\pi}{9}\right]$. You may notice that in all three cube roots, you have the same value of r, and θ increases by $\dfrac{6\pi}{9}=\dfrac{2\pi}{3}$.

If you plot the three cube roots of $8\left(\cos\dfrac{\pi}{3}+i\sin\dfrac{\pi}{3}\right)$, you'll notice that they are the vertices of an equilateral triangle. The nth roots of a number will form the vertices of a regular n-gon.

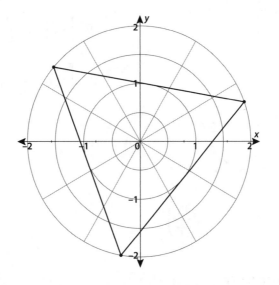

To find the fifth roots of $32\left(\cos\dfrac{\pi}{4}+i\sin\dfrac{\pi}{4}\right)$, evaluate

$$32^{1/5}\left(\cos\frac{1}{5}\left(\frac{\pi}{4}\right)+i\sin\frac{1}{5}\left(\frac{\pi}{4}\right)\right)=2\left(\cos\frac{\pi}{20}+i\sin\frac{\pi}{20}\right)$$

$$32^{1/5}\left(\cos\frac{1}{5}\left(\frac{\pi}{4}+2\pi\right)+i\sin\frac{1}{5}\left(\frac{\pi}{4}+2\pi\right)\right)=2\left(\cos\frac{9\pi}{20}+i\sin\frac{9\pi}{20}\right)$$

$$32^{1/5}\left(\cos\frac{1}{5}\left(\frac{\pi}{4}+4\pi\right)+i\sin\frac{1}{5}\left(\frac{\pi}{4}+4\pi\right)\right)=2\left(\cos\frac{17\pi}{20}+i\sin\frac{17\pi}{20}\right)$$

$$32^{1/5}\left(\cos\frac{1}{5}\left(\frac{\pi}{4}+6\pi\right)+i\sin\frac{1}{5}\left(\frac{\pi}{4}+6\pi\right)\right)=2\left(\cos\frac{25\pi}{20}+i\sin\frac{25\pi}{20}\right)$$

$$32^{1/5}\left(\cos\frac{1}{5}\left(\frac{\pi}{4}+8\pi\right)+i\sin\frac{1}{5}\left(\frac{\pi}{4}+8\pi\right)\right)=2\left(\cos\frac{33\pi}{20}+i\sin\frac{33\pi}{20}\right)$$

Here all the roots have an r value of 2, and the value of θ increases by $\dfrac{8\pi}{20}=\dfrac{2\pi}{5}$. The five fifth roots are the vertices of a regular pentagon.

EXERCISE
8·5

Evaluate each power and give your answer in simplest form.

1. $\left[3\left(\cos\dfrac{\pi}{4}+i\sin\dfrac{\pi}{4}\right)\right]^4$

2. $\left[2\left(\cos\dfrac{\pi}{6}+i\sin\dfrac{\pi}{6}\right)\right]^5$

3. $\left[4\left(\cos\dfrac{7\pi}{4}+i\sin\dfrac{7\pi}{4}\right)\right]^3$

4. $\left[-5\left(\cos\dfrac{2\pi}{9}+i\sin\dfrac{2\pi}{9}\right)\right]^3$

5. $\left[10\left(\cos\pi+i\sin\pi\right)\right]^4$

6. $\left[\dfrac{1}{2}\left(\cos\dfrac{5\pi}{12}+i\sin\dfrac{5\pi}{12}\right)\right]^6$

7. $\left[6\left(\cos\dfrac{\pi}{2}+i\sin\dfrac{\pi}{2}\right)\right]^2$

8. $\left[4\left(\cos\dfrac{7\pi}{15}+i\sin\dfrac{7\pi}{15}\right)\right]^3$

9. $\left[-\dfrac{1}{2}\left(\cos\dfrac{3\pi}{4}+i\sin\dfrac{3\pi}{4}\right)\right]^8$

10. $\left[5\left(\cos\dfrac{5\pi}{6}+i\sin\dfrac{5\pi}{6}\right)\right]^4$

Find all the indicated roots in simplest form.

11. The square roots of $36\left(\cos\dfrac{\pi}{2}+i\sin\dfrac{\pi}{2}\right)$

12. The cube roots of $27\left(\cos\dfrac{3\pi}{4}+i\sin\dfrac{3\pi}{4}\right)$

13. The fourth roots of $81\left(\cos\dfrac{8\pi}{3}+i\sin\dfrac{8\pi}{3}\right)$

14. The fifth roots of $1{,}024\left(\cos\dfrac{5\pi}{3}+i\sin\dfrac{5\pi}{3}\right)$

Change each number to trigonometric form and find all of the indicated roots.

15. The fourth roots of 81

16. The sixth roots of 64

17. The cube roots of -1

18. The fourth roots of $81i$

19. The sixth roots of $-64i$

20. The fifth roots of 32

Vectors in the plane

A vector is a directed distance, a movement from an initial point to a terminal point. The following figure shows a vector with its initial point at (2, 3) and its terminal point at (5, 7). The vector from point P to point Q can be represented as $\overrightarrow{PQ}$, using the notation for a ray in geometry, but vectors are commonly denoted by boldface lowercase letters, such as u and v.

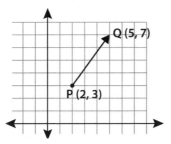

A vector may be used to represent a force acting on an object. The length of the vector represents the magnitude of the force, while the orientation of the vector shows the direction of the force. A vector that represents the force of gravity acting on an object would show a downward movement, perpendicular to the earth's surface, with a magnitude equal to the acceleration due to gravity (9.8 meters per second squared or 32 feet per second squared) times the mass of the object.

Representing vectors

A vector can be specified by identifying its initial and terminal points, by specifying its magnitude and direction, or by resolving the movement into its horizontal and vertical components. Each of these representations has advantages in different situations, and you'll want to be able to convert from one representation to another.

A polar coordinate style of notation $\mathbf{v} = [r, \theta]$ can be used to give the magnitude or length of the vector and its direction. The notation $\mathbf{u} = \left[5, \dfrac{\pi}{4} \right]$ tells you that the vector is 5 units long and makes an angle of $\dfrac{\pi}{4}$ radians (or 45°) with the horizontal. The vector $\mathbf{v} = \left[98, -\dfrac{\pi}{2} \right]$ has a magnitude or length of 98 units and is moving downward at right angles to the horizontal.

Alternately, a vector can be represented by its horizontal and vertical components, the separate movements in each direction. Although the direction of the vector may be oblique, that movement can be accomplished by moving first left or right and then up or down. If you think about counting out the slope of a line, you'll see how this oblique movement can resolve into horizontal and vertical components. This component representation is in keeping with a rectangular coordinate system, but each number in the vector representation is the difference of coordinates, not the coordinates themselves. The vector $\mathbf{v}$ that has initial point (x_1, y_1) and terminal point (x_2, y_2) is represented as $\mathbf{v} = \langle x_2 - x_1, y_2 - y_1 \rangle$ or $\mathbf{v} = \langle \Delta x, \Delta y \rangle$.

If you are familiar with matrix arithmetic, you can think of a vector in component form as a small matrix. Generally, vectors are represented either as row matrices or as column matrices. Understanding vectors in this way may help you with some of the arithmetic of vectors.

If you know the initial and terminal points of the vector, you can find the magnitude by using the distance formula, $d = \sqrt{(x_2 - x_1)^2 + (y_2 - y_1)^2}$. To find the angle that represents the direction of the vector, start with the slope of the vector, $m = \dfrac{y_2 - y_1}{x_2 - x_1}$, and take $\tan^{-1}\left(\dfrac{y_2 - y_1}{x_2 - x_1}\right)$. This will give you the angle for vectors that move up or down to the right, or northeast or southeast. For vectors that move left, that is, northwest or southwest, add π (or 180° if you're working in degrees) to the value of $\tan^{-1}\left(\dfrac{y_2 - y_1}{x_2 - x_1}\right)$.

The vector that has its initial point at P (1, −3) and its terminal point at Q (−3, 1) has a magnitude of $r = \sqrt{(-3-1)^2 + (1+3)^2} = \sqrt{16+16} = 4\sqrt{2}$. To find its direction, first take $\tan^{-1}\left(\dfrac{-3-1}{1+3}\right) = \tan^{-1}(-1) = -\dfrac{\pi}{4}$. But $\overrightarrow{PQ}$ moves to the upper left, so add π to $-\dfrac{\pi}{4}$ to get a direction angle of $\dfrac{3\pi}{4}$. $\overrightarrow{PQ} = \left[4\sqrt{2}, \dfrac{3\pi}{4}\right]$.

If you know the initial and terminal points of the vector, you can find the component form by subtracting the coordinates: $\mathbf{v} = \langle \Delta x, \Delta y \rangle = \langle x_2 - x_1, y_2 - y_1 \rangle$. The vector that has its initial point at P (1, −3) and its terminal point at Q (−3, 1) can be expressed in component form as $\overrightarrow{PQ} = \langle -3-1, 1+3 \rangle = \langle -4.4 \rangle$.

The vector from the origin, O, to point $P\left(3, -3\sqrt{3}\right)$ can be denoted as $\overrightarrow{OP}$ and specified by the magnitude and direction $\left[6, -\dfrac{\pi}{3}\right]$ or by the components $\langle 3, -3\sqrt{3} \rangle$.

Unit vectors

A unit vector is a vector with a magnitude, or length, of 1 unit. The vector $\mathbf{v}$, from $P(-3,1)$ to $Q\left(-\dfrac{6+\sqrt{2}}{2}, \dfrac{2+\sqrt{2}}{2}\right)$, is a unit vector because the magnitude of the vector, denoted $\left\|\overrightarrow{PQ}\right\|$ or $\|\mathbf{v}\|$, is

$$\|\mathbf{v}\| = \sqrt{\left(-\frac{6+\sqrt{2}}{2} + 3\right)^2 + \left(\frac{2+\sqrt{2}}{2} - 1\right)^2}$$

$$= \sqrt{\left(\frac{-\sqrt{2}}{2}\right)^2 + \left(\frac{\sqrt{2}}{2}\right)^2}$$

$$= \sqrt{\frac{1}{2} + \frac{1}{2}} = 1$$

The unit vector from the origin, moving 1 unit to the right, which is written in component form as $\langle 1,0 \rangle$ or in trigonometric form as $[1,0]$, is traditionally denoted as **i**. The vertical unit vector from the origin, written in component form as $\langle 0,1 \rangle$ or in trigonometric form as $\left[1, \dfrac{\pi}{2} \right]$, is denoted as **j**. These unit vectors serve as basic components and allow you to write other vectors as linear combinations of **i** and **j**. The vector **v** with initial point $(4,-2)$ and terminal point $(-1,7)$ can be written in component form as $\langle -5,9 \rangle$ or as $-5\mathbf{i} + 9\mathbf{j}$.

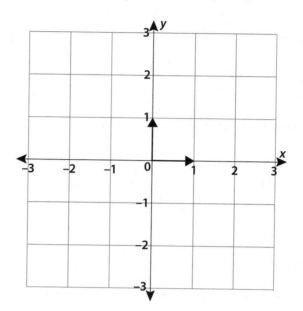

EXERCISE
9·1

Find the magnitude and direction of each vector and write the vector in trigonometric form.

1. From $(0,0)$ to $(-4,-4)$

2. From $(0,0)$ to $(3,3\sqrt{3})$

3. From $(0,0)$ to $(2\sqrt{2},-2\sqrt{2})$

4. From $(0,0)$ to $(-8\sqrt{3},-8)$

5. From $(5,8)$ to $(2,12)$

6. From $(-3,-7)$ to $(2,-19)$

7. From $(0,0)$ to $(6\sqrt{6},-6\sqrt{2})$

8. From $(0,0)$ to $(\sqrt{27},\sqrt{73})$

9. From $(5,4)$ to $(4,1)$

10. From $(-11,18)$ to $(-15,18)$

Write each vector in component form.

11. From $(0,0)$ to $(-4,-4)$

12. From $(0,0)$ to $(3,3\sqrt{3})$

13. From $(0,0)$ to $(2\sqrt{2},-2\sqrt{2})$

14. From $(0,0)$ to $(-8\sqrt{3},-8)$

15. From $(5,8)$ to $(2,12)$

16. From $(-3,-7)$ to $(2,-19)$

17. From $(0,0)$ to $(6\sqrt{6},-6\sqrt{2})$

18. From $(0,0)$ to $(\sqrt{27},\sqrt{73})$

19. From $(5,4)$ to $(4,1)$

20. From $(-11,18)$ to $(-15,18)$

Determine whether the given vector is a unit vector.

21. From $(0,0)$ to $(-0.5, 0.6)$

22. From $(0,0)$ to $\left(\dfrac{1}{5}, \dfrac{2\sqrt{6}}{5}\right)$

23. From $\left(\dfrac{1}{12}, -\dfrac{5}{12}\right)$ to $\left(-\dfrac{1}{2}, \dfrac{7}{12}\right)$

24. From $\left(\dfrac{2}{3}, \dfrac{1}{3}\right)$ to $\left(-\dfrac{1}{3}, -1\right)$

25. From $\left(\dfrac{1}{4}, -\dfrac{1}{4}\right)$ to $\left(\dfrac{1}{12}, -\dfrac{19}{20}\right)$

Write each vector as a linear combination of the form $a\boldsymbol{i} + b\boldsymbol{j}$.

26. From $(0,0)$ to $(8,5)$

27. From $(0,0)$ to $(-2,4)$

28. From $(0,0)$ to $(3,-6)$

29. From $(1,2)$ to $(-3,5)$

30. From $(7,-2)$ to $(-6,3)$

Changing forms

To represent a directed distance, you need to specify both the distance and the direction. Those pieces of information can easily be communicated in trigonometric form, with r giving the distance and θ the direction. If you're working from the initial and terminal points of the vector, finding the magnitude and direction can be complicated calculations. If you're given a vector in trigonometric form, it can be hard to measure out the distance and direction. On the other hand, if you know the initial and terminal points of the vector, the component form is easy to find, and easy to draw, but doesn't directly communicate the distance and direction. So each form has its advantages and disadvantages, and you'll sometimes want to change form.

To resolve a vector that is given in trigonometric notation into its horizontal and vertical components, use the same strategy you used to convert coordinates from trigonometric to rectangular form. The horizontal component is $x = r\cos\theta$, and the vertical component is $y = r\sin\theta$. A vector expressed in trigonometric form as $[r, \theta]$ can be expressed in component form as $\langle r\cos\theta, r\sin\theta \rangle$ or written as a linear combination of unit vectors as $r\cos\theta\,\boldsymbol{i} + r\sin\theta\,\boldsymbol{j}$. So the vector $\mathbf{u} = \left[8, \dfrac{4\pi}{3}\right]$ can also be represented as $\mathbf{u} = \left\langle 8\cos\dfrac{4\pi}{3}, 8\sin\dfrac{4\pi}{3} \right\rangle = \langle -4, -4\sqrt{3} \rangle$ or as $\mathbf{u} = -4\boldsymbol{i} - 4\sqrt{3}\boldsymbol{j}$.

To convert a vector in component form $\langle a, b \rangle$ or in $a\boldsymbol{i} + b\boldsymbol{j}$ form to trigonometric form, recall that $r = \sqrt{a^2 + b^2}$. This is just a modified version of the distance formula. To find θ, the angle that indicates direction, first find $\tan^{-1}\dfrac{b}{a}$. If $a > 0$, the vector is moving to the right, so $\theta = \tan^{-1}\dfrac{b}{a}$. If $a < 0$, the vector is moving to the left, so $\theta = \tan^{-1}\dfrac{b}{a} + \pi$. So the vector $\mathbf{u} = 4\boldsymbol{i} - 3\boldsymbol{j}$ has a magnitude of $r = \sqrt{4^2 + (-3)^2} = 5$. Because the horizontal component is positive, the angle $\theta = \tan^{-1}\left(\dfrac{-3}{4}\right) \approx -0.644$ radians. The vector can be written in trigonometric form as $\mathbf{u} = \langle 5, -0.644 \rangle$. The vector represented in component form as $\mathbf{v} = \langle -3, 3\sqrt{3} \rangle$ has a magnitude of $r = \sqrt{(-3)^2 + \left(3\sqrt{3}\right)^2} = \sqrt{9 + 27} =$ and, because the horizontal component is negative, or leftward, $\theta = \tan^{-1}\left(\dfrac{3\sqrt{3}}{-3}\right) + \pi = \tan^{-1}\left(-\sqrt{3}\right) + \pi = -\dfrac{\pi}{3} + \pi = \dfrac{2\pi}{3}$. The vector in trigonometric form is $\mathbf{v} = \left[6, \dfrac{2\pi}{3}\right]$.

If $a = 0$, you can't calculate $\tan^{-1}\dfrac{b}{a}$, but the vector is vertical, with $\theta = \dfrac{\pi}{2}$ if $b > 0$ (moving up) and $\theta = -\dfrac{\pi}{2}$ (or $\theta = \dfrac{3\pi}{2}$) if $b < 0$ (moving down). So the vector represented in component form as $\mathbf{u} = \langle 0, 5 \rangle$ is equivalent to $\mathbf{u} = \left[5, \dfrac{\pi}{2}\right]$ in trigonometric form, and the component representation $\mathbf{v} = \langle 0, -5 \rangle$ can be expressed in trigonometric form as $\mathbf{v} = \left[5, -\dfrac{\pi}{2}\right]$ or $\mathbf{v} = \left[5, \dfrac{3\pi}{2}\right]$.

EXERCISE 9·2

Each vector is given in component form. Find the magnitude and direction of each vector and write the vector in trigonometric form.

1. $\langle 3, 3\sqrt{3} \rangle$
2. $\langle 7\sqrt{2}, -7\sqrt{2} \rangle$
3. $\langle -5, -5 \rangle$
4. $\langle \sqrt{15}, 3\sqrt{5} \rangle$
5. $\langle 4, -3 \rangle$

6. $\langle -5, 9 \rangle$
7. $\langle 8, 0 \rangle$
8. $\langle -7, 0 \rangle$
9. $\langle -12, 5 \rangle$
10. $\langle 6\sqrt{5}, -3\sqrt{5} \rangle$

Each vector is given in trigonometric form $[r, \theta]$. Resolve each vector into its component form.

11. $\left[6, -\dfrac{\pi}{3}\right]$
12. $[12, \pi]$
13. $\left[9, \dfrac{5\pi}{6}\right]$
14. $\left[10, -\dfrac{2\pi}{3}\right]$
15. $\left[8, \dfrac{3\pi}{2}\right]$

16. $\left[2, \dfrac{7\pi}{4}\right]$
17. $\left[4, -\dfrac{3\pi}{2}\right]$
18. $\left[8, \dfrac{7\pi}{12}\right]$
19. $[9, \pi]$
20. $\left[\dfrac{1}{2}, \dfrac{\pi}{30}\right]$

Addition of vectors

When two vectors with the same direction are applied to the same object, the second movement follows the first, in the same direction, and the result is a vector whose magnitude is the addition of the magnitudes of the individual vectors and whose direction is the same as that of the individual vectors. If $\mathbf{u} = \left[6, \dfrac{\pi}{3} \right]$ and $\mathbf{v} = \left[5, \dfrac{\pi}{3} \right]$, $\mathbf{u} + \mathbf{v} = \left[11, \dfrac{\pi}{3} \right]$.

If two vectors act on the same object but the directions are opposite, they have a canceling effect on one another, with the larger magnitude winning out. The result is a vector with a magnitude equal to the difference of the magnitudes and a direction that matches that of the vector with the larger magnitude. If $\mathbf{u} = \left[8, \dfrac{\pi}{4} \right]$ and $\mathbf{v} = \left[5, \dfrac{5\pi}{4} \right]$, $\mathbf{u} + \mathbf{v} = \left[3, \dfrac{\pi}{4} \right]$, but if $\mathbf{u} = \left[2, \dfrac{\pi}{3} \right]$ and $\mathbf{v} = \left[9, \dfrac{4\pi}{3} \right]$, $\mathbf{u} + \mathbf{v} = \left[7, \dfrac{4\pi}{3} \right]$.

If the directions of the vectors are neither identical nor opposite, however, trigonometry is necessary to find the sum, or resultant vector. Graphically, addition of two vectors, $\mathbf{u}$ and $\mathbf{v}$, can be represented by placing the initial point of $\mathbf{v}$ at the terminal point of $\mathbf{u}$, then drawing a vector from the initial point of $\mathbf{u}$ to the terminal point of $\mathbf{v}$. This resultant vector represents the sum $\mathbf{u} + \mathbf{v}$.

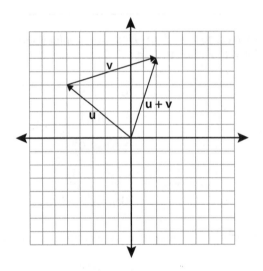

For vectors in component form, if $\mathbf{u} = \langle a, b \rangle$ and $\mathbf{v} = \langle c, d \rangle$, then $\mathbf{u} + \mathbf{v} = \langle a + c, b + d \rangle$. If $\mathbf{u} = \langle 3, -2 \rangle$ and $\mathbf{v} = \langle 4, 5 \rangle$, $\mathbf{u} + \mathbf{v} = \langle 7, 3 \rangle$.

If you are familiar with matrix arithmetic and see each vector as a matrix, this is matrix addition.

For vectors given in trigonometric form, if $\mathbf{u} = [r_1, \theta_1]$ and $\mathbf{v} = [r_2, \theta_2]$, the magnitude, r, of the resultant vector can be found by the law of cosines:

$$r^2 = \left(r_1 \right)^2 + \left(r_2 \right)^2 - 2 r_1 r_2 \cos\left(\pi - \theta_1 + \theta_2 \right)$$

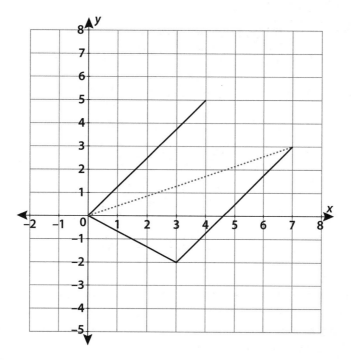

The direction of the resultant vector can be calculated using the equation:

$$\tan\theta = \frac{r_1\sin\theta_1 + r_2\sin\theta_2}{r_1\cos\theta_1 + r_2\cos\theta_2}$$

To add $\mathbf{u} = \left[3, \dfrac{2\pi}{3}\right]$ and $\mathbf{v} = \left[4, \dfrac{5\pi}{4}\right]$, it's a good idea to make at least a rough sketch of the two vectors, so that you have a sense of the magnitude and direction of the resultant vector. The vector $\mathbf{u}$ moves from the origin into the second quadrant, while the vector $\mathbf{v}$ moves from the origin down into the third quadrant. If you place the initial point of $\mathbf{v}$ at the terminal point of $\mathbf{u}$ and draw the resultant, you can see it moves left and just slightly down from the horizontal. Calculate $\mathbf{r}$ with the law of cosines. Don't be tempted by the 3 and 4 to believe that $\mathbf{r}$ is 5. This is not a right triangle, so Pythagorean triples are not relevant:

$$r^2 = \left(r_1\right)^2 + \left(r_2\right)^2 - 2r_1r_2\cos\left(\pi - \theta_1 + \theta_2\right)$$

$$= 3^2 + 4^2 - 2\cdot3\cdot4\cos\left(\pi - \frac{2\pi}{3} + \frac{5\pi}{4}\right)$$

$$= 9 + 16 - 24\cos\frac{19\pi}{12}$$

$$= 25 - 24\cos\frac{19\pi}{12}$$

$$\approx 25 - 24(0.2588)$$

$$\approx 18.788$$

$$r \approx 4.335$$

Then use the tangent to find the direction angle:

$$\tan\theta = \frac{r_1 \sin\theta_1 + r_2 \sin\theta_2}{r_1 \cos\theta_1 + r_2 \cos\theta_2}$$

$$= \frac{3\sin\dfrac{2\pi}{3} + 4\sin\dfrac{5\pi}{4}}{3\cos\dfrac{2\pi}{3} + 4\cos\dfrac{5\pi}{4}}$$

$$= \frac{3\left(\dfrac{\sqrt{3}}{2}\right) + 4\left(-\dfrac{\sqrt{2}}{2}\right)}{3\left(-\dfrac{1}{2}\right) + 4\left(-\dfrac{\sqrt{2}}{2}\right)}$$

$$= \frac{3\sqrt{3} - 4\sqrt{2}}{-3 - 4\sqrt{2}} \approx 0.0532$$

A positive value for tan θ tells you the vector's direction is either up and to the right or down and to the left, and you know from your sketch that it will be down and to the left. So find $\tan^{-1} 0.0532$ and add π. $\tan^{-1} 0.0532 \approx 0.053$, so $\tan^{-1} 0.0532 + \pi \approx 3.195$ radians. The resultant vector $\mathbf{u} + \mathbf{v} = [4.335, 3.195]$ in trigonometric form.

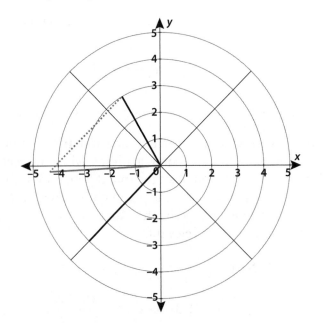

You can see that adding vectors in trigonometric form can be a complicated calculation. It's often simpler, as a result, to resolve the vector into its component form, add, and then find the magnitude and direction of the resultant. This may seem roundabout, but because the individual calculations are generally simpler, it's often the preferred method. To add $\mathbf{u} = \left[3, \dfrac{2\pi}{3}\right]$ and $\mathbf{v} = \left[4, \dfrac{5\pi}{4}\right]$, first convert each vector to component form:

$$\mathbf{u} = \left\langle 3\cos\frac{2\pi}{3}, 3\sin\frac{2\pi}{3} \right\rangle = \left\langle -\frac{3}{2}, \frac{3\sqrt{3}}{2} \right\rangle$$

$$\mathbf{v} = \left\langle 4\cos\frac{5\pi}{4}, 4\sin\frac{5\pi}{4} \right\rangle = \left\langle -2\sqrt{2}, -2\sqrt{2} \right\rangle$$

Then add the vectors by adding the components:

$$\mathbf{u} + \mathbf{v} = \left\langle -\frac{3}{2} - 2\sqrt{2}, \frac{3\sqrt{3}}{2} - 2\sqrt{2} \right\rangle$$

$$= \left\langle \frac{-3 - 4\sqrt{2}}{2}, \frac{3\sqrt{3} - 4\sqrt{2}}{2} \right\rangle$$

$$\approx \left\langle -4.328, -0.230 \right\rangle$$

Finally, if necessary, convert back to trigonometric form by finding the magnitude and direction:

$$r = \sqrt{(-4.328)^2 + (-0.230)^2} = \sqrt{18.784} = 4.334$$

$$\tan^{-1}\left(\frac{-0.230}{-4.328}\right) = \tan^{-1} 0.053 = 0.053 \text{ radians}$$

$$0.053 + \pi = 3.195 \text{ radians}$$

$$\mathbf{u} + \mathbf{v} = [4.334, 3.195]$$

Scalar multiplication

A scalar is a single number that can affect a vector. It gets the name "scalar" because it changes the scale, or magnitude, of the vector. Multiplying by a scalar, c, has the effect of placing c copies of the vector end to end, or adding c copies of the vector.

If a vector represented in trigonometric form, $[r, \theta]$, is multiplied by a scalar, c, the result is $[cr, \theta]$. Multiplying $\left[3, \frac{5\pi}{6}\right]$ by 7 gives you $\left[21, \frac{5\pi}{6}\right]$. If the scalar is positive, the direction of the vector is unchanged. If the scalar is negative, however, the multiplication will change the sign of $\mathbf{r}$, which reverses the vector.

A vector in component form, $\langle a, b \rangle$, multiplied by a scalar, c, gives the vector $\langle ca, cb \rangle$. If you multiply the vector $\langle 4, -7 \rangle$ by 5, you get the vector $\langle 20, -35 \rangle$.

Scalar multiplication corresponds exactly to multiplication of a matrix by a scalar. In matrix arithmetic, each element of the matrix is multiplied by the scalar. If the vector in component form is viewed as a matrix, each component is multiplied by the scalar.

Subtraction of vectors

Subtracting can be viewed as a combination of multiplying one vector by the scalar −1 and adding. For vectors in component form, if $\mathbf{u} = \langle a, b \rangle$ and $\mathbf{v} = \langle c, d \rangle$, then

$$\mathbf{u} - \mathbf{v} = \langle a, b \rangle + -1 \langle c, d \rangle = \langle a, b \rangle + \langle -c, -d \rangle = \langle a - c, b - d \rangle$$

For vectors in trigonometric form, $\mathbf{u} = [r_1, \theta_1]$ and $\mathbf{v} = [r_2, \theta_2]$, to subtract vector $\mathbf{v}$ from vector $\mathbf{u}$, multiply $\mathbf{v}$ by the scalar −1 and then add:

$$\mathbf{u} - \mathbf{v} = [r_1, \theta_1] - [r_2, \theta_2] = [r_1, \theta_1] + [-r_2, \theta_2]$$

In component form, $\mathbf{u} = \langle 9, -5 \rangle$, $\mathbf{v} = \langle -6, 4 \rangle$, and $\mathbf{w} = \langle 0, -5 \rangle$. Perform each calculation.

1. $\mathbf{u} + \mathbf{v}$

2. $\mathbf{v} + \mathbf{w}$

3. $2\mathbf{u} + \mathbf{w}$

4. $\mathbf{v} + 4\mathbf{w}$

5. $6\mathbf{u} + 2\mathbf{v} + 7\mathbf{w}$

6. $\mathbf{v} - \mathbf{u}$

7. $\mathbf{u} - \mathbf{w}$

8. $4\mathbf{v} - 2\mathbf{w}$

9. $9\mathbf{w} - 3\mathbf{u} + 5\mathbf{v}$

10. $5\mathbf{u} + 8\mathbf{v} - 7\mathbf{w}$

In trigonometric form, $\mathbf{u} = \left[8, \dfrac{3\pi}{4}\right]$, $\mathbf{v} = \left[4, \dfrac{5\pi}{3}\right]$, and $\mathbf{w} = [6, \pi]$. Perform each calculation.

11. $\mathbf{u} + \mathbf{v}$

12. $\mathbf{v} + \mathbf{w}$

13. $2\mathbf{u} + \mathbf{w}$

14. $\mathbf{v} + 4\mathbf{w}1$

15. $6\mathbf{u} + 2\mathbf{v} + 7\mathbf{w}$

16. $\mathbf{v} - \mathbf{u}$

17. $\mathbf{u} - \mathbf{w}$

18. $4\mathbf{v} - 2\mathbf{w}$

19. $9\mathbf{w} - 3\mathbf{u} + 5\mathbf{v}$

20. $5\mathbf{u} + 8\mathbf{v} - 7\mathbf{w}$

Multiplication of vectors

There are two ways to multiply vectors: one that produces a scalar and one that produces a vector. The multiplication that produces a scalar is called the dot product, while the multiplication that produces a vector is called the cross product. Because the cross product results in a vector that is not in the same plane as the two original vectors, it doesn't fall within the scope of this chapter. The dot product, however, is a scalar and gives information about the two vectors in the plane.

Dot products

The dot product gives information about the angle between the vectors. If the angle is acute, the dot product will be positive. If the angle is obtuse, the dot product will be negative. Vectors at right angles have a dot product of 0.

If $\mathbf{u}$ and $\mathbf{v}$ are vectors in component form with $\mathbf{u} = \langle a, b \rangle$ and $\mathbf{v} = \langle c, d \rangle$, then the dot product $\mathbf{u} \cdot \mathbf{v}$ is a scalar given by $\mathbf{u} \cdot \mathbf{v} = ac + bd$. The dot product of $\mathbf{u} = \langle 5, 3 \rangle$ and $\mathbf{v} = \langle 4, -1 \rangle$ is $\mathbf{u} \cdot \mathbf{v} = 5 \cdot 4 + 3 \cdot -1 = 20 - 3 = 17$.

If you're familiar with matrices, you may recognize this as the product of a row matrix and a column matrix: $\begin{bmatrix} 5 & 3 \end{bmatrix} \begin{bmatrix} 4 \\ -1 \end{bmatrix} = [5 \cdot 4 + 3 \cdot -1] = [17]$. In matrix multiplication, the product of a single row and a single column is a single element, and in vector arithmetic, the dot product of two vectors is a single scalar.

For vectors in trigonometric form, $\mathbf{u} = [r_1, \theta_1]$ and $\mathbf{v} = [r_2, \theta_2]$, the dot product is found by multiplying the magnitudes by the cosine of the angle between the vectors:

$$\mathbf{u} \cdot \mathbf{v} = r_1 r_2 \cos\left(\theta_1 - \theta_2\right)$$

The dot product of $\mathbf{u} = \left[3, \dfrac{\pi}{4}\right]$ and $\mathbf{v} = \left[5, -\dfrac{\pi}{3}\right]$ is

$$\mathbf{u} \cdot \mathbf{v} = 3 \cdot 5 \cos\left(\frac{\pi}{4} - -\frac{\pi}{3}\right)$$
$$= 15 \cos\frac{7\pi}{12}$$
$$= 15(-0.259)$$
$$= -3.882$$

Angle between two vectors

The dot product of two vectors is useful for finding the angle between two vectors. Using $\mathbf{u} \cdot \mathbf{v} = r_1 r_2 \cos\left(\theta_1 - \theta_2\right)$ and dividing by $r_1 r_2$ gives

$$\frac{\mathbf{u} \cdot \mathbf{v}}{r_1 r_2} = \cos\left(\theta_1 - \theta_2\right)$$

The cosine of the angle between $\mathbf{u}$ and $\mathbf{v}$ is equal to the dot product of $\mathbf{u}$ and $\mathbf{v}$ divided by the product of their magnitudes:

$$\cos\left(\theta_1 - \theta_2\right) = \frac{\mathbf{u} \cdot \mathbf{v}}{\|\mathbf{u}\| \cdot \|\mathbf{v}\|}$$

To find the angle between the vectors $\mathbf{u} = \langle 9, -5 \rangle$ and $\mathbf{v} = \langle -6, 4 \rangle$, first find the dot product of the vectors:

$$\mathbf{u} \cdot \mathbf{v} = 9 \cdot (-6) + (-5) \cdot 4 = -54 - 20 = -74$$

Calculate the magnitude of each vector:

$$\|\mathbf{u}\| = \sqrt{9^2 + (-5)^2} = \sqrt{81 + 25} = \sqrt{106}$$
$$\|\mathbf{v}\| = \sqrt{(-6)^2 + 4^2} = \sqrt{36 + 16} = \sqrt{52} = 2\sqrt{13}$$

Then find the cosine of the angle between the vectors:

$$\cos\left(\theta_1 - \theta_2\right) = \frac{\mathbf{u} \cdot \mathbf{v}}{\|\mathbf{u}\| \cdot \|\mathbf{v}\|}$$
$$= \frac{9 \cdot -6 + -5 \cdot 4}{\sqrt{106} \cdot 2\sqrt{13}}$$
$$\approx \frac{-74}{74.243}$$
$$\approx -0.997$$

Finally, find $\cos^{-1}(-0.997) = 3.061$ radians. The angle between $\mathbf{u}$ and $\mathbf{v}$ is approximately 3.061 radians.

*Find each dot product, **u** · **v**, for the vectors given in component form.*

1. $\mathbf{u} = \langle 4, -3 \rangle$, $\mathbf{v} = \langle 2, 7 \rangle$

2. $\mathbf{u} = \langle -5, 6 \rangle$, $\mathbf{v} = \langle -3, -3 \rangle$

3. $\mathbf{u} = \langle 5, 3 \rangle$, $\mathbf{v} = \langle -1, -2 \rangle$

4. $\mathbf{u} = \langle -7, 5 \rangle$, $\mathbf{v} = \langle 8, -9 \rangle$

5. $\mathbf{u} = \langle 6, -4 \rangle$, $\mathbf{v} = \langle -5, 0 \rangle$

*Find each dot product, **u**•**v**, for the vectors given in trigonometric form.*

6. $\mathbf{u} = \left[3, \dfrac{\pi}{4} \right]$, $\mathbf{v} = \left[4, \dfrac{5\pi}{4} \right]$

7. $\mathbf{u} = \left[6, \dfrac{5\pi}{6} \right]$, $\mathbf{v} = \left[2, \dfrac{\pi}{6} \right]$

8. $\mathbf{u} = \left[9, \dfrac{\pi}{6} \right]$, $\mathbf{v} = \left[4, \dfrac{2\pi}{3} \right]$

9. $\mathbf{u} = \left[5, \dfrac{4\pi}{3} \right]$, $\mathbf{v} = \left[7, \dfrac{3\pi}{4} \right]$

10. $\mathbf{u} = \left[8, \dfrac{\pi}{2} \right]$, $\mathbf{v} = \left[8, \dfrac{5\pi}{4} \right]$

Find the angle between the given vectors.

11. $\mathbf{u} = \langle 4, -3 \rangle$, $\mathbf{v} = \langle 2, 7 \rangle$

12. $\mathbf{u} = \langle 5, 3 \rangle$, $\mathbf{v} = \langle -5, 0 \rangle$

13. $\mathbf{u} = \langle -7, 5 \rangle$, $\mathbf{v} = \langle -3, -3 \rangle$

14. $\mathbf{u} = \langle -5, 6 \rangle$, $\mathbf{v} = \langle 8, -9 \rangle$

15. $\mathbf{u} = \langle 5, 3 \rangle$, $\mathbf{v} = \langle -1, -2 \rangle$

16. $\mathbf{u} = \langle 6, -4 \rangle$, $\mathbf{v} = \langle 8, -9 \rangle$

17. $\mathbf{u} = \langle 4, -3 \rangle$, $\mathbf{v} = \langle -1, -2 \rangle$

18. $\mathbf{u} = \langle -5, 6 \rangle$, $\mathbf{v} = \langle -3, -3 \rangle$

19. $\mathbf{u} = \langle 6, -4 \rangle$, $\mathbf{v} = \langle -5, 0 \rangle$

20. $\mathbf{u} = \langle -7, 5 \rangle$, $\mathbf{v} = \langle 2, 7 \rangle$

Orthogonal vectors

Two vectors, **u** and **v**, are orthogonal if the dot product $\mathbf{u} \cdot \mathbf{v} = 0$. If the dot product $\mathbf{u} \cdot \mathbf{v} = r_1 r_2 \cos(\theta_1 - \theta_2) = 0$, then $\cos(\theta_1 - \theta_2) = 0$, because the magnitudes of the vectors will be nonzero. The cosine of the angle between the vectors is equal to 0 when the angle is $\dfrac{\pi}{2}$. The angle between orthogonal vectors therefore is $\dfrac{\pi}{2}$, so the vectors are perpendicular.

To determine if two vectors in component form are orthogonal, calculate the dot product. The vectors $\mathbf{u} = \langle 5, -3 \rangle$ and $\mathbf{v} = \langle 2, 7 \rangle$ have a dot product $\mathbf{u} \cdot \mathbf{v} = 5 \cdot 2 - 3 \cdot 7 = 10 - 21 = -11$ and therefore are not orthogonal, but the vectors $\mathbf{r} = \langle 4,-2 \rangle$ and $\mathbf{t} = \langle 3,6 \rangle$ are orthogonal because their dot product $\mathbf{r} \cdot \mathbf{t} = 4 \cdot 3 - 2 \cdot 6 = 0$.

Determining whether vectors given in trigonometric form are orthogonal is a simpler matter, because you know the direction angle of each vector. You can calculate the angle between the vectors directly. If either angle is greater than 2π, find the coterminal angle between 0 and 2π. Subtract the angles. If the result is $\frac{\pi}{2}$ (or $-\frac{\pi}{2}$), the vectors are orthogonal.

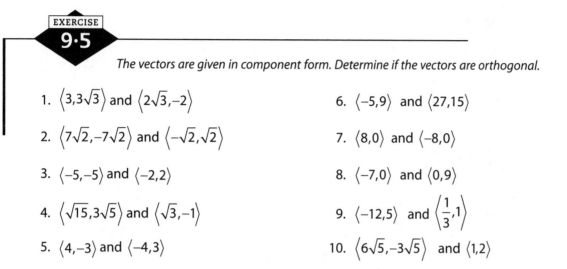

EXERCISE
9·5

The vectors are given in component form. Determine if the vectors are orthogonal.

1. $\langle 3,3\sqrt{3} \rangle$ and $\langle 2\sqrt{3},-2 \rangle$

2. $\langle 7\sqrt{2},-7\sqrt{2} \rangle$ and $\langle -\sqrt{2},\sqrt{2} \rangle$

3. $\langle -5,-5 \rangle$ and $\langle -2,2 \rangle$

4. $\langle \sqrt{15},3\sqrt{5} \rangle$ and $\langle \sqrt{3},-1 \rangle$

5. $\langle 4,-3 \rangle$ and $\langle -4,3 \rangle$

6. $\langle -5,9 \rangle$ and $\langle 27,15 \rangle$

7. $\langle 8,0 \rangle$ and $\langle -8,0 \rangle$

8. $\langle -7,0 \rangle$ and $\langle 0,9 \rangle$

9. $\langle -12,5 \rangle$ and $\left\langle \frac{1}{3},1 \right\rangle$

10. $\langle 6\sqrt{5},-3\sqrt{5} \rangle$ and $\langle 1,2 \rangle$

The vectors are given in trigonometric form. Determine if the vectors are orthogonal.

11. $\left[6,-\frac{\pi}{3} \right]$ and $\left[4,\frac{5\pi}{6} \right]$

12. $[12,\pi]$ and $[15,3\pi]$

13. $\left[9,\frac{5\pi}{6} \right]$ and $\left[7,\frac{\pi}{3} \right]$

14. $\left[10,-\frac{2\pi}{3} \right]$ and $\left[9,\frac{\pi}{6} \right]$

15. $\left[8,\frac{3\pi}{2} \right]$ and $\left[11,\frac{\pi}{4} \right]$

16. $\left[2,\frac{7\pi}{3} \right]$ and $\left[8,\frac{5\pi}{3} \right]$

17. $\left[4,-\frac{3\pi}{2} \right]$ and $[-4,2\pi]$

18. $\left[8,\frac{7\pi}{12} \right]$ and $\left[3,\frac{\pi}{12} \right]$

19. $[9,3\pi]$ and $\left[8,\frac{7\pi}{2} \right]$

20. $\left[8,\frac{7\pi}{2} \right]$ and $\left[\frac{1}{2},\frac{30\pi}{4} \right]$

Answer key

1 Right triangle trigonometry

1·1
1. Acute
2. Obtuse
3. Acute
4. Acute
5. Obtuse
6. Obtuse
7. Obtuse
8. Acute
9. Acute
10. Acute
11. Complement: 43°, supplement: 133°
12. Complement: not possible, supplement: 50°
13. Complement: 71°, supplement: 161°
14. Complement: 1°, supplement: 91°
15. Complement: not possible, supplement: 88°
16. Complement: not possible, supplement: 57°
17. Complement: not possible, supplement: 29°
18. Complement: 49.5°, supplement: 139.5°
19. Complement: 80.8°, supplement: 170.8°
20. Complement: 76.2°, supplement: 166.2°

1·2
1. 22.75°
2. 18.2°
3. 39.8°
4. 137.45°
5. 96.85°
6. 81.1125°
7. 1.72°
8. 178.375°
9. 11.125°
10. 78.376°
11. 25°18′
12. 18°45′
13. 37°6′
14. 135°32′42″
15. 94°44′6″
16. 86°54′
17. 3°15′
18. 167°36′
19. 19°15′
20. 74°18′

1.3
1. *A*: 67° *B*: 54° *C*: 59°
2. *A*: 76° *B*: 45° *C*: 59°
3. *A*: 152° *B*: 9° *C*: 19°
4. *A*: 94° *B*: 18° *C*: 68°
5. *A*: 35° *B*: 102° *C*: 43°
6. *A*: 68° *B*: 73° *C*: 39°
7. *A*: 45° *B*: 54° *C*: 81°
8. *A*: 12° *B*: 61° *C*: 107°
9. *A*: 26° *B*: 153° *C*: 1°
10. *A*: 109° *B*: 1° *C*: 70°

1.4
1. 37°, 90°, 53°
2. 12°48′, 90°, 77°12′
3. 37°
4. 50°
5. 19°36′
6. 84°36′
7. 167°3′
8. 1°50′
9. 4°7′
10. 1°9′

1·5
1. 7 in. and 7 in.
2. 4 cm and $4\sqrt{2}$ cm
3. $6\sqrt{2}$ ft and $6\sqrt{2}$ ft
4. $5\sqrt{6}$ m and $10\sqrt{3}$ m
5. $8\sqrt{7}$ cm and $8\sqrt{7}$ cm
6. 25 m and $25\sqrt{3}$ m
7. 18 cm and $9\sqrt{3}$ cm
8. 7 in. and 14 in.
9. $28\sqrt{6}$ ft and $42\sqrt{2}$ ft
10. $2\sqrt{21}$ cm and $6\sqrt{7}$ cm
11. $\dfrac{\sqrt{2}}{2}$
12. $\dfrac{\sqrt{3}}{3}$
13. $\dfrac{1}{2}$
14. 1
15. 2
16. 2
17. $\dfrac{\sqrt{3}}{3}$
18. $\dfrac{\sqrt{2}}{2}$
19. $\dfrac{1}{2}$
20. $\sqrt{2}$

1·6

1. 12
2. 34.8
3. 44.4 ft and 61.1 ft
4. 333.2 ft and 342.7 ft
5. 92.8 m and 109.5 m
6. 57.5 ft
7. 7.3 ft
8. 4,727.3 ft
9. 67.6 ft
10. 52 ft
11. 22.2 ft
12. 119.9 ft
13. 17.7 ft
14. 204.4 m
15. 6.4 ft
16. 11.3 ft
17. 20.7 ft
18. 227.2 ft
19. 428.7 ft
20. $QT = 363.6$ ft, $TR = 290.8$ ft, so $QR = QT + TR = 363.6 + 290.8 = 654.4$ ft

1·7

1. 24.6°, 65.4°, 90°
2. 8.4°, 81.6°, 90°
3. 29.2°, 60.8°
4. 36.9 °, 53.1°, 90°
5. 22.6°, 67.4°, 90°
6. 29.9°
7. 22.6°
8. 40°
9. 32.6°
10. 39.8°
11. 17°
12. 24.6°
13. 48.6°
14. 26° and 64°
15. N 60.6° E
16. 4.8°
17. 24.9°
18. 14°
19. 18.4°
20. 33.7°

1·8

1. 3.4 cm
2. 6.0 in.
3. 9.0 ft
4. 4.7 m
5. 8.3 km
6. 9.1 cm
7. 2.5 yd
8. 2.5 km
9. 4.4 ft
10. 8.4 m
11. 32.1
12. 37.3
13. 18.8
14. 20.6
15. 3.8
16. 7.9
17. 33.8
18. 15.2
19. 17.4
20. 11.9

2 Trigonometric functions

2·1

1. $\dfrac{2\pi}{9}$

2. $\dfrac{3\pi}{4}$

3. $\dfrac{3\pi}{2}$

4. $\dfrac{11\pi}{6}$

5. $\dfrac{5\pi}{2}$

6. $\dfrac{2\pi}{3}$

7. $\dfrac{5\pi}{4}$

8. $\dfrac{5\pi}{3}$

9. $\dfrac{17\pi}{4}$

10. $\dfrac{45\pi}{4}$

11. $45°$

12. $150°$

13. $300°$

14. $-270°$

15. $-315°$

16. $-630°$

17. $765°$

18. $510°$

19. $15°$

20. $-100°$

21. $\dfrac{\pi}{3}$ radians, $75°$, 2 radians

22. $94°$, $\dfrac{5\pi}{6}$ radians, 3 radians

23. $220°$, $\dfrac{5\pi}{4}$ radians, 4 radians

24. $\dfrac{3\pi}{2}$ radians, $280°$, 5.5 radians

25. $12°$, $\dfrac{\pi}{12}$ radians, 1.2 radians

2·2

1.

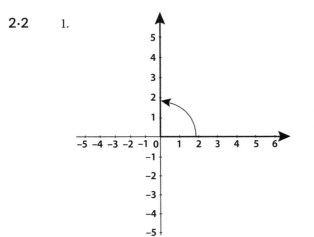

2.

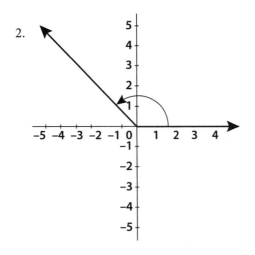

3.

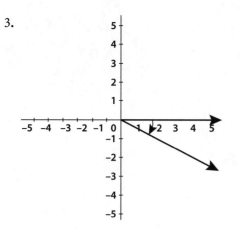

4.

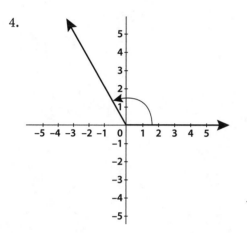

5.

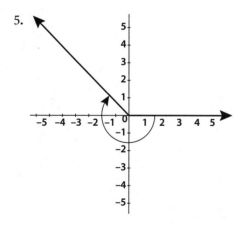

6.

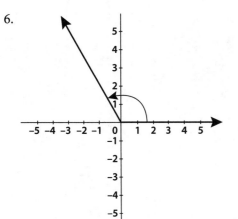

7.

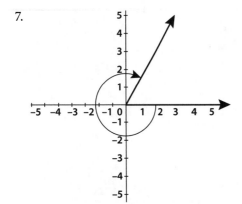

8.

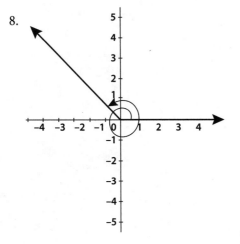

9.

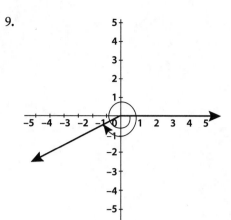

10.

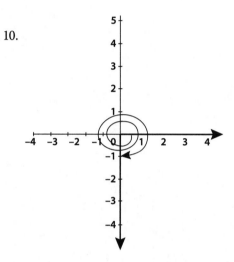

Questions 11–20 have multiple correct answers. Sample answers:

11. $\dfrac{5\pi}{2}, \dfrac{-3\pi}{2}$

12. $\dfrac{23\pi}{6}, \dfrac{-\pi}{6}$

13. $\dfrac{\pi}{3}, -\dfrac{11\pi}{3}$

14. $\dfrac{\pi}{4}, -\dfrac{15\pi}{4}$

15. $5\pi, -\pi$

16. $\dfrac{17\pi}{6}, \dfrac{-7\pi}{6}$

17. $\dfrac{29\pi}{9}, \dfrac{-7\pi}{9}$

18. $\dfrac{5\pi}{3}, -\dfrac{\pi}{3}$

19. $\dfrac{15\pi}{4}, -\dfrac{\pi}{4}$

20. $\dfrac{11\pi}{6}, -\dfrac{\pi}{6}$

2·3

1. $\left(\dfrac{\sqrt{2}}{2}, \dfrac{\sqrt{2}}{2}\right)$

2. $\left(-\dfrac{1}{2}, \dfrac{\sqrt{3}}{2}\right)$

3. $(0, -1)$

4. $\left(-\dfrac{\sqrt{3}}{2}, -\dfrac{1}{2}\right)$

5. $\left(-\dfrac{\sqrt{2}}{2}, \dfrac{\sqrt{2}}{2}\right)$

6. $\left(-\dfrac{1}{2}, \dfrac{\sqrt{3}}{2}\right)$

7. $\left(\dfrac{\sqrt{3}}{2}, \dfrac{1}{2}\right)$

8. $\left(-\dfrac{\sqrt{2}}{2}, \dfrac{\sqrt{2}}{2}\right)$

9. $(0, -1)$

10. $\left(\dfrac{\sqrt{2}}{2}, -\dfrac{\sqrt{2}}{2}\right)$

11. $\dfrac{\sqrt{2}}{2}$

12. $-\dfrac{\sqrt{3}}{2}$

13. $-\dfrac{\sqrt{3}}{3}$

14. $-\dfrac{1}{2}$

15. -1

16. 0

17. $-\dfrac{\sqrt{3}}{2}$

18. $-\dfrac{\sqrt{2}}{2}$

19. $-\dfrac{\sqrt{3}}{3}$

20. 0

2·4

1. $\sin\dfrac{\pi}{3} = \dfrac{\sqrt{3}}{2}, \cos\dfrac{\pi}{3} = \dfrac{1}{2}, \tan\dfrac{\pi}{3} = \sqrt{3}, \csc\dfrac{\pi}{3} = \dfrac{2\sqrt{3}}{3}, \sec\dfrac{\pi}{3} = 2 \cot\dfrac{\pi}{3} = \dfrac{\sqrt{3}}{3}$

2. $\sin\left(-\dfrac{3\pi}{4}\right) = -\dfrac{\sqrt{2}}{2}, \cos\left(-\dfrac{3\pi}{4}\right) = -\dfrac{\sqrt{2}}{2}, \tan\left(-\dfrac{3\pi}{4}\right) = 1, \csc\left(-\dfrac{3\pi}{4}\right) = -\sqrt{2}, \sec\left(-\dfrac{3\pi}{4}\right) = -\sqrt{2}, \cot\left(-\dfrac{3\pi}{4}\right) = 1$

3. $\sin\dfrac{7\pi}{6} = -\dfrac{1}{2}, \cos\dfrac{7\pi}{6} = -\dfrac{\sqrt{3}}{2}, \tan\dfrac{7\pi}{6} = \dfrac{\sqrt{3}}{3}, \csc\dfrac{7\pi}{6} = -2, \sec\dfrac{7\pi}{6} = -\dfrac{2\sqrt{3}}{3}, \cot\dfrac{7\pi}{6} = \sqrt{3}$

4. $\sin\dfrac{3\pi}{2} = -1, \cos\dfrac{3\pi}{2} = 0, \tan\dfrac{3\pi}{2}$ is undefined, $\csc\dfrac{3\pi}{2} = -1, \sec\dfrac{3\pi}{2}$ is undefined, $\cot\dfrac{3\pi}{2} = 0$

5. $\sin(-\pi) = 0, \cos(-\pi) = -1, \tan(-\pi) = 0, \csc(-\pi)$ is undefined, $\sec(-\pi) = -1, \cot(-\pi)$ is undefined

6. $\sin\left(-\dfrac{13\pi}{6}\right) = -\dfrac{1}{2}, \cos\left(-\dfrac{13\pi}{6}\right) = \dfrac{\sqrt{3}}{2}, \tan\left(-\dfrac{13\pi}{6}\right) = -\dfrac{\sqrt{3}}{3}, \csc\left(-\dfrac{13\pi}{6}\right) = -2, \sec\left(-\dfrac{13\pi}{6}\right) = \dfrac{2\sqrt{3}}{3},$

   $\cot\left(-\dfrac{13\pi}{6}\right) = -\sqrt{3}$

7. $\sin(8\pi) = 0, \cos(8\pi) = 1, \tan(8\pi) = 0, \csc(8\pi)$ is undefined, $\sec(8\pi) = 1, \cot(8\pi)$ is undefined

8. $\sin\dfrac{9\pi}{2}=1$, $\cos\dfrac{9\pi}{2}=0$, $\tan\dfrac{9\pi}{2}$ is undefined, $\csc\dfrac{9\pi}{2}=1$, $\sec\dfrac{9\pi}{2}$ is undefined, $\cot\dfrac{9\pi}{2}=0$

9. $\sin\dfrac{11\pi}{6}=-\dfrac{1}{2}$, $\cos\dfrac{11\pi}{6}=\dfrac{\sqrt{3}}{2}$, $\tan\dfrac{11\pi}{6}=-\dfrac{\sqrt{3}}{3}$, $\csc\dfrac{11\pi}{6}=-2$, $\sec\dfrac{11\pi}{6}=\dfrac{2\sqrt{3}}{3}$, $\cot\dfrac{11\pi}{6}=-\sqrt{3}$

10. $\sin\left(-\dfrac{7\pi}{3}\right)=-\dfrac{\sqrt{3}}{2}$, $\cos\left(-\dfrac{7\pi}{3}\right)=\dfrac{1}{2}$, $\tan\left(-\dfrac{7\pi}{3}\right)=-\sqrt{3}$, $\csc\left(-\dfrac{7\pi}{3}\right)=-\dfrac{2\sqrt{3}}{3}$, $\sec\left(-\dfrac{7\pi}{3}\right)=2$,

$\cot\left(-\dfrac{7\pi}{3}\right)=-\dfrac{\sqrt{3}}{3}$

11. Sine: $-\dfrac{\sqrt{2}}{2}$, cosine: $\dfrac{\sqrt{2}}{2}$, tangent: -1

12. Sine: 1, cosine: 0, tangent: undefined

13. Sine: $\dfrac{\sqrt{3}}{2}$, cosine: $-\dfrac{1}{2}$, tangent: $-\sqrt{3}$

14. Sine: $-\dfrac{2\sqrt{7}}{7}$, cosine: $\dfrac{\sqrt{21}}{7}$, tangent: $-\dfrac{2\sqrt{3}}{3}$

15. Sine: 0, cosine: 1, tangent: 0

16. Sine: $\dfrac{3\sqrt{73}}{73}$, cosine: $\dfrac{8\sqrt{73}}{73}$, tangent: $\dfrac{3}{8}$

17. Sine: $\dfrac{5\sqrt{29}}{29}$, cosine: $-\dfrac{2\sqrt{29}}{29}$, tangent: $-\dfrac{5}{2}$

18. Sine: $-\dfrac{\sqrt{5}}{5}$, cosine: $\dfrac{2\sqrt{5}}{5}$, tangent: $-\dfrac{1}{2}$

19. Sine: $\dfrac{4\sqrt{65}}{65}$, cosine: $\dfrac{7\sqrt{65}}{65}$, tangent: $\dfrac{4}{7}$

20. Sine: $-\dfrac{4\sqrt{17}}{17}$, cosine: $-\dfrac{\sqrt{17}}{17}$, tangent: 4

2·5

1. Quadrant II

2. Quadrant III

3. Quadrant I

4. Quadrant III

5. Quadrant II

6. Quadrant I

7. Quadrant IV

8. Quadrant IV

9. Quadrant III

10. Quadrant I

11. $\sin\theta = \dfrac{5}{13}$, $\cos\theta = \dfrac{12}{13}$, $\tan\theta = \dfrac{5}{12}$, $\csc\theta = \dfrac{13}{5}$, $\sec\theta = \dfrac{13}{12}$, $\cot\theta = \dfrac{12}{5}$

12. $\sin\theta = -\dfrac{4}{5}$, $\cos\theta = \dfrac{3}{5}$, $\tan\theta = -\dfrac{4}{3}$, $\csc\theta = -\dfrac{5}{4}$, $\sec\theta = \dfrac{5}{3}$, $\cot\theta = -\dfrac{3}{4}$

13. $\sin\theta = \dfrac{12}{13}$, $\cos\theta = \dfrac{5}{13}$, $\tan\theta = \dfrac{12}{5}$, $\csc\theta = \dfrac{13}{12}$, $\sec\theta = \dfrac{13}{5}$, $\cot\theta = \dfrac{5}{12}$

14. $\sin\theta = -\dfrac{1}{4}$, $\cos\theta = -\dfrac{\sqrt{15}}{4}$, $\tan\theta = \dfrac{\sqrt{15}}{15}$, $\csc\theta = -4$, $\sec\theta = -\dfrac{4\sqrt{15}}{15}$, $\cot\theta = \sqrt{15}$

15. $\sin\theta = -\dfrac{2\sqrt{10}}{7}$, $\cos\theta = \dfrac{3}{7}$, $\tan\theta = -\dfrac{2\sqrt{10}}{3}$, $\csc\theta = -\dfrac{7\sqrt{10}}{20}$, $\sec\theta = \dfrac{7}{3}$, $\cot\theta = -\dfrac{3\sqrt{10}}{20}$

16. $\sin\theta = -\dfrac{8\sqrt{73}}{73}$, $\cos\theta = \dfrac{3\sqrt{73}}{73}$, $\tan\theta = -\dfrac{8}{3}$, $\csc\theta = -\dfrac{\sqrt{73}}{8}$, $\sec\theta = \dfrac{\sqrt{73}}{3}$, $\cot\theta = -\dfrac{3}{8}$

17. $\sin\theta = \dfrac{2}{3}$, $\cos\theta = -\dfrac{\sqrt{5}}{3}$, $\tan\theta = -\dfrac{2\sqrt{5}}{5}$, $\csc\theta = \dfrac{3}{2}$, $\sec\theta = -\dfrac{3\sqrt{5}}{5}$, $\cot\theta = -\dfrac{\sqrt{5}}{2}$

18. $\sin\theta = -\dfrac{3}{5}$, $\cos\theta = \dfrac{4}{5}$, $\tan\theta = -\dfrac{3}{4}$, $\csc\theta = -\dfrac{5}{3}$, $\sec\theta = \dfrac{5}{4}$, $\cot\theta = -\dfrac{4}{3}$

19. $\sin\theta = \dfrac{9\sqrt{97}}{97}$, $\cos\theta = -\dfrac{4\sqrt{97}}{97}$, $\tan\theta = -\dfrac{9}{4}$, $\csc\theta = \dfrac{\sqrt{97}}{9}$, $\sec\theta = -\dfrac{\sqrt{97}}{4}$, $\cot\theta = -\dfrac{4}{9}$

20. $\sin\theta = \dfrac{3\sqrt{17}}{13}$, $\cos\theta = -\dfrac{4}{13}$, $\tan\theta = -\dfrac{3\sqrt{17}}{4}$, $\csc\theta = \dfrac{13\sqrt{17}}{51}$, $\sec\theta = -\dfrac{13}{4}$, $\cot\theta = -\dfrac{4\sqrt{17}}{51}$

21. $\sin\theta = -\dfrac{3\sqrt{10}}{10}$, $\cos\theta = -\dfrac{\sqrt{10}}{10}$, $\tan\theta = 3$, $\csc\theta = -\dfrac{\sqrt{10}}{3}$, $\sec\theta = -\sqrt{10}$, $\cot\theta = \dfrac{1}{3}$

22. $\sin\theta = \dfrac{\sqrt{5}}{5}$, $\cos\theta = -\dfrac{2\sqrt{5}}{5}$, $\tan\theta = -\dfrac{1}{2}$, $\csc\theta = \sqrt{5}$, $\sec\theta = -\dfrac{\sqrt{5}}{2}$, $\cot\theta = -2$

23. $\sin\theta = \dfrac{4-x}{\sqrt{2x^2-8x+16}}$, $\cos\theta = \dfrac{x}{\sqrt{2x^2-8x+16}}$, $\tan\theta = \dfrac{4-x}{x}$, $\csc\theta = \dfrac{\sqrt{2x^2-8x+16}}{4-x}$,

$\sec\theta = \dfrac{\sqrt{2x^2-8x+16}}{x}$, $\cot\theta = \dfrac{x}{4-x}$

24. $\sin\theta = \dfrac{2x-3}{\sqrt{5x^2-12x+9}}$, $\cos\theta = \dfrac{x}{\sqrt{5x^2-12x+9}}$, $\tan\theta = \dfrac{2x-3}{x}$, $\csc\theta = \dfrac{\sqrt{5x^2-12x+9}}{2x-3}$,

$\sec\theta = \dfrac{\sqrt{5x^2-12x+9}}{x}$, $\cot\theta = \dfrac{x}{2x-3}$

25. $\sin\theta = \dfrac{2x-5}{\sqrt{5x^2-20x+25}}$, $\cos\theta = \dfrac{x}{\sqrt{5x^2-20x+25}}$, $\tan\theta = \dfrac{2x-5}{x}$, $\csc\theta = \dfrac{\sqrt{5x^2-20x+25}}{2x-5}$,

$\sec\theta = \dfrac{\sqrt{5x^2-20x+25}}{x}$, $\cot\theta = \dfrac{x}{2x-5}$

3 Graphs of trigonometric functions

1.

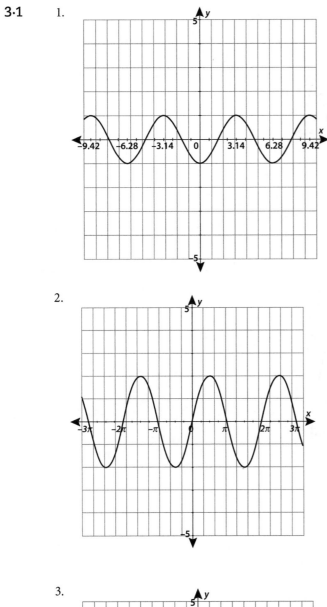

2.

3.

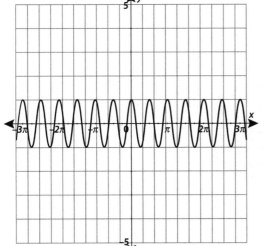

4.

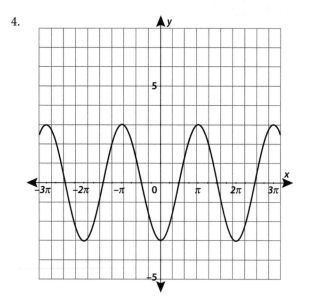

5.

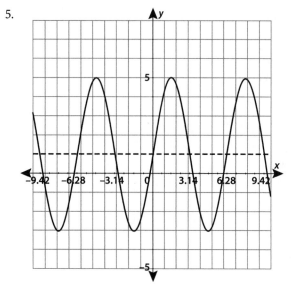

6.

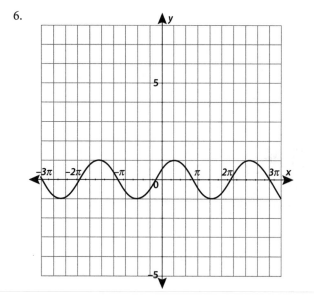

7.

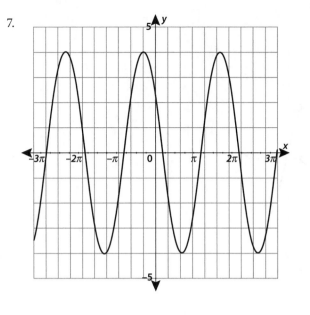

8.

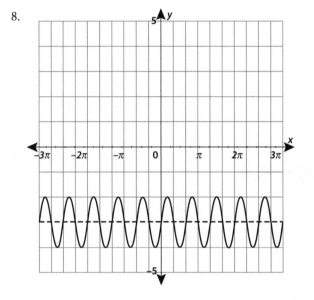

9.

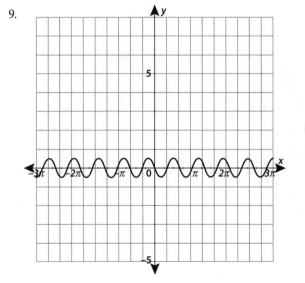

10.

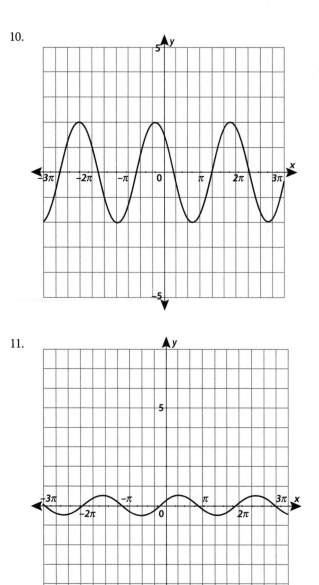

11.

12.

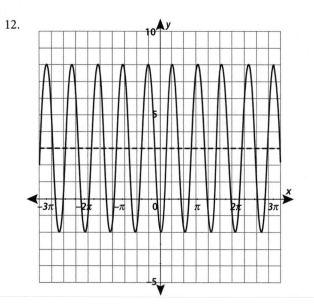

13.

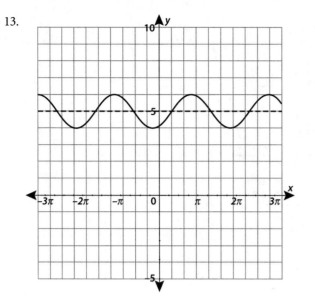

14.

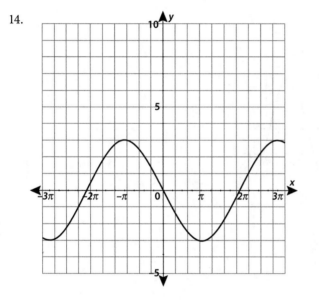

15.

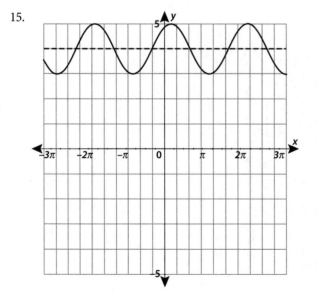

16.

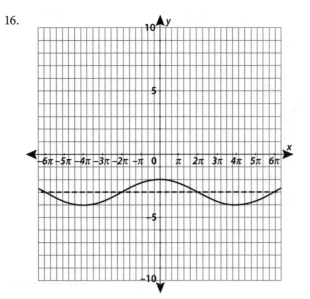

17.

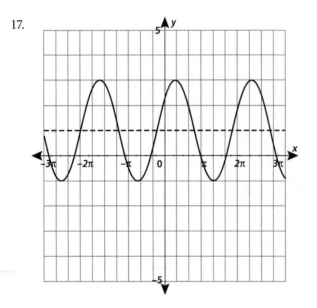

18.

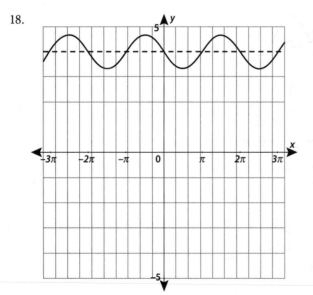

19.

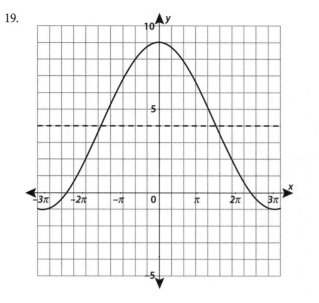

20.

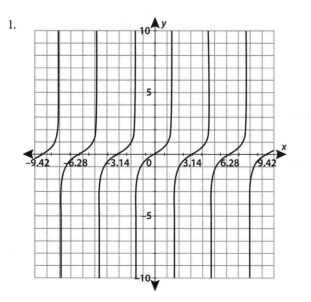

3·2 1.

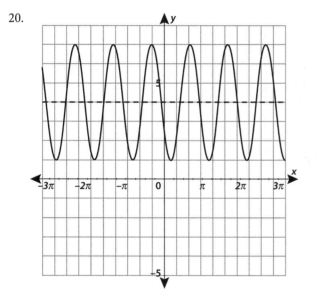

2.

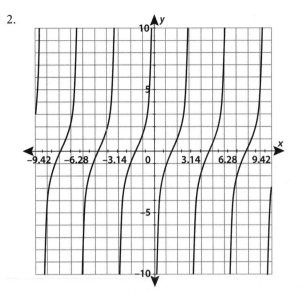

3.

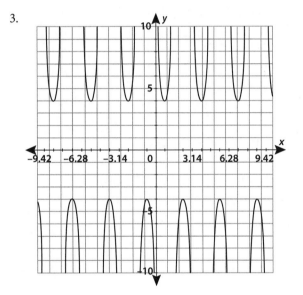

4.

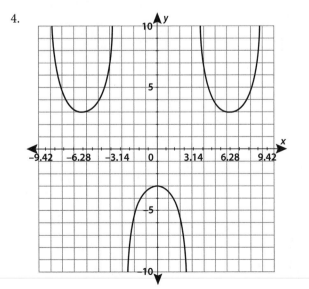

5.

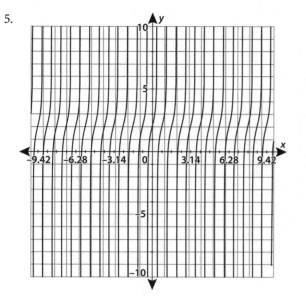

6.

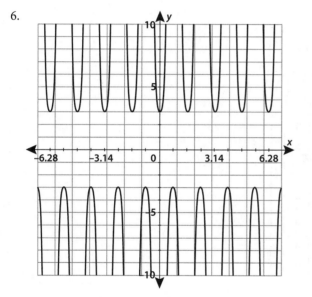

7.

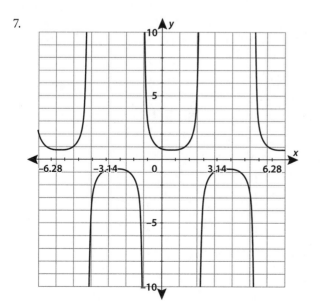

8.

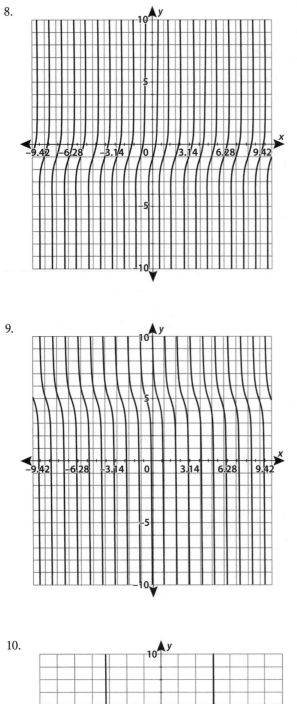

9.

10.

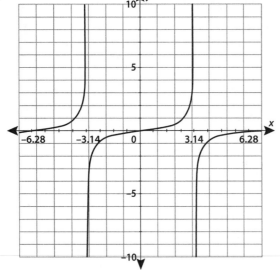

11.

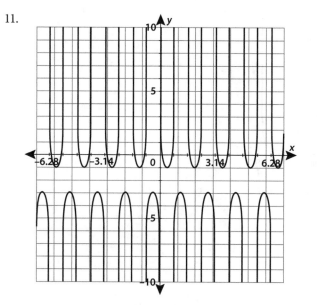

12.

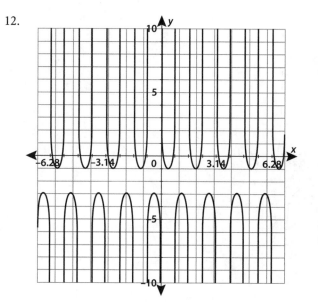

13.

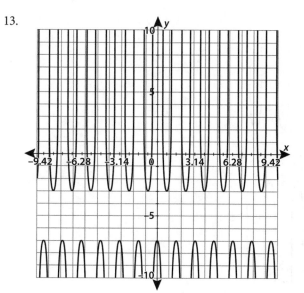

14.

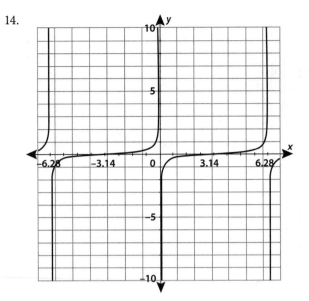

15.

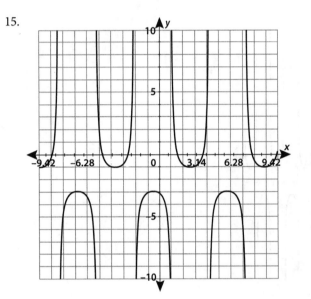

16.

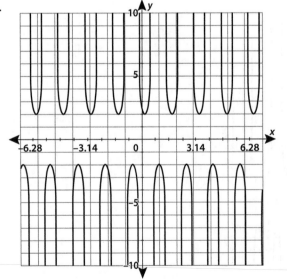

17.

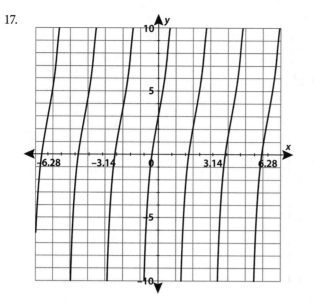

18.

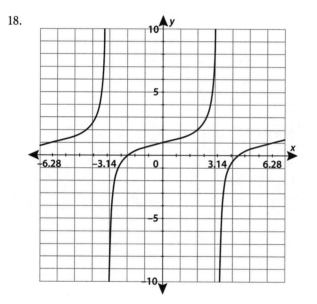

19.

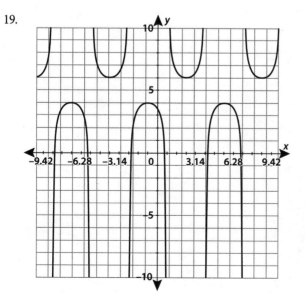

20.

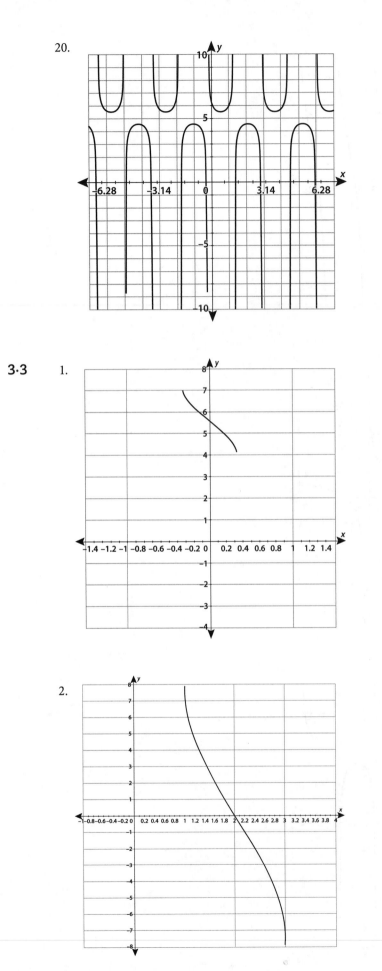

3·3   1.

2.

3.

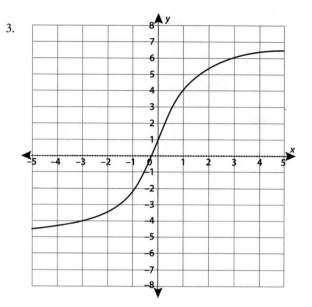

4.

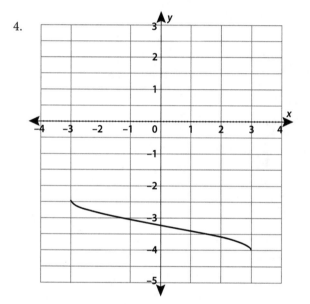

5.

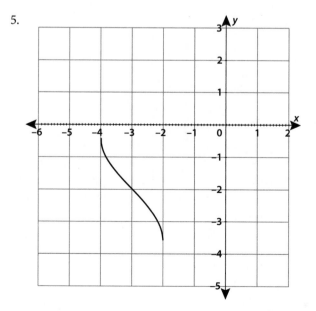

6.

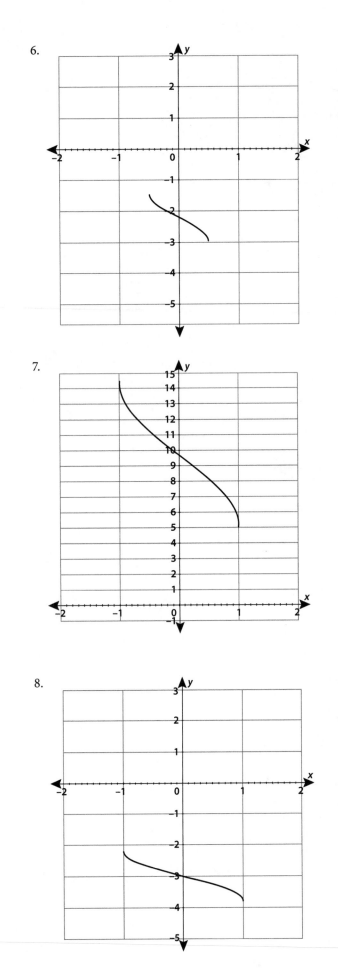

7.

8.

9.

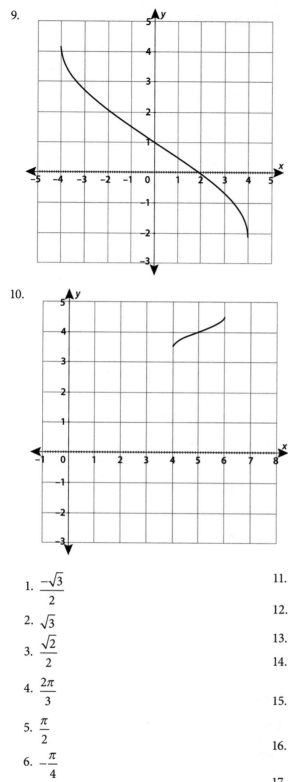

10.

3·4

1. $\dfrac{-\sqrt{3}}{2}$

2. $\sqrt{3}$

3. $\dfrac{\sqrt{2}}{2}$

4. $\dfrac{2\pi}{3}$

5. $\dfrac{\pi}{2}$

6. $-\dfrac{\pi}{4}$

7. 1

8. $-\dfrac{\pi}{4}$

9. 0

10. $-\dfrac{\pi}{6}$

11. $-\sqrt{3}$

12. $\dfrac{\sqrt{3}}{2}$

13. 0

14. $\dfrac{\pi}{3}$

15. $\dfrac{\pi}{6}$

16. $\dfrac{\pi}{2}$

17. $\dfrac{\sqrt{2}}{2}$

18. $-\dfrac{\pi}{2}$

19. $\dfrac{\sqrt{2}}{2}$

20. $\dfrac{\pi}{2}$

4 Applications of sinusoidal functions

4·1

1. Amplitude: 3, frequency: 2, period: π

2. Amplitude: $\dfrac{1}{2}$, frequency: 4, period: $\dfrac{\pi}{2}$

3. Amplitude: 7, frequency: π, period: 2

4. Amplitude: $\dfrac{1}{4}$, frequency: 6, period: $\dfrac{\pi}{3}$

5. Amplitude: $\dfrac{\pi}{4}$, frequency: $\dfrac{2}{3}$, period: 3π

6. Phase shift: $\dfrac{\pi}{3}$ right, vertical shift: 5 up

7. Phase shift: $\dfrac{\pi}{4}$ left, vertical shift: 9 down

8. Phase shift: 5 left, vertical shift: $\dfrac{3}{4}$ down

9. Phase shift: $\dfrac{\pi}{6}$ left, vertical shift: 3 down

10. Phase shift: $\dfrac{\pi}{3}$ right, vertical shift: 1 up

11. $f(x) = -\cos x$

12. $f(x) = 2\sin x$

13. $f(x) = \cos(4x)$

14. $f(x) = \dfrac{1}{2}\sin(3x)$

15. $f(x) = 4\cos\left(x + \dfrac{\pi}{3}\right)$

16. $f(x) = -2\sin\left(x - \dfrac{\pi}{4}\right)$

17. $f(x) = \cos\left(x - \dfrac{\pi}{6}\right) + 4$

18. $f(x) = \sin(\pi x) - 3$

19. $f(x) = -2\cos(x - 4) + 1$

20. $f(x) = 4 - 3\cos\left(2x - \dfrac{\pi}{3}\right)$

4·2

1. $y = 5\sin(\pi t)$

2. $y = -4\sin\left(\dfrac{\pi}{4}t\right)$

3. $y = 5\sin\left(\dfrac{\pi}{2}t\right) + 3$

4. $y = 80\sin\left(\dfrac{2\pi}{5}t - \dfrac{\pi}{2}\right) + 90$

5. $y = 125\sin\left(\dfrac{2\pi}{9}t - \dfrac{\pi}{2}\right) + 15$

6. $y = 70\sin\left(\dfrac{2\pi}{7}t - \pi\right) + 80$

7. $y = \dfrac{212}{\pi}\sin\left(\dfrac{\pi}{15}t - \dfrac{\pi}{2}\right) + 0.1$

8. $y = 8\sin(1{,}000\pi t)$

9. $y = 11\sin(8\pi t)$

10. $y = 3.5\sin(90\pi t)$

11. 90 ft

12. 21.2 ft

13. 98 ft

14. 8 ft

15. 8 min

16. 3 min

17. 7 min

18. 53 ft

19. 53 ft

20. 3 min

4·3

1. $y = 1.5\sin(2\pi t) + 6$

2. 6 ft above the floor

3. 7.5 ft above the floor

4. $\dfrac{3}{4}$ sec

5. $y = 1.5\sin(3\pi t) + 3.5$

6. 3.5 ft above the floor

7. 3.5 ft above the floor

8. Approximately 0.036 sec

9. $y = 5\sin\left(\dfrac{2\pi}{3}t\right)$

10. $\dfrac{5\sqrt{3}}{2} \approx 4.33°$

11. $-\dfrac{5\sqrt{3}}{2} \approx -4.33°$

12. $y = 5\sin\left(\dfrac{2\pi}{3}t + \dfrac{\pi}{2}\right)$

13.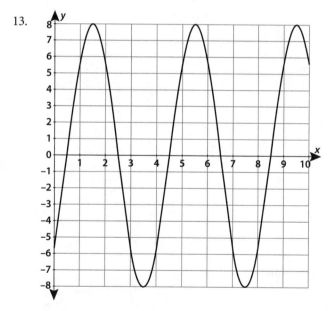

14. $-4\sqrt{2} \approx -5.66°$

15. $4\sqrt{2} \approx 5.66°$

16. 1.5 sec

17. 4 sec

18.

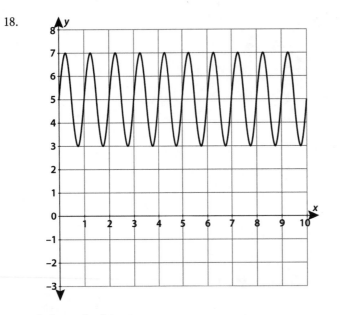

19. 5 ft above the floor

20. 1 sec, 5 ft above the floor

4·4

1. $y = 4\sin\left(\dfrac{\pi}{12}t - \dfrac{\pi}{2}\right) + 7$

2. $y = 4.5\sin\left(\dfrac{\pi}{6}t + \dfrac{\pi}{2}\right) + 3.5$

3. $y = 2.8\sin\left(\dfrac{\pi}{6}t - \dfrac{\pi}{2}\right) + 12$

4. $y = 6.4\sin\left(\dfrac{\pi}{6}t - \dfrac{\pi}{2}\right) + 12$

5. $y = 20.5\sin\left(\dfrac{\pi}{6}t - \dfrac{\pi}{2}\right) + 57.5$

6. $y = 23.5\sin\left(\dfrac{\pi}{6}t - \dfrac{\pi}{2}\right) + 80.5$

7. $y = 60\sin\left(\dfrac{\pi}{45}t\right)$

8. $-30\sqrt{3} \approx -51.96°$ or $51.96°$ south of the equator

9. Approximately 16.6 min and 28.4 min

10. $y = 4{,}140\sin\left(\dfrac{\pi}{45}t\right)$

11. 37.9 in.

12. $y = 5\sin\left(\dfrac{\pi}{30}t\right)$

13. $y = 165\sin\left(\dfrac{\pi}{30}t\right)$

5 Identities and equations

1. $\csc x + \cot x \sec x = 2\csc x$

$$\frac{1}{\sin x} + \frac{\cos x}{\sin x}\frac{1}{\cos x} = 2\csc x$$

$$\frac{1}{\sin x} + \frac{1}{\sin x} = 2\csc x$$

$$\frac{2}{\sin x} = 2\csc x$$

$$2\csc x = 2\csc x$$

2. $\cos x + \sin x \tan x = \sec x$

$$\cos x + \sin x\frac{\sin x}{\cos x} = \sec x$$

$$\frac{\cos^2 x}{\cos x} + \frac{\sin^2 x}{\cos x} = \sec x$$

$$\frac{1}{\cos x} = \sec x$$

$$\sec x = \sec x$$

3. $\dfrac{\cos x \, \csc x}{\cot^2 x} = \tan x$

$$\frac{\cos x \dfrac{1}{\sin x}}{\cot^2 x} = \tan x$$

$$\frac{\cot x}{\cot^2 x} = \tan x$$

$$\frac{1}{\cot x} = \tan x$$

$$\tan x = \tan x$$

4. $$\frac{1}{\sin x} + \frac{1}{\csc x} = \csc x + \sin x$$

$$\frac{\csc x}{\sin x \csc x} + \frac{\sin x}{\sin x \csc x} = \csc x + \sin x$$

$$\frac{\csc x + \sin x}{\sin x \csc x} = \csc x + \sin x$$

$$\frac{\csc x + \sin x}{1} = \csc x + \sin x$$

5. $\cos\left(\dfrac{\pi}{2} - \theta\right)\cot\theta + \tan\theta\sin\left(\dfrac{\pi}{2} - \theta\right) = \cos\theta + \sin\theta$

$$\sin\theta\frac{\cos\theta}{\sin\theta} + \frac{\sin\theta}{\cos\theta}\cos\theta = \cos\theta + \sin\theta$$

$$\cos\theta + \sin\theta = \cos\theta + \sin\theta$$

6.
$$\frac{\tan x}{\sec^2 x} = \cos x \sin x$$

$$\frac{\sin x}{\cos x} \div \frac{1}{\cos^2 x} = \cos x \sin x$$

$$\frac{\sin x}{\cos x} \frac{\cos^2 x}{1} = \cos x \sin x$$

$$\cos x \sin x = \cos x \sin x$$

7. $\tan\left(\frac{\pi}{2} - \theta\right)\left(1 - \cos^2 \theta\right)\sec\theta = \sin\theta$

$$\cot\theta \sin^2 \theta \sec\theta = \sin\theta$$

$$\frac{\cancel{\cos\theta}}{\cancel{\sin\theta}} \frac{\sin^2 \theta}{1} \frac{1}{\cancel{\cos\theta}} = \sin\theta$$

$$\sin\theta = \sin\theta$$

8.
$$\frac{\tan x\left(1 - \sin^2 x\right)}{\sin^2 x} = \cot x$$

$$\frac{\tan x \cos^2 x}{\sin^2 x} = \cot x$$

$$\tan x \cot^2 x = \cot x$$

$$\tan x \cot x \cot x = \cot x$$

$$1 \cot x = \cot x$$

9. $\cos\left(\frac{\pi}{2} - \theta\right)\left(\sin\theta + \cot\theta \cos\theta\right) = 1$

$$\sin\theta\left(\sin\theta + \frac{\cos\theta}{\sin\theta}\cos\theta\right) = 1$$

$$\sin\theta\left(\sin\theta + \frac{\cos^2 \theta}{\sin\theta}\right) = 1$$

$$\sin^2 \theta + \cos^2 \theta = 1$$

10.
$$\frac{\sin x - 1}{\csc x}\left(\csc x + 1\right) = -\cos^2 x$$

$$\left(\sin x - 1\right)\frac{\csc x + 1}{\csc x} = -\cos^2 x$$

$$\left(\sin x - 1\right)\left(1 + \frac{1}{\csc x}\right) = -\cos^2 x$$

$$\left(\sin x - 1\right)\left(1 + \sin x\right) = -\cos^2 x$$

$$\sin^2 x - 1 = -\cos^2 x$$

$$-\left(1 - \sin^2 x\right) = -\cos^2 x$$

$$-\cos^2 x = -\cos^2 x$$

11. $\dfrac{\csc^2\theta\tan\theta - 1}{\csc\theta} = \sec\theta - \sin\theta$

$$\dfrac{\dfrac{1}{\sin^2\theta}\dfrac{\sin\theta}{\cos\theta} - 1}{\dfrac{1}{\sin\theta}} = \sec\theta - \sin\theta$$

$$\dfrac{\dfrac{1}{\sin^{\cancel{2}}\theta}\dfrac{\cancel{\sin\theta}}{\cos\theta} - 1}{\dfrac{1}{\sin\theta}} = \sec\theta - \sin\theta$$

$$\dfrac{\dfrac{1}{\sin\theta\cos\theta} - 1}{\dfrac{1}{\sin\theta}} = \sec\theta - \sin\theta$$

$$\dfrac{\dfrac{1}{\cos\theta} - \sin\theta}{1} = \sec\theta - \sin\theta$$

$$\sec\theta - \sin\theta = \sec\theta - \sin\theta$$

12. $\sin\theta = \sin\left(\dfrac{\pi}{2} - \theta\right)\cot\left(\dfrac{\pi}{2} - \theta\right)$

$\sin\theta = \cos\theta\tan\theta$

$\sin\theta = \cos\theta\dfrac{\sin\theta}{\cos\theta}$

$\sin\theta = \sin\theta$

13. $\sin\theta + \cos\theta\cot\theta = \csc\theta$

$\sin\theta + \cos\theta\dfrac{\cos\theta}{\sin\theta} = \csc\theta$

$\sin\theta + \dfrac{\cos^2\theta}{\sin\theta} = \csc\theta$

$\dfrac{\sin^2\theta}{\sin\theta} + \dfrac{\cos^2\theta}{\sin\theta} = \csc\theta$

$\dfrac{1}{\sin\theta} = \csc\theta$

$\csc\theta = \csc\theta$

14. $\csc\theta\tan\theta - \sin\theta = \dfrac{\tan\theta - \sin^2\theta}{\sin\theta}$

$\csc\theta\tan\theta - \sin\theta = \dfrac{\dfrac{\sin\theta}{\cos\theta} - \sin^2\theta}{\sin\theta}$

$\csc\theta\tan\theta - \sin\theta = \left(\dfrac{\sin\theta}{\cos\theta} - \sin^2\theta\right)\dfrac{1}{\sin\theta}$

$\csc\theta\tan\theta - \sin\theta = \dfrac{1}{\cos\theta} - \sin\theta$

$\csc\theta\tan\theta - \sin\theta = \dfrac{1}{\cos\theta}\dfrac{\sin\theta}{\sin\theta} - \sin\theta$

$\csc\theta\tan\theta - \sin\theta = \dfrac{1}{\sin\theta}\dfrac{\sin\theta}{\cos\theta} - \sin\theta$

$\csc\theta\tan\theta - \sin\theta = \csc\theta\tan\theta - \sin\theta$

15. $\sec\theta\tan\theta - \cot\theta = \dfrac{\tan^2\theta - \cos\theta}{\sin\theta}$

$$\sec\theta\tan\theta - \cot\theta = \dfrac{\dfrac{\sin^2\theta}{\cos^2\theta} - \cos\theta}{\sin\theta}$$

$$\sec\theta\tan\theta - \cot\theta = \dfrac{\sin\theta}{\cos^2\theta} - \cot\theta$$

$$\sec\theta\tan\theta - \cot\theta = \dfrac{1}{\cos\theta}\dfrac{\sin\theta}{\cos\theta} - \cot\theta$$

$$\sec\theta\tan\theta - \cot\theta = \sec\theta\tan\theta - \cot\theta$$

16. $\sec^2\theta\left(\cos^2\theta - 1\right) = -\tan^2\theta$

$$-\sec^2\theta\left(1 - \cos^2\theta\right) = -\tan^2\theta$$

$$-\sec^2\theta\sin^2\theta = -\tan^2\theta$$

$$-\dfrac{1}{\cos^2\theta}\sin^2\theta = -\tan^2\theta$$

$$-\dfrac{\sin^2\theta}{\cos^2\theta} = -\tan^2\theta$$

$$-\tan^2\theta = -\tan^2\theta$$

17. $\dfrac{\sin\theta}{1 - \sin^2\theta} = \csc\left(\dfrac{\pi}{2} - \theta\right)\cot\left(\dfrac{\pi}{2} - \theta\right)$

$$\dfrac{\sin\theta}{1 - \sin^2\theta} = \sec\theta\tan\theta$$

$$\dfrac{\sin\theta}{1 - \sin^2\theta} = \dfrac{1}{\cos\theta}\dfrac{\sin\theta}{\cos\theta}$$

$$\dfrac{\sin\theta}{1 - \sin^2\theta} = \dfrac{\sin\theta}{\cos^2\theta}$$

$$\dfrac{\sin\theta}{1 - \sin^2\theta} = \dfrac{\sin\theta}{1 - \sin^2\theta}$$

18. $\tan^2\theta\sin\theta + \sin\theta = \dfrac{\tan\theta}{\cos\theta}$

$$\sin\theta\left(\tan^2\theta + 1\right) = \dfrac{\tan\theta}{\cos\theta}$$

$$\sin\theta\sec^2\theta = \dfrac{\tan\theta}{\cos\theta}$$

$$\sin\theta\dfrac{1}{\cos^2\theta} = \dfrac{\tan\theta}{\cos\theta}$$

$$\dfrac{\sin\theta}{\cos\theta}\dfrac{1}{\cos\theta} = \dfrac{\tan\theta}{\cos\theta}$$

$$\tan\theta\cdot\dfrac{1}{\cos\theta} = \dfrac{\tan\theta}{\cos\theta}$$

$$\dfrac{\tan\theta}{\cos\theta} = \dfrac{\tan\theta}{\cos\theta}$$

19. $\cos^2\theta - \csc\theta = \dfrac{\sin\theta\cos\theta - \sec\theta}{\sec\theta\sin\theta}$

$\cos^2\theta - \csc\theta = \dfrac{\sin\theta\cos\theta - \dfrac{1}{\cos\theta}}{\dfrac{1}{\cos\theta}\sin\theta}$

$\cos^2\theta - \csc\theta = \dfrac{\sin\theta\cos^2\theta - 1}{\sin\theta}$

$\cos^2\theta - \csc\theta = \cos^2\theta - \dfrac{1}{\sin\theta}$

$\cos^2\theta - \csc\theta = \cos^2\theta - \csc\theta$

20. $\sec\theta\tan\theta - \csc^2\theta = \dfrac{\sin^3\theta - \cos^2\theta}{\left(\sin\theta\cos\theta\right)^2}$

$\sec\theta\tan\theta - \csc^2\theta = \dfrac{\sin^3\theta}{\sin^2\theta\cos^2\theta} - \dfrac{\cos^2\theta}{\sin^2\theta\cos^2\theta}$

$\sec\theta\tan\theta - \csc^2\theta = \dfrac{\sin\theta}{\cos^2\theta} - \dfrac{1}{\sin^2\theta}$

$\sec\theta\tan\theta - \csc^2\theta = \dfrac{1}{\cos\theta}\dfrac{\sin\theta}{\cos\theta} - \dfrac{1}{\sin^2\theta}$

$\sec\theta\tan\theta - \csc^2\theta = \sec\theta\tan\theta - \csc^2\theta$

5·2

1. $x = \dfrac{\pi}{3}$, $x = \dfrac{2\pi}{3}$, $x = \dfrac{4\pi}{3}$, $x = \dfrac{5\pi}{3}$

2. $x = 0$, $x = \pi$, $x = 2\pi$, $x = \dfrac{\pi}{3}$, $x = \dfrac{5\pi}{3}$

3. $x = \dfrac{7\pi}{6}$, $x = \dfrac{11\pi}{6}$, $x = \dfrac{3\pi}{2}$

4. $x = \dfrac{\pi}{3}$, $x = \dfrac{4\pi}{3}$, $x = \pi$

5. $x = \dfrac{\pi}{3}$, $x = \dfrac{2\pi}{3}$, $x = \dfrac{4\pi}{3}$, $x = \dfrac{5\pi}{3}$, $x = \dfrac{3\pi}{4}$, $x = \dfrac{7\pi}{4}$

6. $\theta = \dfrac{\pi}{6}$, $\theta = \dfrac{5\pi}{6}$, $\theta = \dfrac{7\pi}{6}$, $\theta = \dfrac{11\pi}{6}$

7. $\theta \approx 0.84$, $\theta \approx 2.42$, $\theta \approx 3.86$, $\theta \approx 5.44$

8. $\theta \approx 2.21$, $\theta \approx 4.07$, $\theta = \dfrac{\pi}{2}$, $\theta = \dfrac{3\pi}{2}$

9. $\theta = \dfrac{\pi}{4}$, $\theta = \dfrac{3\pi}{4}$, $\theta = \dfrac{5\pi}{4}$, $\theta = \dfrac{7\pi}{4}$

10. $\theta = \dfrac{\pi}{6}$, $\theta = \dfrac{5\pi}{6}$, $\theta = \dfrac{7\pi}{6}$, $\theta = \dfrac{11\pi}{6}$

11. $x = \dfrac{\pi}{4} + 2n\pi$, $x = \dfrac{5\pi}{4} + 2n\pi$, $x = \dfrac{5\pi}{6} + 2n\pi$, $x = \dfrac{11\pi}{6} + 2n\pi$

12. $x = \dfrac{\pi}{4} \pm n\pi$

13. $x = \dfrac{\pi}{2} \pm 2n\pi$

14. $x = \dfrac{5\pi}{4} \pm 2n\pi$, $x = \dfrac{7\pi}{4} \pm 2n\pi$, $x = \dfrac{\pi}{6} \pm 2n\pi$, $x = \dfrac{5\pi}{6} \pm 2n\pi$

15. $x = \dfrac{\pi}{4} + 2n\pi$, $x = \dfrac{5\pi}{4} + 2n\pi$, $x = \dfrac{7\pi}{4} + 2n\pi$

16. $\theta = \dfrac{\pi}{2} \pm 2n\pi$, $\theta = \dfrac{7\pi}{6} \pm 2n\pi$, $\theta = \dfrac{11\pi}{6} \pm 2n\pi$

17. $\theta = \pm 1.35 \pm 2n\pi$

18. $\theta = \pm n\pi$, $\theta = \dfrac{\pi}{6} \pm n\pi$, $\theta = \dfrac{5\pi}{6} \pm n\pi$

19. $\theta = \pm 2n\pi$, $\theta = \dfrac{\pi}{6} \pm 2n\pi$, $\theta = \dfrac{5\pi}{6} \pm 2n\pi$

20. $\theta = \dfrac{\pi}{4} \pm \dfrac{n\pi}{2}$

5·3

1.
$$\sin(\alpha + \beta) + \sin(\alpha - \beta) = 2\sin\alpha\cos\beta$$
$$\sin\alpha\cos\beta + \cos\alpha\sin\beta + \sin\alpha\cos\beta - \cos\alpha\sin\beta = 2\sin\alpha\cos\beta$$
$$\sin\alpha\cos\beta + \sin\alpha\cos\beta = 2\sin\alpha\cos\beta$$
$$2\sin\alpha\cos\beta = 2\sin\alpha\cos\beta$$

2.
$$\cos(\alpha - \beta) - \cos(\alpha + \beta) = 2\sin\alpha\sin\beta$$
$$\cos\alpha\cos\beta + \sin\alpha\sin\beta - (\cos\alpha\cos\beta - \sin\alpha\sin\beta) = 2\sin\alpha\sin\beta$$
$$\cos\alpha\cos\beta + \sin\alpha\sin\beta - \cos\alpha\cos\beta + \sin\alpha\sin\beta = 2\sin\alpha\sin\beta$$
$$\sin\alpha\sin\beta + \sin\alpha\sin\beta = 2\sin\alpha\sin\beta$$
$$2\sin\alpha\sin\beta = 2\sin\alpha\sin\beta$$

3.
$$\frac{\sin(\alpha - \beta)}{\sin(\alpha + \beta)} = \frac{\cot\beta - \cot\alpha}{\cot\beta + \cot\alpha}$$

$$\frac{\sin\alpha\cos\beta - \sin\beta\cos\alpha}{\sin\alpha\cos\beta + \sin\beta\cos\alpha} = \frac{\cot\beta - \cot\alpha}{\cot\beta + \cot\alpha}$$

$$\frac{\dfrac{\cancel{\sin\alpha}\cos\beta}{\cancel{\sin\alpha}} - \dfrac{\sin\beta\cos\alpha}{\sin\alpha}}{\dfrac{\cancel{\sin\alpha}\cos\beta}{\cancel{\sin\alpha}} + \dfrac{\sin\beta\cos\alpha}{\sin\alpha}} = \frac{\cot\beta - \cot\alpha}{\cot\beta + \cot\alpha}$$

$$\frac{\dfrac{\cos\beta}{\sin\beta} - \dfrac{\cancel{\sin\beta}\cos\alpha}{\sin\alpha\,\cancel{\sin\beta}}}{\dfrac{\cos\beta}{\sin\beta} + \dfrac{\cancel{\sin\beta}\cos\alpha}{\sin\alpha\,\cancel{\sin\beta}}} = \frac{\cot\beta - \cot\alpha}{\cot\beta + \cot\alpha}$$

$$\frac{\dfrac{\cos\beta}{\sin\beta} - \dfrac{\cos\alpha}{\sin\alpha}}{\dfrac{\cos\beta}{\sin\beta} + \dfrac{\cos\alpha}{\sin\alpha}} = \frac{\cot\beta - \cot\alpha}{\cot\beta + \cot\alpha}$$

$$\frac{\cot\beta - \cot\alpha}{\cot\beta + \cot\alpha} = \frac{\cot\beta - \cot\alpha}{\cot\beta + \cot\alpha}$$

4.

$$\sin(\alpha+\beta)\sin(\alpha-\beta)=\sin^2\alpha-\sin^2\beta$$
$$(\sin\alpha\cos\beta+\cos\alpha\sin\beta)(\sin\alpha\cos\beta-\cos\alpha\sin\beta)=\sin^2\alpha-\sin^2\beta$$
$$\sin^2\alpha\cos^2\beta+\cos\alpha\sin\beta\sin\alpha\cos\beta-\cos\alpha\sin\beta\sin\alpha\cos\beta-\cos^2\alpha\sin^2\beta=\sin^2\alpha-\sin^2\beta$$
$$\sin^2\alpha\cos^2\beta-\cos^2\alpha\sin^2\beta=\sin^2\alpha-\sin^2\beta$$
$$\sin^2\alpha\left(1-\sin^2\beta\right)-\left(1-\sin^2\alpha\right)\sin^2\beta=\sin^2\alpha-\sin^2\beta$$
$$\sin^2\alpha-\sin^2\alpha\sin^2\beta-\sin^2\beta+\sin^2\alpha\sin^2\beta=\sin^2\alpha-\sin^2\beta$$
$$\sin^2\alpha-\sin^2\beta=\sin^2\alpha-\sin^2\beta$$

5.

$$\sin(\alpha+\beta)\sin(\alpha-\beta)=\cos^2\beta-\cos^2\alpha$$
$$(\sin\alpha\cos\beta+\cos\alpha\sin\beta)(\sin\alpha\cos\beta-\cos\alpha\sin\beta)=\cos^2\beta-\cos^2\alpha$$
$$\sin^2\alpha\cos^2\beta+\cos\alpha\sin\beta\sin\alpha\cos\beta-\cos\alpha\sin\beta\sin\alpha\cos\beta-\cos^2\alpha\sin^2\beta=\cos^2\beta-\cos^2\alpha$$
$$\sin^2\alpha\cos^2\beta-\cos^2\alpha\sin^2\beta=\cos^2\beta-\cos^2\alpha$$
$$\left(1-\cos^2\alpha\right)\cos^2\beta-\cos^2\alpha\left(1-\cos^2\beta\right)=\cos^2\beta-\cos^2\alpha$$
$$\cos^2\beta-\cos^2\alpha\cos^2\beta-\cos^2\alpha+\cos^2\alpha\cos^2\beta=\cos^2\beta-\cos^2\alpha$$
$$\cos^2\beta-\cos^2\alpha=\cos^2\beta-\cos^2\alpha$$

6.

$$\frac{\sin(\alpha+\beta)+\sin(\alpha-\beta)}{\cos(\alpha+\beta)+\cos(\alpha-\beta)}=\tan\alpha$$

$$\frac{\sin\alpha\cos\beta+\cos\alpha\sin\beta+\sin\alpha\cos\beta-\cos\alpha\sin\beta}{\cos\alpha\cos\beta-\sin\alpha\sin\beta+\cos\alpha\cos\beta+\sin\alpha\sin\beta}=\tan\alpha$$

$$\frac{2\sin\alpha\,\cancel{\cos\beta}}{2\cos\alpha\,\cancel{\cos\beta}}=\tan\alpha$$

$$\tan\alpha=\tan\alpha$$

7.

$$\sin\left(\frac{\pi}{2}-x-y\right)=\cos(x+y)$$
$$\sin\left(\frac{\pi}{2}-x\right)\cos y-\cos\left(\frac{\pi}{2}-x\right)\sin y=\cos(x+y)$$
$$\left(\sin\frac{\pi}{2}\cos x-\cos\frac{\pi}{2}\sin x\right)\cos y-\left(\cos\frac{\pi}{2}\cos x+\sin\frac{\pi}{2}\sin x\right)\sin y=\cos(x+y)$$
$$(1\cos x-0\sin x)\cos y-(0\cos x+1\sin x)\sin y=\cos(x+y)$$
$$\cos x\cos y-\sin x\sin y=\cos(x+y)$$
$$\cos(x+y)=\cos(x+y)$$

8.
$$\tan\left(\frac{\pi}{2}-\theta\right)=\cot\theta$$

$$\frac{\sin\left(\frac{\pi}{2}-\theta\right)}{\cos\left(\frac{\pi}{2}-\theta\right)}=\cot\theta$$

$$\frac{\sin\frac{\pi}{2}\cos\theta-\cos\frac{\pi}{2}in\theta}{\cos\frac{\pi}{2}\cos\theta+\sin\frac{\pi}{2}\sin\theta}=\cot\theta$$

$$\frac{1\cos\theta-0\sin\theta}{0\cos\theta+1\sin\theta}=\cot\theta$$

$$\frac{\cos\theta}{\sin\theta}=\cot\theta$$

$$\cot\theta=\cot\theta$$

9.
$$\sin\left(\frac{\pi}{2}-\theta\right)=\cos\theta$$

$$\sin\frac{\pi}{2}\cos\theta-\cos\frac{\pi}{2}\sin\theta=\cos\theta$$

$$1\cos\theta-0\sin\theta=\cos\theta$$

$$\cos\theta=\cos\theta$$

10.
$$\csc\left(\frac{\pi}{2}-\theta\right)=\sec\theta$$

$$\frac{1}{\sin\left(\frac{\pi}{2}-\theta\right)}=\sec\theta$$

$$\frac{1}{\sin\frac{\pi}{2}\cos\theta-\cos\frac{\pi}{2}\sin\theta}=\sec\theta$$

$$\frac{1}{1\cos\theta-0\sin\theta}=\sec\theta$$

$$\frac{1}{\cos\theta}=\sec\theta$$

$$\sec\theta=\sec\theta$$

11. $\dfrac{\sqrt{6}-\sqrt{2}}{4}$

12. $\dfrac{\sqrt{2}-\sqrt{6}}{4}$

13. $2+\sqrt{3}$

14. $\dfrac{\sqrt{2}+\sqrt{6}}{4}$

15. $\dfrac{\sqrt{2}-\sqrt{6}}{4}$

16. $2+\sqrt{3}$

17. $2-\sqrt{3}$

18. $\dfrac{\sqrt{2}+\sqrt{6}}{4}$

19. $2-\sqrt{3}$

20. $\dfrac{-\sqrt{2}-\sqrt{6}}{4}$

21. $\theta \approx 0.322,\ \theta \approx 3.463,\ \theta \approx 0.464,\ \theta \approx 3.605$

22. $\theta = \dfrac{7\pi}{6},\ \theta = \dfrac{11\pi}{6}$

23. $\beta = \dfrac{\pi}{2},\ \beta = \dfrac{3\pi}{2}$

24. No solution

25. $\alpha = \dfrac{\pi}{2},\ \alpha = \dfrac{3\pi}{2},\ \beta = 0,\ \beta = \pi$

5·4

1. $\sec(2\alpha) = 1 + \tan\alpha \tan\alpha$

$$\sec(2\alpha) = 1 + \tan\alpha \left(\frac{2\tan\alpha}{1-\tan^2\alpha} \right)$$

$$\sec(2\alpha) = 1 + \frac{2\tan^2\alpha}{1-\tan^2\alpha}$$

$$\sec(2\alpha) = \frac{1-\tan^2\alpha}{1-\tan^2\alpha} + \frac{2\tan^2\alpha}{1-\tan^2\alpha}$$

$$\sec(2\alpha) = \frac{1+\tan^2\alpha}{1-\tan^2\alpha}$$

$$\sec(2\alpha) = \frac{1+\dfrac{\sin^2\alpha}{\cos^2\alpha}}{1-\dfrac{\sin^2\alpha}{\cos^2\alpha}} \frac{\cos^2\alpha}{\cos^2\alpha}$$

$$\sec(2\alpha) = \frac{\cos^2\alpha+\sin^2\alpha}{\cos^2\alpha-\sin^2\alpha}$$

$$\sec(2\alpha) = \frac{1}{\cos(2\alpha)}$$

$$\sec(2\alpha) = \sec(2\alpha)$$

2. $$\csc(2\theta) = \frac{\sec\theta\csc\theta}{2}$$

$$\frac{1}{\sin(2\theta)} = \frac{\sec\theta\csc\theta}{2}$$

$$\frac{1}{2\sin\alpha\cos\alpha} = \frac{\sec\theta\csc\theta}{2}$$

$$\frac{1}{2}\frac{1}{\sin\alpha}\frac{1}{\cos\alpha} = \frac{\sec\theta\csc\theta}{2}$$

$$\frac{\sec\theta\csc\theta}{2} = \frac{\sec\theta\csc\theta}{2}$$

3. $$\cot\alpha - \tan\beta = 2\cot(2\beta)$$

$$\cot\alpha - \tan\beta = \frac{2}{\tan(2\beta)}$$

$$\cot\alpha - \tan\beta = \frac{2}{\left(\dfrac{2\tan\beta}{1-\tan^2\beta}\right)}$$

$$\cot\alpha - \tan\beta = \frac{\cancel{2}\left(1-\tan^2\beta\right)}{\cancel{2}\tan\beta}$$

$$\cot\alpha - \tan\beta = \frac{1}{\tan\beta} - \frac{\tan^2\beta}{\tan\beta}$$

$$\cot\alpha - \tan\beta = \cot\alpha - \tan\beta$$

4. $$\tan\alpha = \frac{\sin(2\alpha)}{1+\cos(2\alpha)}$$

$$\tan\alpha = \frac{2\sin\alpha\cos\alpha}{1+\cos^2\alpha - \sin^2\alpha}$$

$$\tan\alpha = \frac{2\sin\alpha\cos\alpha}{1-\sin^2\alpha + \cos^2\alpha}$$

$$\tan\alpha = \frac{2\sin\alpha\cos\alpha}{\cos^2\alpha + \cos^2\alpha}$$

$$\tan\alpha = \frac{2\sin\alpha\cos\alpha}{2\cos^2\alpha}$$

$$\tan\alpha = \frac{\sin\alpha}{\cos\alpha}$$

$$\tan\alpha = \tan\alpha$$

5. $$\frac{2\tan x}{\tan(2x)} = 2 - \sec^2 x$$

$$2\tan x \div \frac{2\tan x}{1-\tan^2 x} = 2 - \sec^2 x$$

$$1 - \tan^2 x = 2 - \sec^2 x$$

$$1 - \left(\sec^2 x - 1\right) = 2 - \sec^2 x$$

$$2 - \sec^2 x = 2 - \sec^2 x$$

6.

$$\sin x = \frac{2\tan\dfrac{x}{2}}{1+\tan^2\dfrac{x}{2}}$$

$$\sin x = \frac{2\sqrt{\dfrac{1-\cos x}{1+\cos x}}}{1+\dfrac{1-\cos x}{1+\cos x}}$$

$$\sin x = \frac{2(1+\cos x)\sqrt{\dfrac{1-\cos x}{1+\cos x}}}{1+\cos x+1-\cos x}$$

$$\sin x = \frac{2(1+\cos x)\sqrt{\dfrac{1-\cos x}{1+\cos x}}}{2}$$

$$\sin x = (1+\cos x)\frac{\sqrt{1-\cos x}}{\sqrt{1+\cos x}}\frac{\sqrt{1+\cos x}}{\sqrt{1+\cos x}}$$

$$\sin x = (1+\cos x)\frac{\sqrt{1-\cos^2 x}}{1+\cos x}$$

$$\sin x = \sqrt{1-\cos^2 x}$$

$$\sin x = \sqrt{\sin^2 x}$$

$$\sin x = \sin x$$

7.

$$\cot\theta = \frac{\cos(2\theta)+1}{\sin(2\theta)}$$

$$\cot\theta = \frac{2\cos^2\theta-1+1}{2\sin\theta\cos\theta}$$

$$\cot\theta = \frac{2\cos^2\theta}{2\sin\theta\cos\theta}$$

$$\cot\theta = \frac{\cos\theta}{\sin\theta}$$

$$\cot\theta = \cot\theta$$

8.

$$\sin(3\theta) = 3\sin\theta - 4\sin^3\theta$$

$$\sin(\theta+2\theta) = 3\sin\theta - 4\sin^3\theta$$

$$\sin\theta\cos(2\theta) + \cos\theta\sin(2\theta) = 3\sin\theta - 4\sin^3\theta$$

$$\sin\theta(\cos^2\theta-\sin^2\theta) + \cos\theta(2\sin\theta\cos\theta) = 3\sin\theta - 4\sin^3\theta$$

$$\sin\theta\cos^2\theta - \sin^3\theta + 2\sin\theta\cos^2\theta = 3\sin\theta - 4\sin^3\theta$$

$$3\sin\theta\cos^2\theta - \sin^3\theta = 3\sin\theta - 4\sin^3\theta$$

$$3\sin\theta(1-\sin^2\theta) - \sin^3\theta = 3\sin\theta - 4\sin^3\theta$$

$$3\sin\theta - 3\sin^3\theta - \sin^3\theta = 3\sin\theta - 4\sin^3\theta$$

$$3\sin\theta - 4\sin^3\theta = 3\sin\theta - 4\sin^3\theta$$

9.

$$\cos(3\theta) = 4\cos^3\theta - 3\cos\theta$$

$$\cos(\theta + 2\theta) = 4\cos^3\theta - 3\cos\theta$$

$$\cos\theta\cos(2\theta) - \sin\theta\sin(2\theta) = 4\cos^3\theta - 3\cos\theta$$

$$\cos\theta\left(\cos^2\theta - \sin^2\theta\right) - \sin\theta\left(2\sin\theta\cos\theta\right) = 4\cos^3\theta - 3\cos\theta$$

$$\cos^3\theta - \cos\theta\sin^2\theta - 2\cos\theta\sin^2\theta = 4\cos^3\theta - 3\cos\theta$$

$$\cos^3\theta - 3\cos\theta\sin^2\theta = 4\cos^3\theta - 3\cos\theta$$

$$\cos^3\theta - 3\cos\theta\left(1 - \cos^2\theta\right) = 4\cos^3\theta - 3\cos\theta$$

$$\cos^3\theta - 3\cos\theta + 3\cos^3\theta = 4\cos^3\theta - 3\cos\theta$$

$$4\cos^3\theta - 3\cos\theta = 4\cos^3\theta - 3\cos\theta$$

10.

$$\tan(3\theta) = \frac{3\tan\theta - \tan^3\theta}{1 - 3\tan^2\theta}$$

$$\tan(\theta + 2\theta) = \frac{3\tan\theta - \tan^3\theta}{1 - 3\tan^2\theta}$$

$$\frac{\tan\theta + \tan(2\theta)}{1 - \tan\theta\tan(2\theta)} = \frac{3\tan\theta - \tan^3\theta}{1 - 3\tan^2\theta}$$

$$\frac{\tan\theta + \dfrac{2\tan\theta}{1 - \tan^2\theta}}{1 - \tan\theta\left(\dfrac{2\tan\theta}{1 - \tan^2\theta}\right)} = \frac{3\tan\theta - \tan^3\theta}{1 - 3\tan^2\theta}$$

$$\frac{\tan\theta\left(1 - \tan^2\theta\right) + 2\tan\theta}{1\left(1 - \tan^2\theta\right) - \tan\theta\left(2\tan\theta\right)} = \frac{3\tan\theta - \tan^3\theta}{1 - 3\tan^2\theta}$$

$$\frac{\tan\theta - \tan^3\theta + 2\tan\theta}{1 - \tan^2\theta - 2\tan^2\theta} = \frac{3\tan\theta - \tan^3\theta}{1 - 3\tan^2\theta}$$

$$\frac{3\tan\theta - \tan^3\theta}{1 - 3\tan^2\theta} = \frac{3\tan\theta - \tan^3\theta}{1 - 3\tan^2\theta}$$

11. $\dfrac{\sqrt{2 - \sqrt{3}}}{2}$

12. $\dfrac{\sqrt{2 + \sqrt{3}}}{2}$

13. $\sqrt{\dfrac{2 - \sqrt{3}}{2 + \sqrt{3}}} = 2 - \sqrt{3}$

14. $\dfrac{\sqrt{2 + \sqrt{3}}}{2}$

15. $\dfrac{\sqrt{2 - \sqrt{3}}}{2}$

16. $\theta = \dfrac{\pi}{8} \pm n\pi, \ \theta = \dfrac{3\pi}{8} \pm n\pi$

17. $\theta = \dfrac{\pi}{3} \pm 2n\pi, \ \theta = \dfrac{5\pi}{3} \pm 2n\pi, \ \theta = \pm(2n+1)\pi$

18. $\theta = \dfrac{\pi}{2} \pm 2n\pi$, $\theta = \dfrac{3\pi}{2} \pm 2n\pi$, $\theta = \dfrac{\pi}{6} \pm 2n\pi$, $\theta = \dfrac{5\pi}{6} \pm 2n\pi$

19. $\theta = \dfrac{\pi}{3} \pm 2n\pi$, $\theta = \dfrac{5\pi}{3} \pm 2n\pi$

20. $\theta = \dfrac{\pi}{3} \pm 2n\pi$, $\theta = \dfrac{5\pi}{3} \pm 2n\pi$, $\theta = \pm(2n+1)\pi$

5·5

1. $\cot\alpha = \dfrac{\cos(\alpha+\beta) + \cos(\alpha-\beta)}{\sin(\alpha+\beta) + \sin(\alpha-\beta)}$

 $\cot\alpha = \dfrac{\cos\alpha\cos\beta - \sin\alpha\sin\beta + \cos\alpha\cos\beta + \sin\alpha\sin\beta}{\sin\alpha\cos\beta + \cos\alpha\sin\beta + \sin\alpha\cos\beta - \cos\alpha\sin\beta}$

 $\cot\alpha = \dfrac{2\cos\alpha \,\cancel{\cos\beta}}{2\sin\alpha \,\cancel{\cos\beta}}$

 $\cot\alpha = \cot\alpha$

2. $\sin(2A)\tan A = 2\sin^2 A$

 $2\sin A\cos A\dfrac{\sin A}{\cos A} = 2\sin^2 A$

 $2\sin^2 A = 2\sin^2 A$

3. $1 - \cos^2\theta = 4\sin^2\dfrac{\theta}{2}\cos^2\dfrac{\theta}{2}$

 $1 - \cos^2\theta = 4\dfrac{1-\cos\theta}{2}\dfrac{1+\cos\theta}{2}$

 $1 - \cos^2\theta = 1 - \cos^2\theta$

4. $\dfrac{\sin(9A)}{\sin(3A)} - \dfrac{\cos(9A)}{\cos(3A)} = 2$

 $\dfrac{\sin(9A)\cos(3A) - \cos(9A)\sin(3A)}{\sin(3A)\cos(3A)} = 2$

 $\dfrac{\sin(6A)}{\dfrac{1}{2}\sin(6A)} = 2$

 $2 = 2$

5. $2\cos\alpha\tan\beta = \sin\alpha + \cos\alpha(2\tan\beta - \tan\alpha)$

 $2\cos\alpha\tan\beta = \sin\alpha + 2\cos\alpha\tan\beta - \cos\alpha\tan\alpha$

 $2\cos\alpha\tan\beta = \sin\alpha + 2\cos\alpha\tan\beta - \cos\alpha\dfrac{\sin\alpha}{\cos\alpha}$

 $2\cos\alpha\tan\beta = \sin\alpha + 2\cos\alpha\tan\beta - \sin\alpha$

 $2\cos\alpha\tan\beta = 2\cos\alpha\tan\beta$

6. $4\sin\alpha\sin\beta\cos\alpha\cos\beta = \sin^2(\alpha+\beta)-\sin^2(\alpha-\beta)$

$4\sin\alpha\sin\beta\cos\alpha\cos\beta = (\sin\alpha\cos\beta+\cos\alpha\sin\beta)^2 - (\sin\alpha\cos\beta-\cos\alpha\sin\beta)^2$

$4\sin\alpha\sin\beta\cos\alpha\cos\beta = \sin^2\alpha\cos^2\beta + 2\sin\alpha\cos\beta\cos\alpha\cos\beta + \cos^2\alpha\sin^2\beta$
$\qquad\qquad\qquad\qquad\qquad -\left(\sin^2\alpha\cos^2\beta - 2\sin\alpha\cos\beta\cos\alpha\cos\beta + \cos^2\alpha\sin^2\beta\right)$

$4\sin\alpha\sin\beta\cos\alpha\cos\beta = \sin^2\alpha\cos^2\beta + 2\sin\alpha\cos\beta\cos\alpha\cos\beta + \cos^2\alpha\sin^2\beta$
$\qquad\qquad\qquad\qquad\qquad - \sin^2\alpha\cos^2\beta + 2\sin\alpha\cos\beta\cos\alpha\cos\beta - \cos^2\alpha\sin^2\beta$

$4\sin\alpha\sin\beta\cos\alpha\cos\beta = 4\sin\alpha\cos\beta\cos\alpha\cos\beta$

7. $\tan^2\theta\cos(2\theta) + \cos(2\theta) = 2 - \sec^2\theta$

$\cos(2\theta)\left(\tan^2\theta + 1\right) = 2 - \sec^2\theta$

$\left(2\cos^2\theta - 1\right)\sec^2\theta = 2 - \sec^2\theta$

$2\cos^2\theta\sec^2\theta - \sec^2\theta = 2 - \sec^2\theta$

$2 - \sec^2\theta = 2 - \sec^2\theta$

8. $2\sin\theta\cos\theta = \tan\theta + \tan\theta\cos(2\theta)$

$2\sin\theta\cos\theta = \tan\theta\left(1+\cos(2\theta)\right)$

$2\sin\theta\cos\theta = \dfrac{\sin\theta}{\cos\theta}\left(1 + 2\cos^2\theta - 1\right)$

$2\sin\theta\cos\theta = \dfrac{\sin\theta}{\cos\theta}\left(2\cos^2\theta\right)$

$2\sin\theta\cos\theta = 2\sin\theta\cos\theta$

9. $2\sin^2\theta\cos^2\theta = 1 - \sin^2\theta - \cos(2\theta) + \sin^2\theta\cos(2\theta)$

$2\sin^2\theta\cos^2\theta = \cos^2\theta - \left(\cos^2\theta - \sin^2\theta\right) + \sin^2\theta\left(2\cos^2\theta - 1\right)$

$2\sin^2\theta\cos^2\theta = \cos^2\theta - \cos^2\theta + \sin^2\theta + 2\sin^2\theta\cos^2\theta - \sin^2\theta$

$2\sin^2\theta\cos^2\theta = 2\sin^2\theta\cos^2\theta$

10. $\sin^3(2\theta) = \sin\theta\cos\theta\left(1 - \cos(4\theta)\right)$

$\sin^3(2\theta) = \sin\theta\cos\theta\left(1 - \left(\cos^2(2\theta) - \sin^2(2\theta)\right)\right)$

$\sin^3(2\theta) = \sin\theta\cos\theta\left(1 - \cos^2(2\theta) + \sin^2(2\theta)\right)$

$\sin^3(2\theta) = \sin\theta\cos\theta\left(\sin^2(2\theta) + \sin^2(2\theta)\right)$

$\sin^3(2\theta) = \sin\theta\cos\theta\left(2\sin^2(2\theta)\right)$

$\sin^3(2\theta) = 2\sin\theta\cos\theta\left(2\sin\theta\cos\theta\right)^2$

$\sin^3(2\theta) = 2\sin\theta\cos\theta\left(4\sin^2\theta\cos^2\theta\right)$

$\sin^3(2\theta) = 8\sin^3\theta\cos^3\theta$

$\sin^3(2\theta) = \left(2\sin\theta\cos\theta\right)^3$

$\sin^3(2\theta) = \sin^3(2\theta)$

6 Law of sines and law of cosines

1. 39.58 in.
2. 23.50 m
3. 17.14 ft
4. 231.81 yd
5. 727.90 yd
6. 1,464.60 in.
7. 0.53 cm
8. 5,379.02 ft
9. 77.48 in.
10. 30.13 cm
11. 17.4 in.
12. 10.72 ft
13. 1,501.25 cm
14. 122.77 m
15. 31.91 yd
16. 6.31 in.
17. 143.81 m

18. 4.41 mm
19. 29.06 mi
20. 6.59 km
21. 67.0 cm
22. 12.26 in.
23. $\dfrac{8}{\sin 36°} = \dfrac{x}{\sin 54°}$
    $x \sin 36° = 8 \sin 54°$
    $x = \dfrac{8 \sin 54°}{\sin 36°} \approx 11.01$ cm
24. $\tan 54° = \dfrac{x}{8}$
    $x = 8 \tan 54° \approx 11.01$ cm
25. $\dfrac{a}{\sin A} = \dfrac{c}{\sin C}$
    $a \sin C = c \sin A$
    $\dfrac{\sin C}{\sin A} = \dfrac{c}{a}$
    $\dfrac{\sin C}{\cos C} = \dfrac{c}{a}$
    $\tan C = \dfrac{c}{a}$

1. 33.59°
2. 38.09°
3. 6.87°
4. 1°
5. 39.27°
6. 48.92°
7. 11.48°
8. 71.85°
9. 37.05°
10. 43.88°

11. 31.9°
12. 68.3°
13. 50.3°
14. 32.7°
15. 23.7°
16. 51.3°
17. 34.5°
18. 47.1°
19. 47.6°
20. 66.6°

6·3

1. Two triangles
2. No triangle
3. Two triangles
4. One triangle
5. One triangle
6. Two triangles
7. Two triangles
8. One triangle
9. One triangle
10. No triangle
11. Two triangles
12. Two triangles
13. One triangle
14. Two triangles
15. One triangle
16. No triangle
17. One triangle
18. One triangle
19. One triangle
20. No triangle

6·4

1. 66.93° or 113.07°
2. 12.43°
3. No triangle possible
4. 13.58°
5. 38.83°
6. No triangle possible
7. 30.21°
8. 46.06°
9. 9.34°
10. 34.29° or 145.71°
11. 54.35° or 125.65°
12. No triangle possible
13. 15.06°
14. 29.69°
15. 66.08°
16. 26.35°
17. 30.71°
18. 24.37°
19. 65.97°
20. 38.37°

6·5

1. 5.70 cm
2. 49.87 in.
3. 169.13 ft
4. 8.34 yd
5. 23.02 m
6. 17.66 km
7. 280.67 in.
8. 22.29 cm
9. 87.08 ft
10. 27.65 m
11. 49.96 ft
12. 25.92 in.
13. 67.03 cm
14. 57.31 yd
15. 189.89 m
16. 460.65 ft
17. 667.76 km
18. 76.44 in.
19. 11.38 cm
20. 651.17 ft

6.6

1. 53.62°
2. 52.87°
3. 55.13°
4. 109.84°
5. 27.13°
6. 92.93°
7. 74.51°
8. 75.45°
9. 62.15°
10. 48.34°
11. 28.84°
12. 38.53°
13. 44.09°
14. 39.27°
15. 108.14°
16. 60.74°
17. 100.98°
18. 50.85°
19. 88.91°
20. 55.37°

6.7

1. $\angle C = 57°$, $AC = 10.99$ cm, $AB = 12.21$ cm
2. No triangle possible
3. $\angle X = 23.07°$, $\angle Y = 141.43°$, $\angle Z = 15.50°$
4. 35.11 cm and 73.64 cm
5. 9,348.61 m and 9,652.87 m
6. 95.07 ft
7. 2,279.44 m
8. 116.84 ft
9. 131.78 m
10. 139.58°

7 Polar coordinate system

7·1   1.

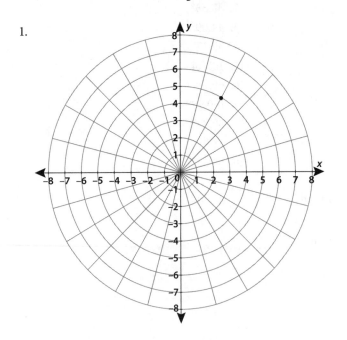

2.

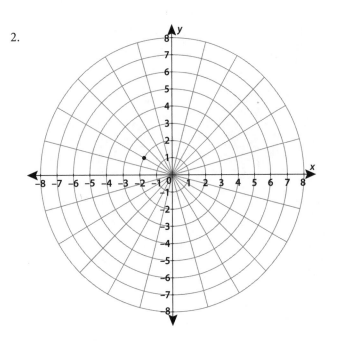

3.

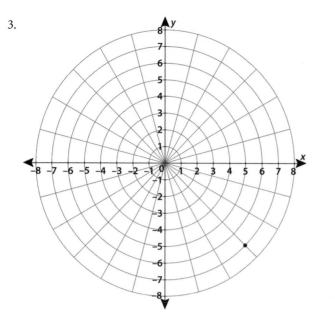

4.

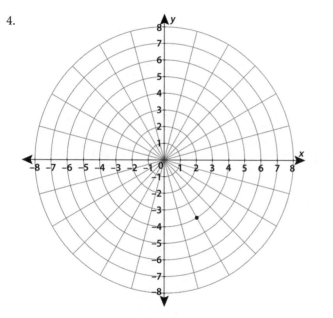

5.

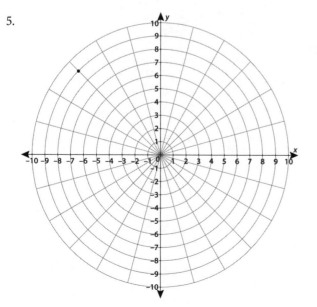

6.

7.

8.

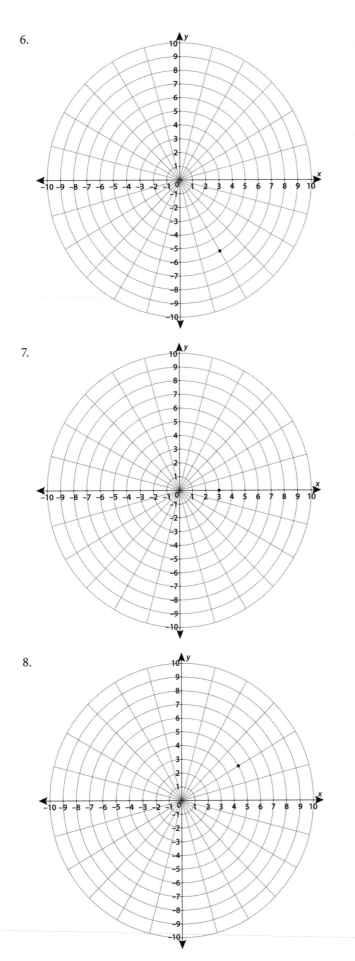

9.

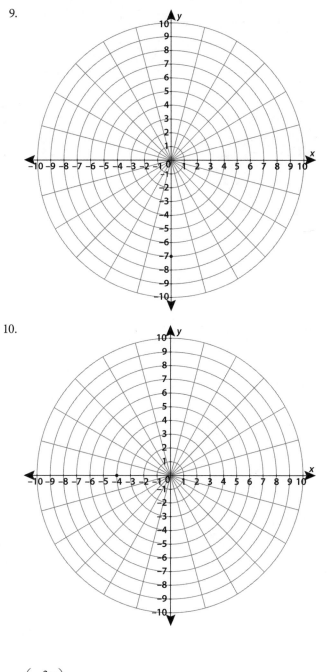

10.

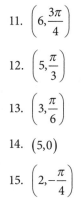

11. $\left(6, \dfrac{3\pi}{4}\right)$

12. $\left(5, \dfrac{\pi}{3}\right)$

13. $\left(3, \dfrac{\pi}{6}\right)$

14. $(5, 0)$

15. $\left(2, -\dfrac{\pi}{4}\right)$

16. $\left(6, \dfrac{11\pi}{6}\right)$

17. $\left(7, \dfrac{3\pi}{2}\right)$

18. $\left(9, \dfrac{4\pi}{3}\right)$

19. $\left(4, \dfrac{5\pi}{4}\right)$

20. $(2, \pi)$

1. $\left(5, \dfrac{\pi}{3}\right)$, $\left(5, -\dfrac{5\pi}{3}\right)$, $\left(5, \dfrac{7\pi}{3}\right)$, $\left(-5, \dfrac{4\pi}{3}\right)$, $\left(-5, -\dfrac{2\pi}{3}\right)$

2. $\left(2, \dfrac{5\pi}{6}\right)$, $\left(2, -\dfrac{7\pi}{6}\right)$, $\left(2, \dfrac{17\pi}{6}\right)$, $\left(-2, \dfrac{11\pi}{6}\right)$, $\left(-2, -\dfrac{\pi}{6}\right)$

3. $\left(7, \dfrac{7\pi}{4}\right)$, $\left(7, -\dfrac{\pi}{4}\right)$, $\left(7, \dfrac{15\pi}{4}\right)$, $\left(-7, \dfrac{3\pi}{4}\right)$, $\left(-7, -\dfrac{5\pi}{4}\right)$

4. $\left(4, \dfrac{5\pi}{3}\right)$, $\left(4, -\dfrac{\pi}{3}\right)$, $\left(4, \dfrac{11\pi}{3}\right)$, $\left(-4, \dfrac{2\pi}{3}\right)$, $\left(-4, -\dfrac{4\pi}{3}\right)$

5. $\left(9, \dfrac{3\pi}{4}\right)$, $\left(9, -\dfrac{5\pi}{4}\right)$, $\left(9, \dfrac{11\pi}{4}\right)$, $\left(-9, \dfrac{7\pi}{4}\right)$, $\left(-9, -\dfrac{3\pi}{4}\right)$

6. $\left(6, \dfrac{5\pi}{3}\right)$, $\left(6, -\dfrac{\pi}{3}\right)$, $\left(6, \dfrac{11\pi}{3}\right)$, $\left(-6, \dfrac{2\pi}{3}\right)$, $\left(-6, -\dfrac{4\pi}{3}\right)$

7. $(3, 0)$, $(3, -2\pi)$, $(3, 4\pi)$, $(-3, \pi)$, $(-3, -\pi)$

8. $\left(5, \dfrac{\pi}{6}\right)$, $\left(5, -\dfrac{11\pi}{6}\right)$, $\left(5, \dfrac{13\pi}{6}\right)$, $\left(-5, \dfrac{7\pi}{6}\right)$, $\left(-5, -\dfrac{5\pi}{6}\right)$

9. $\left(7, \dfrac{3\pi}{2}\right)$, $\left(7, -\dfrac{\pi}{2}\right)$, $\left(7, \dfrac{7\pi}{2}\right)$, $\left(-7, \dfrac{\pi}{2}\right)$, $\left(-7, -\dfrac{3\pi}{2}\right)$

10. $(4, \pi)$, $(4, -\pi)$, $(4, 3\pi)$, $(-4, 0)$, $(-4, -2\pi)$

11. $\left(5, -\dfrac{5\pi}{3}\right)$

12. $(5, -2\pi)$

13. $\left(2, -\dfrac{\pi}{6}\right)$

14. $(2, -\pi)$

15. $\left(-6, \dfrac{7\pi}{4}\right)$

16. $\left(-9, \dfrac{\pi}{3}\right)$

17. $\left(-7, \dfrac{\pi}{2}\right)$

18. $\left(-3, -\dfrac{5\pi}{6}\right)$

19. $\left(-6, -\dfrac{7\pi}{6}\right)$

20. $\left(-4, -\dfrac{7\pi}{4}\right)$

7·3

1. $(5, 0.93)$

2. $(13, -1.18)$

3. $(6, \pi)$

4. $\left(8, \dfrac{4\pi}{3}\right)$

5. $\left(1, \dfrac{3\pi}{2}\right)$

6. $\left(14, \dfrac{5\pi}{3}\right)$

7. $\left(4\sqrt{2}, \dfrac{7\pi}{4}\right)$

8. $\left(12, \dfrac{11\pi}{6}\right)$

9. $\left(3\sqrt{2}, \dfrac{5\pi}{4}\right)$

10. $\left(18\sqrt{2}, \dfrac{11\pi}{6}\right)$

11. $\left(4, 4\sqrt{3}\right)$

12. $\left(\dfrac{9\sqrt{2}}{2}, -\dfrac{9\sqrt{2}}{2}\right)$

13. $\left(\dfrac{3\sqrt{3}}{2}, -\dfrac{3}{2}\right)$

14. $(0, -2)$

15. $(-7, 0)$

16. $\left(-2\sqrt{2}, -2\sqrt{2}\right)$

17. $\left(-4, 4\sqrt{3}\right)$

18. $\left(-6\sqrt{3}, 6\right)$

19. $\left(8\sqrt{2}, -8\sqrt{2}\right)$

20. $\left(-\dfrac{11\sqrt{2}}{2}, \dfrac{11\sqrt{2}}{2}\right)$

7.4   1.

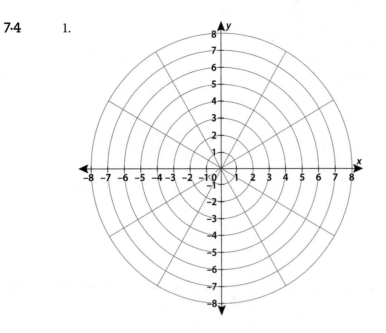

2.

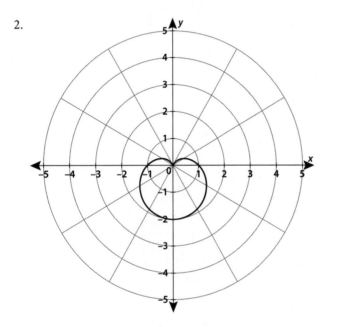

3.

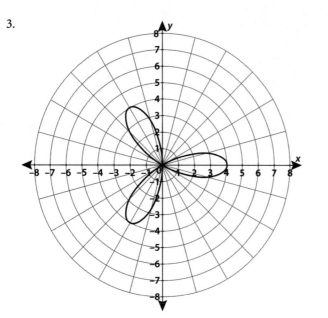

4.

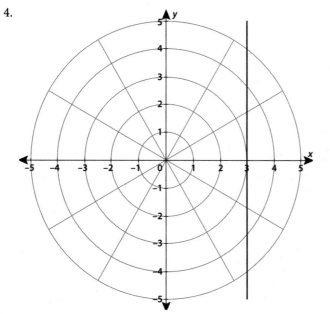

5.

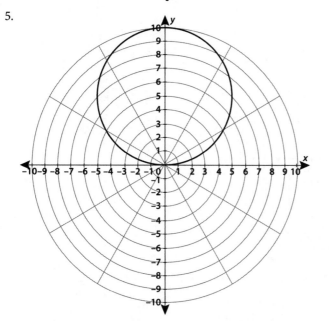

6.

7.

8.

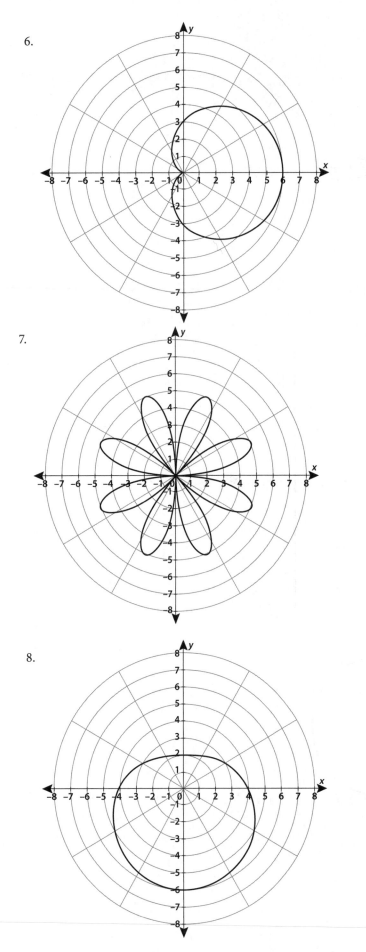

9.

10.

11.

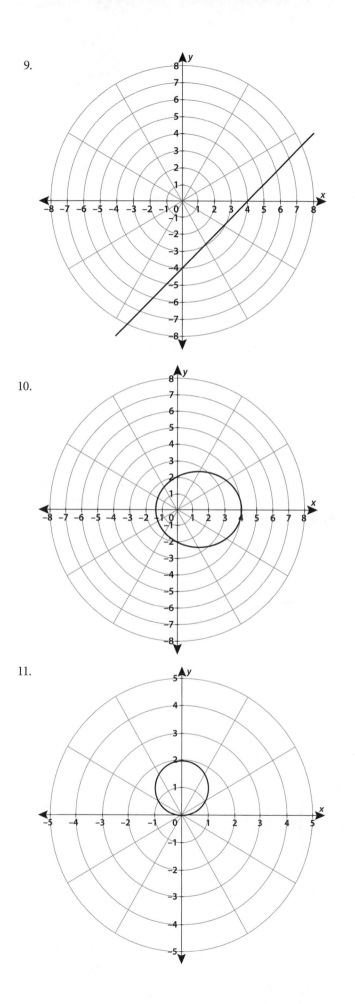

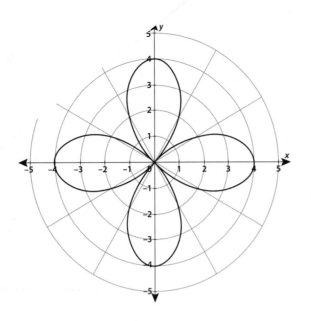

13.

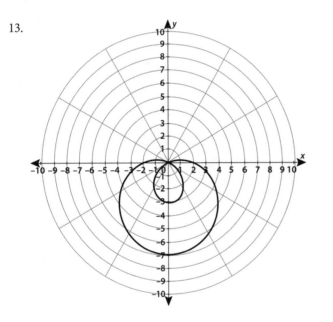

14.

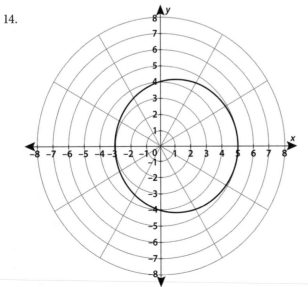

15.

16.

17.

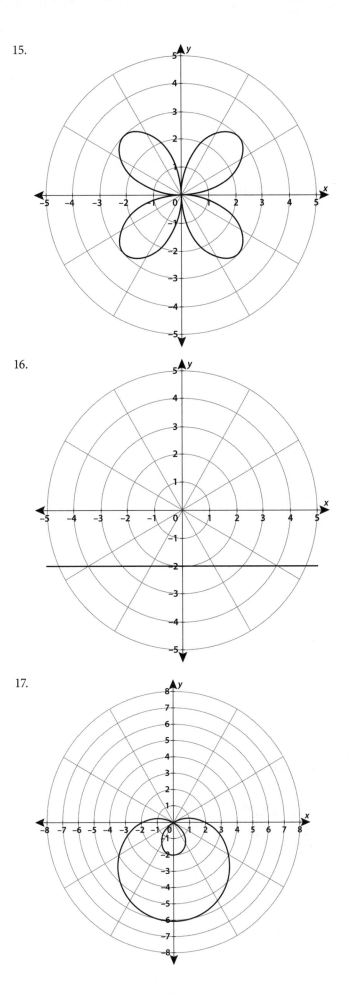

18.

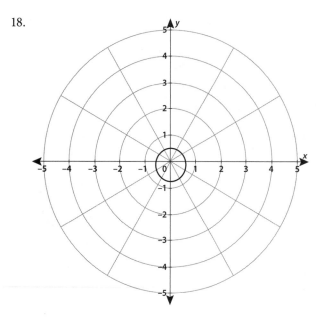

19.

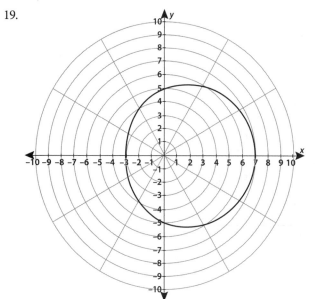

20.

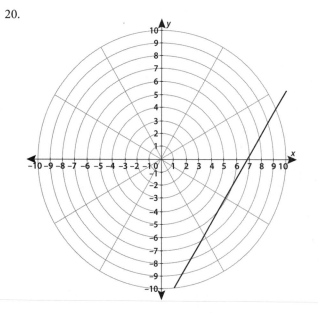

7·5

1. $r = \dfrac{-4}{\sin\theta - 3\cos\theta}$

2. $r^2 - 2r\cos\theta - 24 = 0$

3. $r^2 - r^2\sin^2\theta - r\sin\theta - 4 = 0$

4. $r^2 = \dfrac{36}{4 + 5\sin^2\theta}$

5. $r^2 = \dfrac{16}{5\sin^2\theta - 1}$

6. $r = \dfrac{7}{\cos\theta}$

7. $r^2\sin^2\theta - r\sin\theta - 1 = 0$

8. $r^2 - 4r\cos\theta + 2r\sin\theta = 11$

9. $r^2 - r^2\cos^2\theta - r\cos\theta + 4 = 0$

10. $r = \dfrac{-5}{\sin\theta}$

11. $y = \sqrt{3}x$

12. $(x-6)^2 + y^2 = 36$

13. $y = 3$

14. $\left(x^2 + y^2 + y\right)^2 = x^2 + y^2$

15. $x^2 + y^2 = \dfrac{9}{4}(7-y)^2$

16. $\left(x^2 + 3x + y^2\right)^2 = 4\left(x^2 + y^2\right)$

17. $x = 4$

18. $9\left(x^2 + y^2\right) = (5 - 2y)^2$

19. $x^2 + y^2 = 64$

20. $x^2 + y^2 = 8x$

8 Complex numbers

8·1

1.

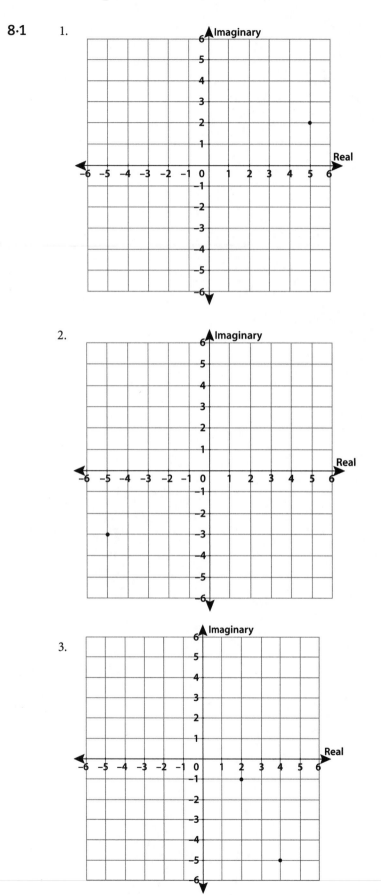

2.

3.

4.

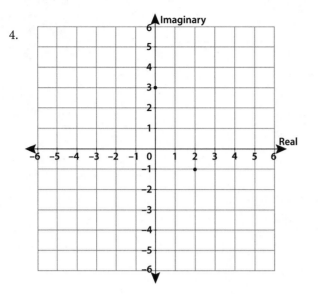

5.

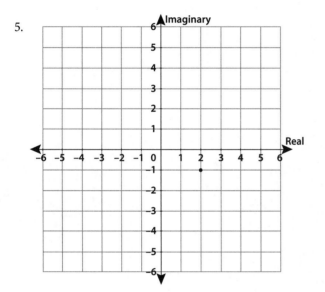

6. $-8 + 2i$

7. $0 + 7i = 7i$

8. $-4 + 0i = -4$

9. $6 - 3i$

10. $5 - 4i$

11. $2 + 7i$

12. $-1 - i$

13. $\sqrt{3} + 2\sqrt{3}i$

14. $-5 + 8i$

15. $-\dfrac{1}{2} - 5i$

16. 13

17. 10

18. 2

19. $5\sqrt{2}$

20. $\sqrt{5}$

21. $5\sqrt{5}$

22. 5

23. 15

24. 1

25. 4

8·2

1. $2+15i$

2. $5-2i$

3. $2-10i$

4. $7+5i$

5. $-21+28i$

6. $10+45i$

7. $-53-69i$

8. $-28-23i$

9. -1

10. $-i$

11. $-243i$

12. $38-34i$

13. $-40+34i$

14. 34

15. $3.5-5i$

16. $9-6i$

17. $-\dfrac{7}{5}-\dfrac{2}{5}i$

18. $-\dfrac{19}{13}-\dfrac{30}{13}i$

19. $\dfrac{3}{5}+\dfrac{4}{5}i$

20. $-\dfrac{98}{5}+\dfrac{57}{5}i$

8·3

1. $5\sqrt{2}\left(\cos\dfrac{\pi}{4}+i\sin\dfrac{\pi}{4}\right)$

2. $14\left(\cos\dfrac{5\pi}{6}+i\sin\dfrac{5\pi}{6}\right)$

3. $24\left(\cos\dfrac{4\pi}{3}+i\sin\dfrac{4\pi}{3}\right)$

4. $6\sqrt{5}\left(\cos\dfrac{5\pi}{3}+i\sin\dfrac{5\pi}{3}\right)$

5. $8\sqrt{2}\left(\cos\dfrac{5\pi}{4}+i\sin\dfrac{5\pi}{4}\right)$

6. $5(\cos 2.21+i\sin 2.21)$

7. $5\left(\cos\dfrac{3\pi}{2}+i\sin\dfrac{3\pi}{2}\right)$

8. $6\sqrt{5}\left(\cos 5.82+i\sin 5.82\right)$

9. $3\sqrt{5}\left(\cos 1.11+i\sin 1.11\right)$

10. $9\left(\cos\pi+i\sin\pi\right)$

11. $2+2i\sqrt{3}$

12. $6+2i\sqrt{3}$

13. $-6\sqrt{2}+6i\sqrt{2}$

14. $\dfrac{15}{2}-\dfrac{15\sqrt{3}}{2}i$

15. -9

16. $4\sqrt{2}-4i\sqrt{2}$

17. $-4\sqrt{2}-4i\sqrt{2}$

18. -2

19. $-5i$

20. $11i$

8·4

1. $12\operatorname{cis}\dfrac{\pi}{2}=12i$

2. $18\operatorname{cis}\pi=-18$

3. $6\operatorname{cis}\dfrac{7\pi}{4}=3\sqrt{2}-3i\sqrt{2}$

4. $28\operatorname{cis}\dfrac{\pi}{2}=28i$

5. $40\operatorname{cis}2\pi=40$

6. $30\operatorname{cis}\dfrac{9\pi}{4}=15\sqrt{2}+15i\sqrt{2}$

7. $6\operatorname{cis}\dfrac{5\pi}{2}=6i$

8. $-10\operatorname{cis}\dfrac{11\pi}{6}=10\operatorname{cis}\dfrac{5\pi}{6}=5\sqrt{3}+5i$

9. $\dfrac{1}{4}\operatorname{cis}\dfrac{35\pi}{12}$

10. $-3\operatorname{cis}\dfrac{\pi}{3}=3\operatorname{cis}\dfrac{4\pi}{3}=-\dfrac{3}{2}-\dfrac{3\sqrt{3}}{2}i$

11. $2\operatorname{cis}\dfrac{7\pi}{6}=-\sqrt{3}-i$

12. $-2\operatorname{cis}\left(-\dfrac{\pi}{4}\right)=2\operatorname{cis}\dfrac{3\pi}{4}=-\sqrt{2}+\sqrt{2}i$

13. $2\operatorname{cis}\left(-\dfrac{7\pi}{12}\right)$

14. $4\sqrt{5}\operatorname{cis}\dfrac{14\pi}{3}=4\sqrt{5}\operatorname{cis}\dfrac{2\pi}{3}=-2\sqrt{5}+2\sqrt{15}i$

15. $\dfrac{1}{2}\sqrt{3}\operatorname{cis}\dfrac{3\pi}{4}=-\dfrac{\sqrt{6}}{4}+\dfrac{\sqrt{6}}{4}i$

16. $\dfrac{1}{2}\operatorname{cis}\dfrac{3\pi}{40}$.

17. $4\sqrt{2}\operatorname{cis}\left(-\dfrac{\pi}{2}\right)=4\sqrt{2}\operatorname{cis}\dfrac{3\pi}{2}=-4\sqrt{2}i$

18. $-4\operatorname{cis}\dfrac{4\pi}{3}=2+2i\sqrt{3}$

19. $3\operatorname{cis}\dfrac{3\pi}{4}=-\dfrac{3\sqrt{2}}{2}+\dfrac{3\sqrt{2}}{2}i$

20. $4\operatorname{cis}\left(-4\pi\right)=4\operatorname{cis}0=4$

8·5

1. $81\operatorname{cis}\pi = -81$

2. $32\operatorname{cis}\dfrac{5\pi}{6} = -16\sqrt{3}+16i$

3. $64\operatorname{cis}\dfrac{21\pi}{4} = 64\operatorname{cis}\dfrac{5\pi}{4} = -32\sqrt{2}-32\sqrt{2}$

4. $-125\operatorname{cis}\dfrac{2\pi}{3} = \dfrac{125}{2}-\dfrac{125\sqrt{3}}{2}$

5. $10,000\operatorname{cis}4\pi = 10,000$

6. $\dfrac{1}{64}\operatorname{cis}\dfrac{5\pi}{2} = \dfrac{i}{64}$

7. $36\operatorname{cis}\pi = -36$

8. $64\operatorname{cis}\dfrac{7\pi}{5}$

9. $\dfrac{1}{256}\operatorname{cis}6\pi = \dfrac{1}{256}$

10. $625\operatorname{cis}\dfrac{10\pi}{3} = 625\operatorname{cis}\dfrac{4\pi}{3} = -\dfrac{625}{2}-\dfrac{625\sqrt{3}}{2}i$

11. $6\operatorname{cis}\dfrac{\pi}{4} = 3\sqrt{2}+3i\sqrt{2}$, $6\operatorname{cis}\dfrac{5\pi}{4} = -3\sqrt{2}-3i\sqrt{2}$

12. $3\operatorname{cis}\dfrac{\pi}{4}$, $3\operatorname{cis}\dfrac{11\pi}{12}$, $3\operatorname{cis}\dfrac{19\pi}{12}$

13. $3\operatorname{cis}\dfrac{2\pi}{3}$, $3\operatorname{cis}\dfrac{7\pi}{6}$, $3\operatorname{cis}\dfrac{5\pi}{3}$, $3\operatorname{cis}\dfrac{13\pi}{6}$

14. $4\operatorname{cis}\dfrac{\pi}{3}$, $4\operatorname{cis}\dfrac{11\pi}{15}$, $4\operatorname{cis}\dfrac{17\pi}{15}$, $4\operatorname{cis}\dfrac{23\pi}{15}$, $4\operatorname{cis}\dfrac{29\pi}{15}$

15. $3\operatorname{cis}0$, $3\operatorname{cis}\dfrac{\pi}{2}$, $3\operatorname{cis}\pi$, $3\operatorname{cis}\dfrac{3\pi}{2}$ or $3,\ 3i,\ -3,\ -3i$

16. $2\operatorname{cis}0$, $2\operatorname{cis}\dfrac{\pi}{3}$, $2\operatorname{cis}\dfrac{2\pi}{3}$, $2\operatorname{cis}\pi$, $2\operatorname{cis}\dfrac{4\pi}{3}$, $2\operatorname{cis}\dfrac{5\pi}{3}$ or $2,\ 1+\sqrt{3},\ -1+\sqrt{3},\ -2,\ -1-\sqrt{3},\ 1-\sqrt{3}$

17. $1\operatorname{cis}\dfrac{\pi}{3}$, $1\operatorname{cis}\pi$, $1\operatorname{cis}\dfrac{5\pi}{3}$ or $\dfrac{1}{2}+\dfrac{\sqrt{3}}{2}i,\ -1,\ \dfrac{1}{2}-\dfrac{\sqrt{3}}{2}i$

18. $3\operatorname{cis}\dfrac{\pi}{8}$, $3\operatorname{cis}\dfrac{5\pi}{8}$, $3\operatorname{cis}\dfrac{9\pi}{8}$, $3\operatorname{cis}\dfrac{13\pi}{8}$

19. $2\operatorname{cis}\dfrac{\pi}{4}$, $2\operatorname{cis}\dfrac{7\pi}{12}$, $2\operatorname{cis}\dfrac{11\pi}{12}$, $2\operatorname{cis}\dfrac{5\pi}{4}$, $2\operatorname{cis}\dfrac{19\pi}{12}$, $2\operatorname{cis}\dfrac{23\pi}{12}$

20. $2, 2\operatorname{cis}\dfrac{2\pi}{5}, 2\operatorname{cis}\dfrac{4\pi}{5}, 2\operatorname{cis}\dfrac{6\pi}{5}, 2\operatorname{cis}\dfrac{8\pi}{5}$

9 Vectors in the plane

1. $r = 4\sqrt{2}, \theta = \dfrac{\pi}{4}, \mathbf{v} = \left[4\sqrt{2}, \dfrac{\pi}{4} \right]$

2. $r = 6, \theta = \dfrac{\pi}{3}, \mathbf{v} = \left[6, \dfrac{\pi}{3} \right]$

3. $r = 4, \theta = \dfrac{7\pi}{4}, \mathbf{v} = \left[4, \dfrac{7\pi}{4} \right]$

4. $r = 16, \theta = \dfrac{11\pi}{6}, \mathbf{v} = \left[16, \dfrac{11\pi}{6} \right]$

5. $r = 5, \theta = 2.215, \mathbf{v} = \left[5, 2.215 \right]$

6. $r = 13, \theta = 5.107, \mathbf{v} = \left[13, 5.107 \right]$

7. $r = 12\sqrt{2}, \theta = \dfrac{7\pi}{4}, \mathbf{v} = \left[12\sqrt{2}, \dfrac{7\pi}{4} \right]$

8. $r = 10, \theta = 1.024, \mathbf{v} = \left[10, 1.024 \right]$

9. $r = \sqrt{10}, \theta = 4.391, \mathbf{v} = \left[\sqrt{10}, 4.391 \right]$

10. $r = 4, \theta = \pi, \mathbf{v} = \left[4, \pi \right]$

11. $\langle -4, -4 \rangle$

12. $\langle 3, 3\sqrt{3} \rangle$

13. $\langle 2\sqrt{2}, -2\sqrt{2} \rangle$

14. $\langle -8\sqrt{3}, -8 \rangle$

15. $\langle -3, 4 \rangle$

16. $\langle 5, -12 \rangle$

17. $\langle 6\sqrt{6}, -6\sqrt{2} \rangle$

18. $\langle \sqrt{27}, \sqrt{73} \rangle$

19. $\langle -1, -3 \rangle$

20. $\langle -4, 0 \rangle$

21. No

22. Yes

23. No

24. No

25. No

26. $8\mathbf{i} + 5\mathbf{j}$

27. $-2\mathbf{i} + 4\mathbf{j}$

28. $3\mathbf{i} - 6\mathbf{j}$

29. $-4\mathbf{i} + 3\mathbf{j}$

30. $-13\mathbf{i} + 5\mathbf{j}$

9·2

1. $\left[6, \dfrac{\pi}{3}\right]$

2. $\left[14, \dfrac{7\pi}{4}\right]$

3. $\left[14, \dfrac{7\pi}{4}\right]$

4. $\left[2\sqrt{15}, \dfrac{\pi}{3}\right]$

5. $[5, 5.64]$

6. $\left[\sqrt{106}, 2.078\right]$

7. $[8, 0]$

8. $[7, \pi]$

9. $[13, 2.747]$

10. $[15, 5.820]$

11. $\left\langle 3, -3\sqrt{3} \right\rangle$

12. $\left\langle -12, 0 \right\rangle$

13. $\left\langle -\dfrac{9\sqrt{3}}{2}, \dfrac{9}{2} \right\rangle$

14. $\left\langle -5, -5\sqrt{3} \right\rangle$

15. $\left\langle 0, -8 \right\rangle$

16. $\left\langle \sqrt{2}, -\sqrt{2} \right\rangle$

17. $\left\langle 0, 4 \right\rangle$

18. $\left\langle -2.07, 7.73 \right\rangle$

19. $\left\langle -9, 0 \right\rangle$

20. $\left\langle 0.497, 0.052 \right\rangle$

9·3

1. $\mathbf{u} + \mathbf{v} = \left\langle 3, -1 \right\rangle$

2. $\mathbf{v} + \mathbf{w} = \left\langle -6, -1 \right\rangle$

3. $2\mathbf{u} + \mathbf{w} = \left\langle 18, -15 \right\rangle$

4. $\mathbf{v} + 4\mathbf{w} = \left\langle -6, -16 \right\rangle$

5. $6\mathbf{u} + 2\mathbf{v} + 7\mathbf{w} = \left\langle 42, -57 \right\rangle$

6. $\mathbf{v} - \mathbf{u} = \left\langle -15, 9 \right\rangle$

7. $\mathbf{u} - \mathbf{w} = \left\langle 9, 0 \right\rangle$

8. $4\mathbf{v} - 2\mathbf{w} = \langle -24, 26 \rangle$

9. $9\mathbf{w} - 3\mathbf{u} + 5\mathbf{v} = \langle -57, -10 \rangle$

10. $5\mathbf{u} + 8\mathbf{v} - 7\mathbf{w} = \langle -3, 42 \rangle$

11. $\mathbf{u} + \mathbf{v} \approx [4.264, 2.601]$

12. $\mathbf{v} + \mathbf{w} = [5.292, 3.855]$

13. $2\mathbf{u} + \mathbf{w} = [20.682, 2.563]$

14. $\mathbf{v} + 4\mathbf{w} = [22.271, 3.298]$

15. $6\mathbf{u} + 2\mathbf{v} + 7\mathbf{w} = [76.845, 2.782]$

16. $\mathbf{v} - \mathbf{u} = [11.909, 5.411]$

17. $\mathbf{u} - \mathbf{w} = [5.667, 1.510]$

18. $4\mathbf{v} - 2\mathbf{w} = [24.331, 5.677]$

19. $9\mathbf{w} - 3\mathbf{u} + 5\mathbf{v} = [43.663, 4.045]$

20. $5\mathbf{u} + 8\mathbf{v} - 7\mathbf{w} = [29.721, 0.019]$

9·4
1. -13

2. -3

3. -11

4. -101

5. -30

6. -12

7. -6

8. 0

9. -9.058

10. $-32\sqrt{2}$

11. 1.936 radians

12. 2.601 radians

13. 1.406 radians

14. 3.110 radians

15. 2.575 radians

16. 0.256 radians

17. 1.391 radians

18. 1.661 radians

19. 2.554 radians

20. 1.229 radians

9·5
1. Orthogonal
2. Not orthogonal
3. Orthogonal
4. Orthogonal
5. Not orthogonal
6. Orthogonal
7. Not orthogonal
8. Orthogonal
9. Not orthogonal
10. Orthogonal
11. Orthogonal
12. Not orthogonal
13. Orthogonal
14. Not orthogonal
15. Not orthogonal
16. Not orthogonal
17. Orthogonal
18. Orthogonal
19. Orthogonal
20. Not orthogonal

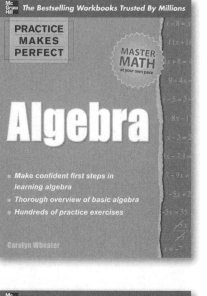

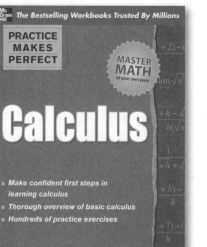